MW00614793

Circulating Genius: John Middleton Murry,
Katherine Mansfield and D. H. Lawrence

To Frederick
– and to Linda, as always

Circulating Genius: John Middleton Murry, Katherine Mansfield and D. H. Lawrence

Sydney Janet Kaplan

Edinburgh University Press

Edinburgh University Press Ltd
22 George Square, Edinburgh

www.euppublishing.com

Typeset in10.5/13 Adobe Sabon
by Servis Filmsetting Ltd, Stockport, Cheshire, and
printed and bound in Great Britain by
CPI Antony Rowe, Chippenham and Eastbourne

A CIP record for this book is available from the British Library

ISBN 978 0 7486 4148 2 (hardback)

Contents

Acknowledgements

I have been fortunate to receive a Fellowship from the National Endowment for the Humanities for this project, and wish to gratefully acknowledge its support. In addition, I would like to thank the University of Washington for supplementing the Fellowship in order to allow me a full year of leave from teaching during the initial stages of developing this book. I also would like to thank the Graduate School for awarding me a grant from the Royalty Research Fund to enable a research trip to Edinburgh and London. I owe a great debt of gratitude to the librarians at Suzzallo Library at the University of Washington, especially Faye Christenberry, and the staff of the Interlibrary Loan department, who facilitated my study of the microfilms of Murry's journals. I am deeply grateful to the Alexander Turnbull Library in New Zealand for allowing me access to the microfilms through interlibrary loan, and to the Department of Special Collections at Edinburgh University Library for access to the John Middleton Murry Collection. Additionally, I would like to thank librarians at the Newberry Library in Chicago, the Berg Collection at the New York Public Library, Washington State University Library, the British Library, and City University in London. For their kind assistance in producing this book, I am indebted to the staff at Edinburgh University Press, especially my editor, Jackie Jones, and copy-editor, Stephanie Pickering. I would also like to acknowledge my thanks to the participants at the Katherine Mansfield Centenary Conference in 2008 at Birkbeck College for allowing me to share my ideas about the relationship between John Middleton Murry and Katherine Mansfield and for giving me such sound and knowledgeable advice, in particular, Gerri Kimber, Janet Wilson, Delia da Sousa Correa, and Nancy Gray. My grateful thanks go to my students and colleagues at the University of Washington with whom I have discussed many of the issues addressed in this book, and to Ivan and Carol Doig for their words of encouragement during the long course of its writing.

Finally, this book could never have been completed without the loving support of Linda Bierds.

* * *

Brief portions of this book have appeared in different versions in *Katherine Mansfield Studies* 1 (2009), and in the *Virginia Woolf Miscellany* 76 (Fall/Winter 2009).

* * *

The author and publisher wish to thank the following copyright holders for permission to use material:

The Alexander Turnbull Library in Wellington, New Zealand, for permission to quote from 'The Diaries and Notebooks of John Middleton Murry' (MS-Group-0411).

The Society of Authors as the Literary Representative of the Estate of John Middleton Murry.

The Society of Authors as the Literary Representative of the Estate of Katherine Mansfield.

Extracts from *The Letters of D. H. Lawrence* are reproduced by permission of Pollinger Limited and the Estate of Frieda Lawrence Ravagli.

Extracts from *The Letters of Virginia Woolf* and *The Diary of Virginia Woolf* are reprinted by permission of the Random House Group Ltd.

Abbreviations

A	J. M. Murry (1920), *Aspects of Literature*
BTW	J. M. Murry (1935), *Between Two Worlds*
D	J. M. Murry (1924), *Discoveries*
DR	J. M. Murry (1989), *Defending Romanticism*
DVW	V. Woolf (1977–84), *The Diary of Virginia Woolf*, 5 vols
E	J. M. Murry (1920), *The Evolution of an Intellectual*
KMCL	K. Mansfield (1984–2008), *The Collected Letters of Katherine Mansfield*, 5 vols
KMCS	K. Mansfield (1945), *Collected Stories of Katherine Mansfield*
KMN	K. Mansfield (2002), *The Katherine Mansfield Notebooks*, 2 vols in 1
KW	M. Kinkead-Weekes (1996), *D. H. Lawrence: Triumph to Exile, 1912–1922*
L	F. A. Lea (1959), *The Life of John Middleton Murry*
LDHL	D. H. Lawrence (1979–2000), *The Letters of D. H. Lawrence*, 8 vols
LKMJM	K. Mansfield and J. M. Murry (1988), *Letters Between Katherine Mansfield and John Middleton Murry*
LJMM	J. M. Murry (1983), *The Letters of John Middleton Murry to Katherine Mansfield*
LVW	V. Woolf (1975–80), *The Letters of Virginia Woolf*
MSX	'The Diaries and Notebooks of John Middleton Murry', MS-Group-0411, Alexander Turnbull Library, Wellington, New Zealand
RDHL	J. M. Murry (1933), *Reminiscences of D. H. Lawrence*
SL	J. M. Murry (1916), *Still Life*
SW	J. M. Murry (1931), *Son of Woman: The Story of D. H. Lawrence*
WL	D. H. Lawrence (1987), *Women in Love*

Introduction

There must be a certain perversity in writing a book centred on John Middleton Murry (1889–1957), the editor and critic who was once called 'the best-hated man of letters' (L: 213).[1] After all, didn't Virginia Woolf name him 'the one vile man I have ever known' (LVW 4: 312)? And wasn't he supposed to be the infamous editor Burlap in Aldous Huxley's *Point Counter Point*? And didn't D. H. Lawrence once call him 'an obscene bug sucking my life away' (RDHL: 79)? There was something about Murry that alienated people and even his supporters have prefaced their remarks (as I do here), with qualifications.[2] I must admit that I used to go along with the general critical opinion and even contributed my share to his bad reputation in *Katherine Mansfield and the Origins of Modernist Fiction* (1991), by objecting to his behaviour as her husband and literary executor. Like most Mansfield critics, I found it easy to use Murry as her negative counterpoint.

For years I had been so absorbed in Katherine Mansfield's writing that I had not interrogated her reactions to Murry sufficiently. I had pored over her letters; read biographies, critical studies and memoirs by friends and acquaintances; and travelled to New Zealand to study her notebooks at the Alexander Turnbull Library in Wellington. As it happened, Murry's letters to Mansfield, which had not yet been published, were also housed at the Turnbull Library. Reading through them, I must even then have had an inkling that perhaps I had passed judgment on Murry too quickly. I remember that I was surprised by the frequency of his responses to her letters, and that seemed to belie her claim that he was neglecting her by not corresponding. Moreover, many of his letters were sensitive, warm and moving in ways I had not expected. Nonetheless, since my focus was the writing and not the life of Mansfield, I could easily put my unresolved questions about Murry aside. I did not anticipate that I would ever return to them.

After completing my book on Mansfield, I briefly considered writing a second one, this time focusing on her relationship with Virginia Woolf. Little did I suspect that this project would lead me back to Murry. But my initial investigations involved studying the reviews that both women wrote for the *Athenaeum* under Murry's editorship, between 1919 and 1921, and I needed to understand the background of their participation in that periodical. To that end, I went to London to examine the marked editorial copies of the *Athenaeum* housed at City University,[3] and to the University of Edinburgh to study its collection of Murry's papers. I hoped to find, buried within them, some personal accounts of his experience as editor of the *Athenaeum* which might illuminate some aspects of Woolf's involvement in it. Unfortunately, it turned out that the Edinburgh collection did not include Murry's papers from the two years of his editorship. It did, however, contain a wealth of material from his later career, especially some papers relevant to his debates with T. S. Eliot in the years following the end of Murry's editorship.

At this stage I began to envision a different kind of book from my original intention. I realised that Mansfield's relationship with Woolf might be balanced by Murry's with Eliot. The idea of circularity began to emerge as I considered the interactions amongst these four writers. It was grounded, obviously, in Murry's role as editor, *circulating* the writing of Mansfield, Woolf and Eliot. This practical, 'marketing' function was only at the manifest level, however; the latent social, psychological and political levels were hidden underneath. And, as a literary critic, I was drawn more to the latter. The metaphorical implications of circularity were manifold, and I soon realised that I would have to arbitrarily limit their proliferation if they were not to spiral out of control. This became even more an issue when the project moved to its next stage. I discovered that Murry's unpublished journals had recently been purchased by the Alexander Turnbull Library and were finally accessible to researchers. The Murry I found there – in thousands of pages written over a span of more than forty years – frequently contradicted the Murry portrayed by his detractors. He emerged as a person far more complicated and dynamic, more intellectually vigorous and emotionally sympathetic than those detractors claimed. I am not suggesting that the journals revealed the 'real' Murry. No matter how 'honest' any journal might be, it is nonetheless a literary construction and thereby subject to certain narrative conventions. Its 'truth' can never be ascertained completely, just as the 'self' it reveals can never be delimited.

Luckily, since writing a biography of Murry had never been my plan, I did not have to circumscribe the 'real' Murry.[4] His journals could be used as 'texts' in correspondence with the other texts I would analyse in the course of the development of this book. Studying Murry's journals convinced me that I could no longer ignore the figure that had lurked behind my tentative four-sided construct. I had suppressed the significance of D. H. Lawrence in order to focus on the interactions of Murry and Mansfield with Bloomsbury. But the journals revealed so fully the enormous significance of Lawrence to both of them that I knew I would have to bring him into the discussion. What had been four now became five. And here I needed once again to control that proliferating impulse and shrink the circle if I were to write a book of a manageable size. The journals made clear to me that the book's centre of energy had to be Murry's interactions with Mansfield and Lawrence, with Woolf and Eliot more on the periphery. This decision was made easier for me with the publication of two important books, which separately address the pairings I had proposed in my initial explorations: Angela Smith's *Katherine Mansfield and Virginia Woolf: A Public of Two* (1999); and David Goldie's *A Critical Difference: T. S. Eliot and John Middleton Murry in English Literary Criticism, 1919–1928* (1998).[5]

Goldie's book, in particular, helped me to define the parameters of my own more decisively. While I had long been intrigued by Murry's critical dialogue with Eliot on romanticism and classicism, a dialogue once described as 'probably the most serious intellectual controversy in England during the period' (Rees 1963: 44), I recognised that I could not treat it comprehensively in the book without it subsuming my other concerns. Goldie fully explores the dynamics of the debates, and by giving serious consideration to Murry's critical powers and recognising his importance in literary history, helps to restore the balance between him and Eliot. He suggests that the two men should be treated 'as they were treated by their contemporaries, as equals worthy of being taking seriously on their own merits' (Goldie 1998: 5).

Nonetheless, in terms of lasting influence, Eliot prevailed. His views on tradition, impersonality and authority have dominated the critical discourse on modernism until quite recently. Murry's notoriety as the defender of romanticism seemed to position him as somehow outside modernism altogether. This had not always been the case, as C. A. Hankin, the editor of Murry's letters to Mansfield, suggests:

Historically, Murry is an important figure because he was present at, indeed assisted in, the birth of English modernism. Pound and Eliot were virtually unknown, James Joyce had published no fiction, D. H. Lawrence had not written *Sons and Lovers*, nor Virginia Woolf her first novel, when in 1911 Murry co-founded *Rhythm*, an avant-garde magazine of art and literature. (LJMM: 4)

Thus when Murry was only twenty-two and still an undergraduate at Oxford, he was at the forefront of the modernist venture in England. He had gone immediately from reading Classics at Oxford to reading Bergson in Paris, discovering the tumultuous world of artists and writers, and experiencing his sexual awakening in a relationship with a young Frenchwoman named Marguéritte, with whom he fell in love. The inaugural issue, in June 1911, of *Rhythm*, which he had founded with Michael Sadleir after his return to England, contained his artistic 'manifesto', 'Art and Philosophy', in which he declared that

> Modernism is not the capricious outburst of intellectual dipsomania. It penetrates beneath the outward surface of the world, and disengages the rhythms that lie at the heart of things, rhythms strange to the eye, unaccustomed to the ear, primitive harmonies of the world that is and lives. (DR: 55)

Murry later described *Rhythm* as 'a strange hotch-potch of a quarterly magazine . . . full of post-impressionist drawings and decorations . . . To us, I believe fell the unmerited honour of being the first to reproduce a Picasso in England' (Murry 1956a: 33). *Rhythm*'s purpose, according to Murry, was to recognise the philosophy of Bergson as 'a living artistic force'. He attacked the old dispensation for operating 'under the cloak of a morbid humanitarianism' (DR: 53).

Thus Murry started his literary career precisely as a 'modernist'. He did not have the kind of long, slow evolution into modernism that is evident in the careers of some of his contemporaries, Virginia Woolf in particular. Like Woolf, Murry discovered that 'human character' changed in December 1910. And like Woolf, his awakening was hastened by an encounter with post-Impressionism. (He had spent his Christmas vacation that year in Paris and soon after met the Fauvist painter John Duncan Fergusson, whose influence helped determine the name and the aesthetics of *Rhythm*.)[6] The difference between them was that Murry was still so unformed and amorphous, so pliable and open to change at the age of twenty-one, and so less hindered by the standards of Victorian family control than the young Virginia Stephen, that his discovery of the avant-garde could become the foundation of his adult self-creation. His break from his lower-middle-class background was a process that his education as a scholarship student had by now nearly completed. So dissociated was he from his familial environment by the time he reached Oxford that he felt he 'was nothing but a bundle of antennae, feeling out for a new social persona' (Murry 1956a: 32).

It was through his editorship of *Rhythm* that Murry first became acquainted with both Mansfield and Lawrence. A few months after publishing one of Mansfield's stories in the journal, he moved into her flat, first as a lodger, then soon afterwards, as her lover.[7] Although she was only ten months older than he, she was far more sophisticated and experienced. Aside from the vagaries of her personal life – she had been pregnant, suffered a miscarriage, had several affairs, and was still legally married to a man she did not live with – her writing career was well on its way. Even before publishing her first book, *In a German Pension* (1911), she had been writing stories and articles for the prominent journal *The New Age*.[8] It was Mansfield who made the first contact with Lawrence. She had become Murry's assistant editor and in January 1913 wrote to ask Lawrence for something to publish in *Rhythm*. Lawrence's personal situation was similarly complicated. He had eloped with Frieda von Richthofen Weekley on 3 May 1912, and was living with her in Italy.[9]

On 9 July 1913, a few weeks after Lawrence and Frieda had returned from the continent, they visited Murry and Mansfield at the journal office. The two couples were fascinated with each other. Lawrence and Frieda were surprised to find the editors so young and so bohemian in their lifestyle, and later that month, invited them for a visit to their borrowed country cottage, where they all bathed naked together in the sea. Murry and Mansfield took home with them a copy of *Sons and Lovers*, which they began to read together on the train journey back to London on 29 July. By 1 August, Mansfield was enthusiastically outlining her own plan for a novel influenced by *Sons and Lovers*.[10] Murry also must have started to think about a novel, but he was too immersed in the failure of *The Blue Review* (which only survived through three issues) and his struggle to earn enough through his sporadic journalism to focus his energies on writing fiction. Soon afterwards, Lawrence and Frieda returned to Italy and Lawrence began to urge Murry to give up reviewing and join them there, to live, if necessary, on Mansfield's income (she received £150 a year from her father; but Lawrence did not realise that Murry had committed this money to paying off his debt for *Rhythm*). On 17 November he wrote Murry the now famous letter in which he remarked: 'a woman who loves a man would sleep on a board' (LDHL 2: 111).

Only partially following Lawrence's advice – choosing Paris rather than Italy – Murry and Mansfield moved across the Channel, where Murry began to review French books for the *Times Literary Supplement*. Another immersion in the bohemian atmosphere of Paris would reawaken Murry's fascination with Fauvist art and allow him to become familiar with a considerable range of modern French literature. Mansfield's experiences in Paris during that period of less than two months would affect her writing as well, as I will show in subsequent chapters of this book.

These early encounters with continental modernism were important to both Murry and Mansfield in terms of both their responses to experimentation in art and their commitment to experimental ways of living. This book begins at the point when both of them were attempting to incorporate these responses into their respective modes of writing. It can justifiably be argued that while modernism was avant-garde, Murry and Mansfield were among its earliest proponents, but by the time Murry was to edit the *Athenaeum* in 1919, 'he was as much a traditionalist as a revolutionary' (L: 70). Ironically, the 'humanitarianism' Murry started out hating gradually came to dominate his critical responses. His later reputation began its decline as he became disengaged from the central movements of literary modernism because of his defence of romanticism and his increasing fondness for the confessional mode of criticism. His reputation had already begun to decline in the mid-twenties when he was editor of the *Adelphi*, and engaged in his long literary debate on romanticism and classicism with T. S. Eliot. By 1927, he recognised that the fashionable intellectual elite was beginning to call him an 'emotional crank' (DR: 46).[11] His subsequent career as a 'moral' critic would eventually take him through several idiosyncratic versions of Marxism, Christian Socialism and pacifism as the twentieth century advanced. Malcolm Woodfield, the editor of the most recent collection of Murry's writing, *Defending Romanticism* (1989), remarks that

> Murry did not begin at the margins and move towards the centres of intellectual, political or cultural power. On the contrary, he began at the centre and moved towards what the culture called and what cultural history has continued to call the margins. (DR: 1)

It is in that marginality that Murry might be compared with other writers who have lost their footing on the trail to canonisation. That may account, in part, for my attraction to him. Murry's opposition to Eliot's ideology was significant. His defence of romantic idealism, intuition and the role of the personal, as well as his more generous conception of literary tradition, revealed an egalitarian approach to literary studies and a deepening suspicion of hierarchical authority.

In this respect, my interest in Murry is a continuation of the concerns which have held my attention from the beginning of my career: the redefinition of the concept of modernism, the enlarging of its parameters, and the re-interpretation of its cultural impact. I had been engaged in shifting the focus of critical attention away from what Katherine Mansfield once satirically described – with particular reference to T. S. Eliot – as those 'dark young men – so proud of their plumes and their black and silver cloaks' (KMCL 2: 318). Instead, I had first directed my attention to the achievements of the women in their midst: most notably Dorothy Richardson, May Sinclair and Virginia Woolf.[12] This effort was part of a widespread, ongoing reassessment of modernist literary history that was provoked by the insistence of feminist critics that the standard story of modernism's development had left out the contributions of women. By now, most critics take for granted that women writers contributed significantly to the development of modernism and that the dynamics of gender were central to both its aesthetics and its ideology.

Not surprisingly, a large part of the initial effort of reassessing modernism had involved reconsiderations of canonical writers. Beginning with Kate Millet's *Sexual Politics* in 1970, investigations of the misogyny of leading male modernists had been a popular form of feminist criticism. More productive, however, once this basic fact had been revealed, was to investigate how both men and women had been affected by the changes in sexual relationships produced by the pressures of modernity. Sandra Gilbert and Susan Gubar's massive study *No Man's Land* (1988–94) exemplifies this direction in feminist criticism. Additionally, in the movement away from New Critical formalism, critics began to look once again at the interactions between writers, critics and their readers. An interest in intertextuality in its various formations began to diminish the domination of the 'major' writers and make room for other participants in the intellectual life of modernism, such as Murry, who had been forgotten once the canon had cohered around a few figures.

My attempt to understand Murry's engagement in modernism became even more difficult when I tried to disentangle the numerous strands of his personal associations. The more I looked at the intersections between his writing and his interactions with those around him, the more I realised how profoundly acts of literary criticism are embedded in the daily lives of the critic. The filaments of intertextuality are finer and more tangled than I once supposed. I am not suggesting that literary criticism is itself autobiographical in any common sense, but rather that a critic's positions are affected not only by ideology and the nuances of personal history and circumstance, but also by a host of contingencies that periodically alter any theoretical surety. This applies to myself, as well as to Murry, as this abbreviated account of my discovery of the focus for this book should suggest. There turns out to be a certain irony in the fact that in providing this explanation of the genesis of the book, I am guilty of something similar to what Katherine Mansfield complained of to Murry when she objected to the intrusion of the personal into his discussion of the evolution of his ideas in the preface to *Aspects of Literature*

(1920). Mansfield exclaimed that it was 'indecent – no less – to say such things' (KMCL 4: 141).

Clearly, Mansfield was offended by Murry's 'confessional' style as a critic, and so were many of their contemporaries. Yet, Murry's emphasis on the personal, or, in the jargon of postmodern critical theorists, his 'subject position', should strike a familiar note to readers of the twenty-first century. As he admitted in 1922: 'After all I believe that criticism is a personal affair, and that the less we critics try to disguise this from ourselves the better' (D: 17). Murry's emphasis on the personal – in the midst of the era of modernist 'impersonality' – might actually be the suppressed element in modernism which would break open in the years following the Second World War, with the rise of confessional poetry and the subsequent outpourings of autobiographical fiction and non-fiction in the latter decades of the twentieth century. Herbert Read, commenting on 'the fashion in our times to reveal the intimacies of an author's life, perhaps even before he is dead and certainly while our memory of him is still vivid', notes the 'considerable extent' to which 'Murry himself, in relation to Katherine Mansfield and D. H. Lawrence, was responsible for this fashion, for he always stood before the public ready to display his own stigmata' (Read 1960: 64). In the field of literary criticism, confessionalism reaches perhaps its fullest expression in what David Simpson calls 'the habit of speaking personally [which] is now taking over professionalized academic discourse' (Simpson 1995: 76). Such a 'habit' may reflect more than an eccentricity of academic narcissism, and Simpson recognises the historical dimensions of this impulse to reveal the personal: 'One might see academic storytelling as a return to latent traditions temporarily discredited by the heydays of New Criticism, deconstruction, and other impersonal theoreticisms' (Simpson 1995: 61).

Murry's was not the kind of 'academic storytelling' that Simpson describes, but his confessionalism had a similar origin in that particularly English strand of Protestant individualism and romanticist self-creation, exactly the locus of Eliot's disdain when he acidly remarked upon 'the shadowy Protestant underworld' in which Murry (and also Lawrence) 'seem gracefully to move' (Eliot 1931: 769). Murry's critical approach was one of the 'latent traditions' suppressed by the more fashionable modes of modernist criticism. That Murry was unfashionable, no one can deny. He admitted it himself; as he explained in *Things to Come* in 1928, 'nowadays you can be orthodox and fashionable, or sceptical and fashionable. You cannot be what I am and be fashionable' (Murry 1928: 5).

I have no interest in making Murry 'fashionable' at long last. This book is not an attempt to declare him a proto-postmodernist, even if some of his concerns seem to point in that direction. As Malcolm Woodfield has so well stated:

> Murry is decidedly pre-modernist in situating his critical commentary, as a search for truth, on the same level as the work being commented upon and bearing on the same object. His critical language does not belong to the category of metalanguage. Nevertheless, he did recognize that reflection on literature and criticism was not only a part but also a feature of the ideological movements of his time as it is of ours. (DR: 3)

Murry believed that 'the true literary critic must have a humanistic philosophy' and that critical 'inquiries must be modulated subject to an intimate organic governance, by an ideal of the good life' (A: 7).[13] Early in his career he attacked the 'dead mechanical framework of rules about the unities', which he believed French criticism had initiated in its 'sterilised and lifeless Artistotelianism' (A: 6), and near the end of his life he expressed his frustration with the New Criticism, calling it 'a blind alley: a kind of occupational disease', and worried that it was 'trying to expand literary criticism into something analogous to Theology in the Middle Ages – and the Queen of the Sciences' (MSX 4161: 13).

This book is not a general study of Murry as a critic, however.[14] Although it may suggest some of the range and diversity of his criticism, it is always within the context of its connections with his immediate intellectual and emotional concerns.[15] Accordingly, given its focus on his relations with Mansfield and Lawrence, I do not discuss, except in passing, the many other aspects of Murry's extraordinary personal life and career, which are so admirably analysed in Lea's biography, such as his three later marriages; his considerable involvement in the Independent Labour Party; his creation of the Adelphi Centre, a utopian community 'for Socialists of all denominations' (L: 223);[16] his complicated religious enthusiasms and voluminous writing on religious topics; his emotional and controversial commitment to pacifism (and his later rejection of it); and his experiences in running a communal farm.[17] Neither will I discuss here Murry's most well-known books on major literary figures: *Keats and Shakespeare* (1925), *Studies in Keats* (1930), *William Blake* (1933), *Shakespeare* (1936), and *Jonathan Swift* (1954). It may well be time for new evaluations of Murry's critical *oeuvre* and new investigations of his contributions to British political and social criticism, and I hope future critics will consider doing so.

My concern here is rather to pay attention to the ways that modernist literary history looks different when Murry is at its centre. Murry interacted, both professionally and emotionally, with so many figures of importance in modernism: Mansfield, of course, and Lawrence, but also significantly with Henri Gaudier-Brzeska, T. S. Eliot, Virginia Woolf and Aldous Huxley. Therefore, when I suggest putting him at centre, it is not to imply that he is 'major' in some hierarchical order of modernists, but instead to investigate how much more we can learn about the dynamics of early twentieth-century literary relations when Murry is used as its fulcrum. I am interested in how both his love and his friendship were complicated by his intersecting relations with Bloomsbury and by the dynamics of literary politics and personal competition. Thus I revisit some of the well-known controversies associated with Murry during the years of his tumultuous partnership with Mansfield and his fractured friendship with Lawrence, but this time from his own perspective, rather than from the unavoidably partisan interpretations of their respective biographers.[18] I should emphasise here that Murry's 'perspective' is only partly available to us through his journals and letters. These must be read in tandem with his published writings: his literary and social criticism, his autobiography and his fiction. The latter proves to be a particularly fertile ground for exploration in that it reveals the tension between Murry's submerged desires and his strategies for artistic control. His novels also provide additional pathways towards an understanding of Katherine Mansfield's character and talent, especially when they are read intertextually with her own writing.

I am also aware that my attention to Murry's writing process might appear to some readers as a regression to the traditional concept of 'author' that has been so widely discredited in contemporary critical theory, what Jack Stillinger calls 'the romantic myth of the author as solitary genius' (Stillinger 1991: 202). Now Murry himself declared that he was certainly no 'genius', yet because he actually was one of the most significant perpetuators of that 'romantic myth' in his role as literary critic, it seems fitting to utilise some of his own techniques and turn them back on himself. Of course, such an approach needs to incorporate more contemporary theories about the ways that literary texts are produced through a conjunction of various discourses – cultural, social, economic and psychological – operating at different levels of alternating significance. The crux of the difference between contemporary approaches to literary criticism and Murry's is, fundamentally, their emphasis on 'discourse' rather than his purportedly naïve use of 'experience'. A biographically informed literary criticism, however, cannot avoid making use of 'experience', despite its contested and overly mediated representations. A book such as this one, which attempts to explore the intensity and pressure of the daily life out of which its subjects produced their fiction and criticism, needs to retain at least some semblance of consistent and coherent 'authors', regardless of any theoretical claims of their demise.

The intersections between the lives and writings of Murry, Mansfield, and Lawrence begin the process of circularity around which this book coheres. Behind it lurks the more general question of how literature is produced: out of which conjunctions of outward circumstance and inward necessity? And, in turn, the questions of how literature itself produces changed lives, and how the lives shaped by fiction shape again the lives of their producers, and finally, of those who circulate their ideas, and their lives.

Notes

1. This remark, quoted by Lea, was made by Rayner Heppenstall, the author of the first book on Murry, published in 1934, which is oddly titled *Middleton Murry: A Study in Excellent Normality*.
2. Richard Rees once remarked that Murry 'kept his worst faults on the surface, which may partly explain the amount of venom he aroused' (Rees 1963: 24).
3. The marked copies identify the authors of all unsigned articles and reviews.
4. The only biography of Murry is the 'authorised' one by F. A. Lea, published in 1959. Although Lea is more reticent than biographers today, he still managed to convey the contradictions in Murry's temperament and the emotional turmoil he lived through. Lea had access to Murry's journals and used them judiciously and cautiously. His biography remains an impressive example of the genre. Murry's autobiography, *Between Two Worlds* (1935), includes long, highly edited excerpts from his journals.
5. See also two books that preceded Smith's, both published in 1996: *Katherine Mansfield and Virginia Woolf: A Personal and Professional Bond* by Nóra Séllei, and *Word of Mouth: Body Language in Katherine Mansfield and Virginia Woolf* by Patricia Moran.
6. See Angela Smith, *Katherine Mansfield: A Literary Life* (2000), for a finely nuanced discussion of the influence of Fauvism on Mansfield's writing. Her analysis of the contents of *Rhythm* convincingly reveals its Fauvist and Bergsonian foundation. Smith also provides an interesting account of Murry's and Mansfield's friendship with Fergusson. Fergusson's centrality to modernist art in Scotland is elaborated in *Colour, Rhythm & Dance: Paintings & Drawings by J D Fergusson and His Circle in Paris*, published in Edinburgh by the Scottish Arts Council in 1985.
7. The story was 'The Woman at the Store'. Murry had been so impressed with it that he persuaded a literary acquaintance, W. L. George, to arrange an introduction to its author at a dinner party in December 1911.
8. These events are chronicled by Mansfield's biographers, Antony Alpers (1953: 134–41); Jeffrey Meyers (1978: 65–7); and Claire Tomalin (1988: 95–6); also by Murry's biographer, F. A. Lea (L: 29–31); and most fully by Murry himself in *Between Two Worlds* (1935: 184–211).

9. Lawrence wrote two reviews for the struggling publication, which by the time the second one (on Thomas Mann) appeared in July 1913, had become *The Blue Review*. This change occurred after the publisher of *Rhythm* absconded and left the printer's debt to Murry, resulting in his bankruptcy.

10. I discuss Mansfield's attempts at a novel during this time in *Katherine Mansfield and the Origins of Modernist Fiction* (Kaplan 1991: 97–102). (See also Tomlin 1988: 120.)

11. Woodfield (Murry 1989) quotes this passage from the preface to the 1927 edition of Murry's *The Evolution of an Intellectual*.

12. My first book, *Feminine Consciousness in the Modern British Novel* (Urbana: Illinois University Press, 1975), was an early attempt to redress the absence of women from the modernist canon.

13. This comment appears in an unsigned article by Murry in the *Times Literary Supplement* (*TLS*), 'The Function of Criticism', which appeared on 13 May 1920. It is reprinted in *Aspects of Literature* (Murry 1920).

14. There have been two book-length general studies of Murry's criticism: *John Middleton Murry*, by Ernest G. Griffin (1969b), and *John Middleton Murry: The Critic as Moralist*, by Sharron Greer Cassavant (1982). Malcolm Woodfield's introduction to *Defending Romanticism* (Murry 1989) provides a concise yet provocative overview of Murry's work. Other important brief studies are those by René Wellek (1986) and Chris Baldrick (1996).

15. Murry's productivity was enormous: George P. Lilley's bibliography lists sixty-six books and more than 1,500 contributions to periodicals, not counting the dozens of introductions to the works of others. Additionally, in 1991, David Bradshaw identified more than 400 unsigned pieces by Murry in the *TLS*.

16. For a more recent interpretation of the Adelphi Centre within a larger, historical framework, see Dennis Hardy (2000).

17. Murry's *Community Farm* (1952) describes his experiences running the farm so well that it might be considered his most lively and accessible book.

18. The negativity towards Murry in Mansfield scholarship is most vehement in Jeffrey Meyers' biography of Mansfield (1978). Its index lists under the category of Murry's 'background and character' only the following qualities: 'egoism', 'guilt', 'immaturity', 'ineptitude', 'jealousy', 'passivity', and 'self-pity' (Meyers 1978: 304).

Chapter 1

'My Blundering Way of Learning': Murry's *Still Life*

I

John Middleton Murry's first novel, *Still Life*, published in 1916, was considered a failure by friends and critics alike. Lawrence complained that it was 'the kind of wriggling self-abuse I can't make head or tail of' (LDHL 3: 53). His complaint conceals a troubled history of his relations with Murry, but it astutely addresses one of modernism's most significant critical problems: how to combine the new psychological awareness of the moderns with a literary form that would control the inevitable tendency to self-disclosure, a subject Murry was interrogating in his concurrent critical writing. The density of his novel results from Murry's refusal to simplify, condense or symbolise, a function of his need not to ignore any aspect of what he believed to be 'the psychological truth'.[1]

I should say at the start that I am not suggesting that *Still Life* is a lost masterpiece nor that Murry's fictional talents should have been encouraged. Murry himself recognised his limitations. Although he persevered through the writing of two more novels after *Still Life*, he came to the conclusion that writing fiction was 'merely my blundering way of learning – as always by hard experience – that I was not a novelist' (BTW: 259). His failure partially stems from a conception of the novel still dependent upon nineteenth-century narrative conventions. Murry's narrative practice stumbled behind his critical theory. If he failed to achieve 'significant form' in his very long (464 pages) and very dense novel, it is, nonetheless, well worth examining now as a document of the attempt to create modernist fiction by a writer living in the midst of one of its nodes of crisis.

Murry's emphasis on 'hard experience' is the key to both his struggle with the aesthetic problems of writing fiction and his attempt to understand himself in relation to the tumultuous personal and political events occurring at the time of its writing. Consequently, his writing process becomes as significant as the finished novel in illuminating the quagmire of desperation, anomie and emotional paralysis that affected him as well as so many others of his generation. His major artistic problem was how to depict the psychology of that generation: modern, urban people whose direct feelings were suppressed by their over-stimulated intellects. He would make that the central dilemma for his novel's protagonist, who 'examined himself so often and instinctively that his whole life seemed to be histrionic, broken by one only impulse to throw himself into another's keeping, and thus be rid of the unending necessity of choosing and acting the part he chose' (SL: 8–9). Self-examination thus becomes self-immobilising, the achieved novel diagnostic rather than revelatory.

It is ironic that only six months before he began to write *Still Life*, Murry was questioning the value of fiction based on autobiography. In 'Mr. Bennett, Stendhal and the Modern Novel', he declared that 'autobiographical fiction is not only the result of an entirely false deduction from the constant relation between the writer and the created character, but an evidence of an extraordinary self-conceit' (DR: 60).[2] Yet he understood the cultural impetus for such fiction, attributing its origins to 'the intellectual unrest of the middle classes' and the accompanying 'insurgence of individuality against the tradition of the family and the obtaining social order' (DR: 61). He scorned the critics' extravagant praise of young writers who were producing these novels and concluded that 'it is a virtue . . . not to have written a novel at the age of twenty-three' (DR: 61).

At the age of twenty-four, however, Murry had to face what he had just rejected. Despite his criticism of autobiographical fiction, he certainly did not go to any great pains to conceal how closely the novel resembled his own life. He named his protagonist Maurice Temple ('Morry' to his friends), and gave the name of Madeleine to the young French woman obviously patterned after Marguéritte. The personal subtext of the novel is the persistence of Murry's guilt over abandoning Marguéritte in 1911. Lea suggests that 'the pang of that betrayal was to haunt him for twenty-eight years, the shame of it to the end of his life' (L: 26).

A brief overview of the story Murry tries to tell in *Still Life* is necessary at this point if readers are to follow the arguments I make here and in further chapters of this book. The novel begins at the point when Maurice abandons Madeleine in Paris, returns to London, and takes up work as a freelance journalist. A year later, when he is twenty-four, he meets a thirty-two-year-old married woman, Anne Cradock, and within a record amount of time – less than two days – after their first encounter, she leaves her husband and elopes with Maurice to a borrowed cottage in Sussex. Their elopement is reminiscent of that of the Lawrences, but the break-up of the Cradock marriage is far less complicated because no children are involved and Anne has her own money. Anne's resemblance to Katherine Mansfield is unmistakable. Mansfield was also older than Murry (although only by less than ten months); she too was married (although she had long since left her husband, George Bowden, whom she had married to shield her pregnancy from an earlier affair with Garnet Trowell). Additionally, Mansfield's adolescent dream of becoming a cellist figures in Anne Cradock's desire to become a musician.

To complicate the sexual difficulties of Maurice and Anne, who, like Murry and Mansfield, take a long time to finally have intercourse, Murry introduces the character of Dennis Beauchamp, a medical doctor, who combines aspects of Gordon Campbell – a barrister who was Murry's intellectual soulmate during much of the writing of *Still Life* – and Frederick Goodyear, a close friend since his Oxford days, who envied Murry's relationship with Mansfield, and who actually accompanied them to Paris in December 1913.[3] (Incidentally, 'Beauchamp' was Katherine Mansfield's family name.)

Dennis visits the couple in their rural hideaway, arriving the day after they first slept together. The intensity of the threesome in one household alters the once delicately romantic atmosphere of the cottage. Both Anne and Maurice are mysteriously drawn to Dennis and feel overpowered by him. Amidst long scenes of self-disclosure and self-analysis, Maurice eventually tells Anne and Dennis about his earlier abandonment of Madeleine and his lingering feelings of guilt over his cowardice. Soon, emotional claustrophobia takes over and Anne and Maurice decide to move to Paris. Since Anne has her own money, Maurice will no longer have to scramble to make a living, and he should be able to devote himself to serious writing. Maurice, however, is as ambivalent about living on Anne's money as he is about everything else.

In Paris, Maurice links up with his friends from his earlier stay there: the painter, Ramsay (based on Murry's Scottish friend, the Fauvist J. D. Fergusson), Miss Etheredge (based on a lesbian artist who called herself 'George Banks'), and Dupont (based on Francis Carco, the French novelist who would become Katherine Mansfield's lover for a brief time in 1915). Dennis soon follows the couple to Paris, resigning his job at the hospital, determined to begin a new life outside the strictures of conventional society. Life in Paris devolves into scenes of disillusionment amidst the disarray of bohemia. *Still Life* is heavy with an ennui punctuated by vivid moments capturing street life and the Paris underworld, as well as lively arguments about art and gender differences. An undercurrent of suppressed homoeroticism between women makes a few scenes ambiguous and inconclusive. Finally, Maurice decides that his desperation can only be resolved by returning to Madeleine, but she has disappeared, and when he fails to find her in her home village, he approaches a state of nearly suicidal despair. Then, in a state of passive exhaustion, he returns to Paris. Meanwhile, Anne and Dennis recognise themselves in each other and impulsively decide they might as well go off to Avignon together. Thus, under the guise of a workable 'plot', engineered to depict the resolution of Murry's first love affair, intruded the breaking-down of his second.[4]

Murry's treatment of this complicated story reveals how much his understanding of the 'psychological' was in direct conflict with emerging modernist thought. He was still enmeshed in Idealist notions of the realised self that were traditional features of nineteenth-century humanist conceptions of subjectivity. Yet, such conceptions were already being called into question by artists and thinkers alike. (Although Murry was not yet familiar with the ideas of Heidegger and Wittgenstein, he was acquainted with Nietzsche's attack on the western metaphysical tradition). Only months before the outbreak of the war, Murry seems nearly desperate to hold on to an ideal that could not possibly be maintained in his own novel if it were to be true to the conditions of modern life. His journal reveals his struggle to elucidate a definition of psychic integration that could help him understand himself as well as the characters he was in the process of constructing. His entry of 17 January 1914, for example, considers the nature of subjectivity, insisting that despite the complexities of individual experience, one can discern a central self, and that to delineate that self is the real task of the novelist, not the surface details common to Realist fiction. Yet not just any 'self' is worthy of novelistic development. Murry notes that a great writer creates a great protagonist, someone who has achieved 'a harmony of the diverse elements of his soul' (MSX 4147: 24).

In *Still Life*, Murry works these ideas into a conversation at the Cradocks' dinner party, where Maurice first meets Anne. Maurice argues for the superiority of ancient Greek sculpture to fashionable 'modern' art, and sets up an opposition between the 'harmony of the soul' he discerns in classical art and modern fragmented subjectivity. He recognises that he cannot attain such wholeness because his 'life is always tormented by its insecurity', and he keeps looking for someone who can give it to him. What Maurice ignores in his deliberations on the ideal of harmony is readily apparent to a contemporary reader: the problem of sexuality. Dennis understands that better than the naïve Maurice. He responds to Maurice's reiterated speculations with humour, asserting that the ancient Greeks who theorised the concept of harmony omitted women from their conception of it.

Murry's treatment of sexuality in *Still Life* reveals Lawrence's influence, but also Murry's resistance to it. During the same time that he was working out the intricacies of Maurice's uncertain sexual impulses, Lawrence was bombarding him with Freudian concepts, reflecting the influence of his new friendships with a group of Freudians in Hampstead, including Dr David Eder, one of the first psychoanalysts in Britain. Murry, sensing exclusion because of his ignorance of Freud, felt the 'first real taste of an experience that was pretty constant throughout my relation with [Lawrence] – a feeling that I did not really understand what he was 'driving at . . . I felt that I was being indicted, rather unreasonably, for not taking SEX seriously' (BTW: 287). But Lawrence was right. Murry's own sexual immaturity is only dimly recognised in his depiction of Maurice Temple's relations with Anne Cradock in *Still Life*, which are inflected by the same existential anxiety that prevented him from achieving the interior harmony expressed by the Greek sculptures. Murry clearly recognised that such anxiety derives from the increasing division between mind and body associated with industrialism. His use of mechanistic imagery underscores that division when he describes Maurice watching his own 'brain, ticking as a noisy clock, with a metallic sound that echoed into empty spaces beyond', instead of acting upon his 'passionate desire' to leave his lonely bed and go to Anne, who chastely sleeps in a separate room.[5] He continues to lie awake thinking about how he is bounded by the lines of his body, only 'a speck in a vast circumambient universe'. Accordingly, he is stymied by a 'conviction of his own insufficiency', which makes him pretend to be asleep when Anne then silently enters his bedroom and gently plays with his hair. He can feel her breath on his cheek while his 'nerves seemed separately to quiver with their sensitiveness, as though each smallest pulse of sensation, before lost in one indistinguishable, now for the first time had its own quality'. When Anne then kisses him on the lips and whispers: '"Morry, darling . . . How like a little boy he is"', Maurice keeps his eyes shut but cannot 'prevent a smile of happiness from puckering his lips' (SL: 118–19).

Maurice's immediate response to this infantilising moment is to sink into an indulgence in the kind of sensation that Freud, in *Civilization and Its Discontents*, aptly called 'oceanic', in which the ego's sense of boundaries seems dissolved (Freud 1989: 15). As Anne tiptoes away, Maurice feels himself become 'one with all that surrounded him', and 'his consciousness ebbed out into his body and was lost' (SL: 119). When he awakens a short time later, he is suddenly possessed by 'a nameless terror', and like a child seeking his mother for comfort, he dizzily hurries to Anne's bedroom and curls up next to her. The reader expects that the couple will become lovers at this point, but it will take another fifty pages to get them to that moment. The divisions within Maurice keep defeating the rise of sexual desire; he cannot 'lose himself' in Anne and continues to see 'himself, deliberate and conscious' (SL: 128).

As Maurice's secret pleasure in Anne's infantilising nocturnal bedside visit and the emphasis on his desire to lose himself in her suggest, the sexual relations between them are afflicted by what Lawrence, in a letter to Mansfield, called 'Mother-incest'. He insisted that Mansfield's sexual relationship with Murry was fuelled by the interlocking desires of the man 'to [cast] himself as it were into her womb, and she, the Magna Mater, [to receive] him with gratification'. He scolded her by saying: 'it is what Jack does to you, and what repels and fascinates you', but he also admitted that this same conflict had long affected his own struggles with Frieda, 'the devouring mother' (LDHL 3: 301–2). Although this letter was written a couple of years after Murry completed *Still Life*, it none-theless articulates ideas that Lawrence was already propounding during their days in Rose Tree Cottage. Clearly, Murry understood the problem at some level, but he was unable to go any further with it because he could not accept – and was not yet willing to consider – the Freudian theory most relevant to his protagonist's dilemma. His metaphysical approach to the harmony of the soul must have been constantly threat-ened by Lawrence's insistence on probing its unconscious dimensions.

Murry's treatment of the problem emphasises Anne's sexual dissat-isfaction, and it is illuminating in this context to discover that Murry depicts the couple's first sexual intercourse only through her perspec-tive, and on the day *after* it occurred. He does not attempt to reveal Maurice's conscious thoughts about the experience. Even more sugges-tive is the fact that Anne is shown thinking about it at the same time as Maurice is on his way to the railway station to meet Dennis Beauchamp, leading a reader to wonder if it was Dennis's impending visit that had provoked a more intense sexual desire in Maurice. Anne remembers how Maurice 'had been strange with the burden of a half-ashamed desire', which in turn, led her to begin to feel ashamed. Undoubtedly, this diminished her pleasure and resulted in 'the agony with which she had, so vainly, prayed for unconsciousness'. It makes her uneasy to remember how she had been 'utterly involved' in a 'falsity' towards him. Instead, she chooses to concentrate her thoughts on 'how he had rested his head upon her breast and gone to sleep, while she had watched her own poignant unhappiness fade away' (SL: 177). Anne's awareness of her own sense of unfulfilled desire, which she puts aside here in favour of Maurice's satisfaction, will continue to affect her moods and be an unacknowledged cause of the failure of the relationship.

In contrast, Maurice does not seem to recognise that he has failed to satisfy Anne. As he walks towards the railway station to meet Dennis, he is only aware of his own renewed sense of physical vigour, 'the steady harmonious march of his body' as he delights in his agility climbing over the hills and splashing through the muddy ponds. He senses that he is 'gradually' overcoming his 'depression and insecurity' and moving towards 'a future where he simply lived' (SL: 179). When he pauses for a moment on a bridge, transfixed by the view of the stream below, where a brief 'shower mingled with the incessant commotions of the rising fish' (SL: 180), the phallic symbolism is blatant.

The novel then abruptly shifts back to Anne's point of view. As she works in the garden, 'tenderly stroking' the tulips she has just cut, her thoughts alternate between a momentary elation when she considers 'how changed were all the outward circumstances of her life!' and the realisation that she was nonetheless still unchanged: 'the same dimly mysterious Anne that she had always been even to herself' (SL: 178). From elation to fear and back again, her moods shift: 'She passed back into herself, more aloof, more dispassionate and cold. She felt that she was very old', and Murry compares her to a crystal, 'set hard from among the fluid in which her elements had been dispersed, impervious to new influences' (SL: 178). He then adds a coda to her musings: 'Something in the definite little picture pleased her, and she brooded over it, sad for her loneliness and glad that she was alone' (SL: 179). That shift to Anne's catching herself taking pleasure in the artistic shaping of that 'little picture' nicely captures Katherine Mansfield's mixed desires for intimacy and solitude and her ability to enjoy the contradiction: her tendency to aestheticise the moment. Anne's feeling that 'she was very old' corresponds almost exactly with Mansfield's remark in her diary of 2 January 1915:

> The chief thing I feel lately about myself is that I am getting old. I don't feel like a girl any more, or even like a young woman. I feel really past my prime. [She was twenty-six when she wrote this.] At times the fear of death is dreadful. I feel so much older than Jack and that he recognises it I am sure. He never used to but now he often talks like a young man to an older woman. Well, perhaps, its a good thing. (KMN 2: 2)

II

Murry's journal entry of 10 November 1914 mentions that he was at work on the scene of the couple's first day in the Sussex cottage, which suggests to me that Murry would not write about Anne and Maurice's sexual incompatibility until late November or December, considering how slowly he was working. If so, it bolsters my sense that the events in the 'cottage' in the novel, were being shaped by the events in Rose Tree Cottage after 10 November. Murry describes the dynamics of the intellectual discourse at Rose Tree Cottage quite vividly in *Between Two Worlds*, quoting excerpts from his journal to give the reader a sense of the younger Murry's reactions to the confusing emotional atmosphere surrounding him, and of what he describes as his 'strange dislocation of the personality' (BTW: 307).

A journal entry of 18 November, quoted in *Between Two Worlds*, details an intense conversation between Murry, Mansfield and Lawrence about the historical opposition between what Lawrence called 'the idea of Law, and the idea of Love', which Murry suggests might better be called 'the condition of Being and the condition of Knowing'. He then remarks that Lawrence 'has a confusing way of calling them the Male and the Female principles – I forget which is which' (BTW: 315). Murry's confusion over which is which is revealing. He can keep up with Lawrence as long as the discussion remains within the parameters of standard philosophical discourse. When the particularly Lawrentian concern with sexuality intrudes, Murry draws back, on the defensive. He tries to unravel Lawrence's point: 'Man as knowing and comprehending the whole system in himself', or 'Man unconscious, a root-tip of the general Life', and recognises that Lawrence is searching for 'a balance, a living harmony between the conscious and unconscious principles'. However, Murry stubbornly holds fast to his old, Idealist, conception by insisting that he does 'not think it is different, essentially, from my old business of soul harmony; but it was very hard to understand what he meant' (BTW: 315).

As the evening continues, the conversation segues into the personal. They talk about 'the sensuous nature', which Lawrence tells Murry he lacks. Murry recognises that he has been 'terribly stunted' by his father, and worries that the damage might be 'irreparable'. He is surprised that Lawrence has 'a far more passionate indignation against my Father than I had ever been able to summon up myself' (BTW: 315). Clearly, the man who had written *Sons and Lovers* was more astute than Murry about the psychological implications of the oedipal paradigm. Murry recognised that he did not have Lawrence's 'sensuous spontaneity' and felt inferior because of it, so that he needed to assert himself 'more a man than he'. He understood also that because of 'the poverty of his own instinctive nature' he 'took refuge in [his] tower of "intellectual mysticism"' (BTW: 316–17). (Murry uses this image without any degree of humour over its Freudian connotations.) He describes his tendency to do so as 'a queer kind of intellectual sensationalism, because there was an indubitable element of self-indulgence in it – a kind of private drug-taking' (BTW: 311).

On 16 November, when Murry received a letter from his French friend, the writer Francis Carco, Mansfield wrote in her notebook that she wished Carco were her own friend, admiring 'his confidence and his warm sensational life' (KMN 1: 285), exactly the qualities so manifestly absent in Murry. She began her own correspondence with Carco, which by December, had turned into an exchange of love letters. The turning point between fantasies of love and an actual decision to take action occurred on 18 December. Mansfield wrote angrily that she would 'play this game no longer', that she and Murry were 'not going to stay together'. Her remarks were prompted by her secret reading of Murry's journal, where he recounted how he had told Gordon Campbell that he had doubts about his feelings for her. Mansfield's own notebook specifies what she had read there: 'For him I am hardly anything except a gratification & a comfort . . . When once I have left you I will be more remote than you could imagine. I see you & Gordon discussing the extraordinary *time* it lasted' (KMN 1: 286–7).

Unaware of the extent of Mansfield's dissatisfaction, Murry continued to be preoccupied with his competition with Lawrence. Constantly confronted with Lawrence's greater power as a novelist, recognising how slowly he was proceeding with his own book (his journal reveals that he had only finished 280 pages after working on it for a year), Murry tried to boost his confidence by criticising Lawrence's writing (MSX 4147: 47). On 22 December, he refers to 'the crack-brained, sex-obsessed D. H. L.' and mentions that Mansfield, 'who has written better stories than . . . D. H. L.', feels the same way (BTW: 317–18). Some of his negativity derives from hearing strong praise from Frieda about Lawrence's new book in progress: *The Rainbow*, which could only have intensified his frustration over his own novel.

Murry drank too much at the Lawrences' Christmas Eve party, and the handwriting in his journal becomes a messy scrawl. The Christmas festivities continued into the next day with the famous party at Gilbert and Mary Cannan's Mill house in nearby Cholesbury, described by Cannan's biographer as 'the last splendid Christmas in 1914 before the true horror of the war was apparent' (Farr 1978: 113). After dinner and a great deal of drinking, the guests decided to perform little 'plays'. In the third of these, Murry and Mansfield acted out 'a dramatization of the actual situation' between them, 'and in which Mark Gertler, the painter, was cast for the part of [his] successor' (BTW: 321). Mansfield suddenly decided not to follow the scenario – which had her returning to Murry – and insisted on staying with Gertler instead. Lawrence was angered by Murry's passivity and 'indignantly interrupted the drama', then took Murry outside and lectured to him: '"Was I blind?" If not how did I dare to expose myself? "It's not as though we didn't love you"' (BTW: 322).

In his journal, Murry mentions that when he returned to the house he discovered that Gertler 'had been declaring a passion' for Mansfield and that she had kissed him in turn. Frieda had became enraged with Mansfield, telling her she had led Gertler on and that she would not speak to her any more. Gertler then became upset and began to cry, worried about Murry's reaction to what had happened. Afterwards, Murry and Mansfield went to bed and talked about the whole event, and its 'extraordinary atmosphere – very like a Dostoievsky novel' (MSX 4147: 52).

Not only was the atmosphere like that of a novel, but nearly everyone there was *writing* one. Gertler later told Lytton Strachey that the party was 'so interesting' that 'all the writers of Cholesbury feel inspired to use it in their work' (Gertler 1965: 77). Lawrence, of course, was in the middle of *The Rainbow* (but he would later use the Mansfield/ Gertler incident in shaping the Gudrun/Loerke situation in *Women in Love*); Mansfield was struggling with 'Maata', which she eventually abandoned; Gilbert Cannan was garnering facts about Gertler during his stay at the windmill for use in his novel *Mendel* (which, like Murry's *Still Life*, would be published in 1916); even Gordon Campbell, 'the successful barrister', was trying to write a novel (which was never published).[6]

The emotional intensity of the last days of 1914 – with its exuberant parties and confused passions – was in great contrast to the claustrophobic mood of the novel Murry was engaged in. Even the day before the first Christmas party, Murry recognised that he 'must hurry to introduce some subsidiary characters – the Paris people will help there – because the strain of working these three alone is a bit too much' (MSX 4147: 47). At Rose Tree Cottage, the 'strain' of tension between Mansfield, Murry and Gordon Campbell had nearly reached its climax. But unlike the tension in the novel – where the primary threat in Dennis's intrusion into Anne and Maurice's love affair is that it might draw Anne towards Dennis – the tension in Rose Tree Cottage was due to Murry and Campbell drawing away from Mansfield.

Murry had become increasingly absorbed in his friendship with Campbell, a friendship lacking the competitive edge of his relations with Lawrence. In *Still Life*, Murry suggests the intensity of his feelings for

Campbell when he describes Maurice's ecstatic post-coitus ramble over the hills, which is propelled by his eagerness to greet Dennis at the train station. However, Dennis does not reflect the same level of emotion; he 'checked Maurice's exuberance. He was deliberate . . . Nevertheless it chilled him now and he became apprehensive' (SL: 181). Behind Maurice's anxiety was the recognition that 'they were waiting each for the other to say something about the affair with Anne' (SL: 181).

Dennis's manner of cool deliberation might be a product of his professionalism. As a doctor he has learned to be objective and impersonal, characteristics in exact opposition to what Murry called Lawrence's 'sensuous spontaneity'. Yet Murry uses Dennis to explain, in a lecture to his students on the function of the optic nerve, the same problematic inherent in the dualism he was currently debating with Lawrence:

> 'We have bodies and we have consciousness . . . Of course for a great part of the day we do not worry about it. We just accept the fact that we are conscious beings and are grateful . . . That is the way of health. Unfortunately we have begun to be self-conscious.' (SL: 140)

Dennis calls the human dilemma of self-consciousness '"a form of metaphysical depression"' (SL: 141).

Dennis's lecture – which goes on for many pages in *Still Life* – displays the kind of long-winded intellectual analysis that Murry describes in his journal when he recounts his conversations with both Campbell and Lawrence. Mansfield had always been uncomfortable with Murry's indulgence in such conversations. A remark of hers in a book review she wrote for *Rhythm* in July 1912 seems prescient if one considers it in relation to what now was going on during the last months of 1914: 'Mysticism is perverted sensuality; it is "passionate" admiration for that which has no reality at all . . . it is a paraphernalia of clichés' (quoted by Alpers 1953: 194).

Gordon Campbell must have been at a loose end during the last part of the year while his wife, Beatrice, remained at their home in Ireland – still recuperating from the birth of their daughter – and he was more than willing to spend time talking with Murry. In her memoirs, Beatrice Campbell (Lady Glenavy) writes that her husband had found his encounters with Murry to be 'an exciting intellectual experience . . . full of possibilities of revelation and illumination on all sorts of profound subjects', but that he had no interest in Murry's 'personal life', nor was he aware of Murry's escalating feelings for him (Glenavy 1964: 63). He would have been shocked had he actually received the letter Murry wrote after Campbell failed to arrive at the cottage for a planned visit on 1 February 1915, in which Murry exclaimed:

Why in God's name was it important that I was waiting for you to come here on Saturday week, that I rode into Chesham miserable after your telegram came, that I made myself cheerful again coming back with the thought that you would come after all, that I tried to work in the evening, and when I heard a cart stop outside, my heart stopped too, stopped so that I could hardly breathe for a long while – it all seems silly as I write it – were it not that I went through it. (Glenavy 1964: 64)

The passionate nature of Murry's emotions is revealed in the building phrases of the long sentence, a style not typical of his prose. Later in the letter he admits that he has 'asked too much of [Campbell]' and that 'there was some stupid mistake – some romantic imagination of my own . . . Whatever it was, it was a good thing, for now I can see that I must have loved you as one man seldom loves another.' Towards the end of this long letter, with its mixture of confused anger and confounded love, Lawrence's influence intrudes:

We might have pulled off some great thing together, but you were divided – perhaps I was divided too. Perhaps we came together, too late . . . I can hear Lawrence say that it would only have been possible between a man and a woman. I don't think so. It would have been possible for us, had you been other than you are. (Glenavy 1964: 65–6)

Mark Kinkead-Weekes remarks that Murry's letter 'reads for all the world like one from a jilted lover. Indeed, provided that one does not think in too sexual terms, that is what it is' (KW: 194), and Beatrice Campbell insists that the 'whole relationship was enveloped in a sort of innocence which at the present time [1963] might be difficult to understand' (Glenavy 1964: 63). But Murry must have been aware that it was not completely innocent, because he hid the letter away for thirty-seven years. He finally decided to send it to Gordon in 1952, accompanied by the following explanation:

The reason why my affection for you took the extravagant turn it did, I am pretty sure, is that Katherine, at that time, was withdrawing from me, and preparing to leave me: for the very sound reason, that there was no Murry. And when I knew that was happening, I clung desperately in my mind to the idea of you. (Glenavy 1964: 67–8)

Before sending the letter on to Gordon, Murry copied it into his journal. Underneath the signature initials, he has written in smaller letters: 'A strange, pathetic letter. It would (I fear) be called "homosexual". But I never had one *atom* of physical feeling for Gordon; nor he (I am sure) for me' (MSX 4157: 176). Nonetheless, the drift of his entanglement with Campbell seems to suggest what Freudians consider latent homosexuality, although I find Eve Kosofsky Sedgwick's concept of 'homosocial desire' more useful in interpreting this relationship because it makes such clear sense of the kind of 'male bonding' that characterises so much of the behaviour between Campbell and Murry (and later, the conflicts between Lawrence and Murry). Sedgwick recognises that 'in any male-dominated society, there is a special relationship between male homosocial (including homosexual) desires and the structures for maintaining and transmitting patriarchal power' (Sedgwick 1985: 25). She explains that 'to draw the "homosocial" back into the orbit of "desire," of the potentially erotic . . . is to hypothesize the potential unbrokenness of a continuum between homosocial and homosexual – a continuum whose visibility, for men, in our society, is radically disrupted'. Additionally, Sedgwick stipulates that homosocial desire may also 'be characterized by intense homophobia' (Sedgwick 1985: 1–2), which, in Murry's case, is particularly relevant.

Murry's journals reveal considerable defensiveness whenever the subject of homosexuality arises, such as his comment in 1953, in an entry where he considers 'the attitude towards homosexuality among the fashionable *intelligentsia*', that 'homosexuality is a closed and alien world to me, who am in every fibre of my being heterosexual' (MSX 4158: 303). By 1953, however, Murry could understand that his 'almost violent disgust at homosexuality' (what we now call 'homophobia'), was related to an incident that occurred when he was about fourteen, when he was molested by a school dentist, and never told anyone about it. He writes of his fear and loathing, and the 'scar' it left on him for years afterwards (MSX 4157: 310).

Murry's incomplete understanding of the homosocial dynamics of the friendship between Maurice and Dennis in *Still Life* accounts for much of the strange atmosphere of ambiguity in the novel. As the intensity of Murry's feelings for Campbell grew, his grasp of the psychological nuances of his characters' behaviour lessened. He did not know why he found himself including certain details, such as putting 'in a dream for Dennis for some unknown reason, and unscrupulously [making] use of an experience of Gordon's on the Dublin boat 3 weeks ago' (MSX 4147: 46–7).

The way that Dennis Beauchamp supplants Maurice Temple in Anne Cradock's affection seems to be willed by Maurice's withdrawal from her, but it also allows Dennis to be even closer to Maurice by making love to Maurice's lover. The greatest energy in the novel seems to be expressed in the scenes revealing the complex dimensions of the friendship between the two men, not in the love scenes between Maurice and Anne.[7] Within a short while after Dennis's arrival at the cottage, Maurice feels uneasy when a 'silence descended upon them', because 'between him and Dennis silence was unnatural'. Maurice cannot understand what is causing the restraint he feels in both of them, sensing that 'it must be due to some third thing come between them', and asks Dennis: '"this isn't going to make any difference to us, is it?"'. When Dennis abruptly questions him: '"I wish I knew what part of you was in love with Anne"', Maurice responds with puzzlement: '"I don't know. All of me, I suppose"'. Dennis's response accords with the suppressed homosocial desire that affects the entire discussion: '"No, that's not it. I don't see how it could be, anyway. You wouldn't want me, if that were true"'. After reaching this point of illumination, the intensity of their conversation subsides and the terms of the discussion become more vague: 'thing', 'things like this', their referents nearly lost in a rush away from the implications of the revelation, until Dennis finally says: '"There always comes a time when I'm talking like this when the whole thing seems to blow away like smoke"' (SL: 207).

Mansfield's diary records that Beatrice Campbell had arrived from Ireland when she and Murry went to London on 26 January 1915, and it is therefore possible that Beatrice's return made Gordon less interested in visiting Murry (KMN 2: 7). Whatever need Murry fulfilled for Campbell was assuaged by the resumption of family life. It is surprising that Mansfield's diary contains no reference to Murry's abject disappointment over Campbell. Did he not tell her about it? That in itself says a great deal about how far apart they had drifted. Mansfield's diary entries show her completely preoccupied with her feelings for Francis Carco and her need to distance herself from Murry. Her entry of 31 January mentions that she and Murry 'talked of London. Jack understands that I want to live there and apart from him. It is time' (KMN 2: 8). This is the *same* day that Campbell was supposed to arrive and did not.

Murry's repeated use of the word 'curious' in his journal entries during the days before Mansfield's departure for Paris might suggest a dim recognition that he should probe more deeply to reach some hidden truth about himself. He remarks that it is 'curious' that he 'cannot think about anything', including his 'attitude' about *Still Life*, and it is 'curious' that he was not 'jealous of [Mansfield's] happiness nor inclined to wet-blanket it'. He concludes that his 'sensations are surprisingly uncomplex for one who imagines that he is going to be a psychological novelist' (MSX 4147: 55).

Nonetheless, he was unable to lose himself in the novel that was becoming increasingly remote from his current dilemma – at least on the surface. The events of these days would increase the novel's emphasis on abandonment and betrayal. Instead of forcing himself to continue writing in the miserable atmosphere of Rose Tree Cottage, Murry left

the next day to visit the Lawrences at Greatham in Sussex. It was storm-
ing, and he had a cold which was rapidly turning into a severe case of
influenza. By the time he reached them he was in very bad shape, desperate for some physical – and emotional – comforting. These he received
from Lawrence in full. Lawrence put him to bed and nursed him through
his illness and listened to his troubles – and gave him advice.

I think we can date the true beginning of the bonding phase of the
Lawrence/Murry relationship from this moment. Whatever interest
in Murry Lawrence felt previously had been diluted, first through the
initial parallel structure of heterosexual coupling, which gradually broke
apart through Murry and Mansfield's discomfort with Frieda, and sec-
ondly, by Murry's absorption in Gordon Campbell. For those few days
in February, however, Lawrence had Murry all to himself and in a condition of extreme vulnerability. Murry later wrote: 'If Lawrence were to
reject me now that Katherine and Campbell had rejected me . . . it was
unthinkable' (BTW: 335).

The subject of homosexuality was very much on Lawrence's mind
during this period, as evidenced by his letter to Henry Savage, written
only a few months earlier, in which he questions why great artists, especially the Greeks, tended to prefer the bodies of men to those of women
(LDHL 2: 115). Moreover, E. M. Forster had been a guest at Greatham
less than a week before Murry's arrival there, and apparently, Lawrence
was troubled by Forster's homosexuality and argued with him about it
(KW: 191–2). Lawrence's critics tend to assume that he based the scene
in *Aaron's Rod*, where Lilly massages Aaron's 'lower centres', upon his
nursing of Murry in February 1915. Kinkead-Weekes makes a good
argument against this assumption and I tend to agree with him, at least
in terms of the unlikelihood of a massage to the lower body. There is
no evidence in Murry's detailed daily journal for any unconventional
'massage', which would have been profoundly disturbing to the distraught and physically defensive Murry. But Kinkead-Weekes's supposition that 'the insinuation of homosexual feeling is also unlikely' since the
'attraction' was 'predominantly intellectual and "spiritual" rather than
physical' (KW: 802 n60), does not seem to allow for enough consideration of the more unconscious aspects of Lawrence's behaviour, as well
as the broader continuum of 'homosocial desire'.

I suspect that Lawrence was strangely affected by Murry's extreme
reaction to Gordon Campbell's 'rejection'. It must have resonated with
his own disturbed reactions to the homosexuality of Forster. It appears
from Murry's journal entry of 19 February 1915 that Lawrence was
using the Campbell incident as a way of bringing Murry into a closer
dependence upon himself, telling him that his relationship with Campbell

'was the most regrettable part of each of [them]', and calling Campbell '*a callous materialist underneath*' (MSX 4143). With Lawrence influencing his interpretation of the Campbell incident, Murry was also taking on some particularly Lawrentian notions, such as referring to his relationship with Campbell as 'sterile, an unnatural excitement, like drinking absinthe, to season life', and considering that Campbell was using him 'merely as a means for some intellectual sensationalism' (MSX 4143).

Katherine Mansfield returned from Paris on 25 February and Murry left Greatham to meet her and resume their relationship. Lawrence would, nonetheless, continue to meddle in the Murry/Campbell entanglement even after Murry's departure. In a letter to Campbell written around 3 March, Lawrence manages to be both conciliatory and competitive towards Campbell. He praises him for being 'very sound and healthy not to want [Murry's] close love', and that Murry's extreme reaction was that of 'a jilted lover' needing 'to show his superiority for the moment, because he was so deeply insulted and injured'. He assures Campbell that Murry actually was 'only waiting till you can be genuine, healthy friends with each other'. The competitive edge enters Lawrence's letter when he suggests, without saying it directly, that his own influence on Murry is by far the strongest and most significant. He says that Murry 'has burst the skin of his womb-sac and entered into his newer, larger birth. I think he does not trouble about his immediate self any more'. The ending of this letter shows that at the same time that Murry was retreating to his union with Mansfield, attempting to resurrect their love affair with an ever more absorbing isolation *à deux*, Lawrence was envisioning a moving-beyond such atomised couplings:

> I want us to form a league – you and Murry and me and perhaps Forster – and our women – and any one who will be added on to us – so long as we are centred around a core of reality, and carried on one impulse. (LDHL 2: 301–2)

III

Murry's armour was heavy against any threats of physical homosexuality. Yet the erotic possibilities of lesbianism might not have elicited the same reaction. For many men of the early twentieth century, lesbians connoted the power of female sexuality untamed. Both pornography and more serious literature suggested the erotic attraction of lesbian sexuality for men, and the fantasy of winning a woman away from her female partner certainly was a subject of interest, especially to Lawrence, as is evident in both *The Fox* and *The Rainbow*.[8] A late entry in Murry's journal, on 12 March 1956, is particularly suggestive. Musing about an article in *TLS* about homosexuality, he considers society's 'instinctive repugnance' to it, as well as his own as a man who is 'congenitally hetero-sexual', and then remarks:

> What is queer is that I have no such positive repugnance to homosexuality between women; maybe because it is necessarily rather abstract to me. I wonder whether women have the same sort of indifference to homosexuality between men. (MSX 4160: 96)

It might well have been that part of Murry's initial attraction to Katherine Mansfield was her refusal to be typically 'feminine'. His description of his first impression of her shields more than it describes. It suggests some intuitive sense of her underlying androgyny; perhaps that androgyny answered a suppressed question about himself: 'there was something almost boyish about her . . . She was not, somehow, primarily a woman. I was not conscious of her as a woman. She was a perfectly exquisite, perfectly simple human being, whose naturalness made me natural' (BTW: 194). Relying upon his old model of 'the harmony of the soul', Murry emphasises Mansfield's refusal to accept either 'the dominion of the Female, or the physical, and the dominion of the Male, or mental', because she 'really did embody something of the poise and true balance between them which was an idea or an ideal both to Lawrence and myself' (BTW: 316).

What Murry does not state in his autobiography, and in fact never reveals in any of his writing about Katherine Mansfield, is the complicating fact of her *sexual* ambivalence. Unlike Murry, who considered himself 'in every fibre of my being heterosexual', Mansfield did not. It was during the weeks of living at Rose Tree Cottage that Mansfield confided in Frieda Lawrence about her adolescent sexual experiences with women, from which, both Claire Tomalin and Mark Kinkead-Weekes surmise, Lawrence drew the details for the 'Shame' chapter in *The Rainbow*. Kinkead-Weekes suggests that learning about Mansfield's lesbianism at this precise moment was significant for Lawrence in terms of his own concerns about homosexuality (KW: 153).

Although Frieda probably broke confidence by telling Lawrence about Mansfield's sexual history, it is not evident that Lawrence did the same by telling Murry about Katherine's past. I found no evidence in Murry's journals that he knew anything about all this at the time. Yet, by 1935, when Murry wrote *Between Two Worlds*, he would have known about those adolescent lesbian affairs through editing Mansfield's notebooks for his *Journal of Katherine Mansfield* (1927), where he carefully excised the lesbian passages. Such omissions are not surprising, considering the near invisibility of lesbianism in the discourse of the times.[9] He also does not discuss in his autobiography Mansfield's emotionally charged relationship with Ida Baker (L. M.) and how it collided with their own. Although L. M. was in Africa while Murry was writing *Still Life*, Mansfield recorded in her journal, on 1 January 1915, at the height of his escalating obsession with Campbell, this arresting image: 'The ghost of Lesley ran through my heart her hair flying – very pale, with dark startled eyes' (KMN 2: 1). Kinkead-Weekes remarks that Ida Baker's absence might have been the reason the usually self-protective Mansfield 'dropped her defences' and confided her sexual secrets to Frieda Lawrence (KW: 153).

A lesbian subtext becomes apparent only in the second half of *Still Life*, when Maurice Temple returns to Paris with Anne Cradock and eagerly introduces her to Miss Etheredge. Murry modelled this character on the artist Dorothy (known as 'George') Banks, whom he had met during his first visit to Paris in 1910–11. Murry later describes Banks as 'a strange and brilliant woman, whose psychology was quite outside my range', but he never mentions that she was a lesbian. He only hints at it by saying that she had a 'heavy, pale face reminiscent of the photograph of Oscar Wilde, which was tucked in her mantel piece' and mentions how she would 'overwhelm [him] with Wilde and Weininger', whose very names encode homosexuality. Yet Murry quickly deflects that implication by stating flatly that Banks 'must have lived (I now think) in a condition of permanent hysteria due to sexual repression' (BTW: 144–5).

Banks had been helpful to Murry when he was setting up *Rhythm* by introducing him to artists (it was through her that he discovered the work of Picasso, and obtained a drawing from him that would be the first one published in Britain). Mansfield met her on her first trip with Murry to Paris in May 1912, when she was also introduced to Francis Carco.[10] Beatrice Campbell's lively account of that trip to Paris provides details which are strikingly apropos to *Still Life*, such as her reference to

> a big woman who wore men's clothes and looked like Oscar Wilde and was always weeping. At night we went from café to café; there always seemed to be some terrific psychological drama going on, and we had to keep avoiding someone or other. A great discussion was also raging and it seemed to be eternally on the same subject: 'was the Titanic a work of art?'. (Glenavy 1964: 58)

That 'big woman who wore men's clothes' also participated in another incident in Murry's life that relates to suppressed homosexuality. On 12 May 1913, George Banks joined with the sculptor Henri Gaudier-Brzeska in a violent attack on Murry in his *Rhythm* office, ostensibly about not being paid for their contributions to the journal. Murry writes vividly in his autobiography about the attack – how the two conspirators argued with him, how Gaudier 'squeezed his fingers round an imaginary throat' (BTW: 246), and slapped his face. The avenging duo then snatched two drawings off the wall and left, threatening more violence to come. Murry wrote Mansfield a frantic and hysterical letter afterwards: 'I'm crying out of sheer nervous reaction . . . I'm crying again now – O God' (LJMKM: 16). Murry's description of the attack becomes murky when he tries to explain its motivation:

> But I now believe I was completely obtuse in my conception of Gaudier's attitude towards me. And since a like misconception was to play a considerable part in a more important relation to my life (that with D. H. Lawrence), it behoves me to dwell upon it here . . . I confess I am out of my depth in this matter. But I have since come to believe that in both Gaudier and Lawrence there may have been some kind of sexual ambivalence and that this may have been intimately connected with the quite peculiar impression of natural genius which both made on me. (I should make it perfectly clear that I am not at all attributing to them what is generally understood by the word homosexuality.)
>
> But Gaudier was different, and I did not know it . . . and I have come to the conclusion that his later conduct towards me, which I found so inexplicable and frightening, yields to the explanation that it was the spite of miscarried love. (BTW: 245)

Murry also considers 'the spite of miscarried love' as the motive behind George Banks's equally violent behaviour. He suggests that it emerged because of romantic feelings towards himself, which had been suppressed while he was in love with Marguéritte, and then again with Mansfield.

Murry uses this realisation in the novel when he depicts Miss Etheredge's jealousy and allows Maurice 'to construct a romantic story and to convince himself that she was in love with him herself' (SL: 113). Clearly, this simplistic interpretation of Banks also shaped his construction of the 'Epilogue' to *Still Life*, where Maurice comes back to Miss Etheredge's flat after returning from his futile search for Madeleine and realises that Anne has left Paris with Dennis. Miss Etheredge is brisk, unfriendly and hostile: '"When did you run away from Mrs. C.? . . . You'll have to get somebody else to mother you now . . . Or did you think I might be anxious to take on the job."' Murry gives her the last sentence of the novel: '"The fool, the fool . . . the little fool," she said at length and began to cry' (SL: 464).

George Banks's participation in the violent attack on Murry, however, might better suggest a displacement of love object complementing the one between Gaudier and Murry, but hers may have been even more complex and multi-faceted. Embedded in the novel – at a level perhaps only dimly perceived by Murry – is Miss Etheredge's attraction to Anne. This leads me to wonder if George Banks's animosity towards Murry was really aimed at Mansfield? Was it really Katherine Mansfield who was the object of her 'spite of miscarried love'? In Francis Carco's novel *Les Innocents*, published in 1916 (the same year as *Still Life*), the character patterned after Mansfield is murdered by her lesbian friend, who, according to Antony Alpers, physically resembles George Banks (Alpers 1980: 178).[11]

In *Still Life*, Murry constructs a complicated web of emotional connections which entwines not only Anne, Maurice and Miss Etheredge, but Dennis as well. When Maurice returns to Paris with Anne, he is eager to introduce her to Miss Etheredge, yet quickly reacts with jealousy to the two women's immediate establishment of intimacy; simultaneously, Dennis Beauchamp is drawn to Miss Etheredge, 'a woman of an obviously magnificent and unfamiliar kind'. The mutual antagonism between Dennis and Miss Etheredge that quickly ensues suggests each one's underlying attraction to Anne. Dennis is unprepared for 'the sudden thrust' of Miss Etheredge's hostility: 'The surprise of an unexpected bludgeon, where he might have expected a rapier, stunned him. But he was not the man to show it' (SL: 304–5). (Like George Banks, Miss Etheredge has violent propensities; for example, she once threatened the new lover of her former roommate, Netta, with a revolver.)

Through a number of implicitly suggestive verbal manoeuvres, Miss Etheredge attempts to draw Anne to herself and away from *both* Maurice and Dennis. At first, there appears to be a deep affinity between the two women; while Anne listens to Miss Etheredge she feels it is as if 'she heard herself speaking', and that she 'did not even feel that Miss Etheredge was a separate person' (SL: 383). Yet, when she reaches over to comfort her new friend, Anne suddenly becomes aware of 'how large were her shoulders, how incongruous her own embrace' (SL: 383). Murry's repeated emphasis on Miss Etheredge's physicality tends to reinforce the lesbian subtext, but he undercuts it by remarking that 'at the moment when they had come closest together . . . was a suggestion of something hostile' (SL: 387). This hostility emerges when Murry shifts the women's conversation to the problem of Maurice Temple, implying that Anne's interest in Miss Etheredge derives from her intuition that she too had been in love with Maurice, and that he might even have some feelings for her in return. Consequently, a growing intimacy between two women is countered by a return to competitiveness over men. In this, Murry confirms Virginia Woolf's observation in *A Room of One's Own* that in most fiction by male writers, women are 'almost without exception . . . shown in their relation to men' (Woolf 1963: 86).

If Anne could have read Maurice's mind shortly after he had introduced her to Miss Etheredge, she would have found her intuition confirmed. His thoughts keep straying to his memories of his relations with Miss Etheredge three years earlier, and how she 'opened broad vistas of life to him'. He suddenly remembers how she 'would sit in her littered room and weep' when he visited her, and realises that she might have been in love with him, and 'burns' at the thought: 'He felt again the firm warmth of her massive body as he had put his arm round her in an instinctive, frightened attempt to comfort her. He wished he had kissed her. He desired to kiss her now' (SL: 323).

True to Dennis's patterned response of being attracted to whomever Maurice loves, he too is drawn to Miss Etheredge, but he is more astute than Maurice about the nature of this woman's difference, seeing her as '"a woman apart from her kind"' (SL: 320). His gaze focuses on 'a heavy earth-born sensuality in her gait' and 'her large, slow-swinging breasts' (SL: 321), which leads him to indulge in a sexualised exoticism. He exclaims to Maurice:

'She bowls me over . . . She comes clean outside my idea of a woman. One moment I thought what on earth is she doing, painting and messing about here; she ought to be mixed up in some terrific drama of the primitive passions, wherever those things happen.' (324–5)

In relation to this woman, Dennis finds his 'detachment failed him, as it were dissolved away before a desperate desire to prove his own worth by forcing Miss Etheredge to acknowledge his power' (SL: 315). Dennis pursues Miss Etheredge and when Anne hears about it, she is disturbed, not knowing why. Near the end of the novel, after he has reached a state of nearly total dissolution, he tells Anne about his feelings for Miss Etheredge: '"She suddenly solved everything. I was going to marry her . . . I can't say why I wanted to marry her; but it was plain to me that this was the thing I was seeking, that would save me"' (SL: 458).

As if Miss Etheredge could be any man's salvation! This is a woman who says about her relationships:

'If I want to begin, everything seems rotten. I know beforehand that everything will fail. Everything and everybody. It's all the same. The men turn beasts. The women turn nothing at all. They're only a second-rate double of the men they hang on to. The best of them go that way. I can't do that.' [This implication of lesbianism is the most overt in the novel.] (SL: 382)

Dennis's peculiar desire to marry Miss Etheredge is the behaviour of a man nearly totally lacking in psychological insight. The suddenness of his decision is all of a piece with his precipitous escape to Paris to join Maurice and Anne, throwing away a promising career in medicine. He alternates bemused theoretical speculation with dangerously impulsive action. Continually misreading his own emotions, he becomes perplexing to Maurice, who 'began to be frightened of a new and inscrutable Dennis' (SL: 216). Maurice notices 'an insidious malice that seemed at times to emerge in Dennis, and so quickly disappeared that he could never be certain that it had really been' (SL: 210).

Anne's decision at the end of the story to go off with Dennis occurs *after* she realises that he had asked Miss Etheredge to marry him. Her decision, therefore, is as mired in sexual ambiguity as everything else in the novel. In one stunning instance – a major turning point of the story – Anne, Maurice and Dennis engage in conversation with a young prostitute, Josephine, during their visit to Montmartre. Each of them responds to the young woman with some level of desire. Dennis's is tinged with sadism. He grabs her wrist so tightly that she tells him '"I should be really happy if monsieur were not hurting my hand"' and he asks forgiveness and puts his lips to 'the faint-red mark his fingers had left' (SL: 337).

Maurice watches the interplay between Dennis and Josephine and suddenly begins to desire her himself:

> He would never have dared to kiss her, or be kissed by her in front of Anne. Only because he was too much the coward. What difference could it make? Why couldn't he be free? Of course he would come back eventually to Anne; but now he desired to kiss that girl, to be her lover, only for a night. (SL: 337)

At that moment Maurice realises that if he did go off with Josephine he 'wouldn't go back' to Anne, and he is shocked by this knowledge: 'Quite plainly he could see himself deciding not to return . . . He mustn't let Anne know that' (SL: 337–8).

Murry's description of Maurice's attraction to Josephine here might have been his way of introducing into his highly autobiographical novel an incident about which he was deeply ashamed: his contracting gonorrhoea from a prostitute after he had left Marguéritte. It was the primary reason for his sexual avoidance at the beginning of his affair with Mansfield. In *Still Life*, Murry lets Maurice only *think* about going off with the prostitute. But in so doing, he channels the scene's erotic desire three ways. Dennis finally becomes the conduit of all their libidinal energies when he actually takes the woman home. (As it turns out, Dennis does not have sex with her, but Maurice and Anne do not know that.)

Murry's treatment of Anne's attraction to Josephine is the most ambiguous. After Josephine asks Anne to dance with her, she accepts with a kind of ironic pleasure, and quickly begins to enjoy the dance. Anne holds the other woman 'close' and feels how her 'whole body moved in rhythm, it was as though her feet moved not at all'. To the two men watching them intently, the 'girl seemed to partake of a common rapture. In Anne's arms she was soft and languid, dancing in a dream that might have had no end' (SL: 339). After they finish their dance, Josephine tells Anne: '"It is not every day one dances like that," she said. "It is different with men, but Madame dances as a lover"' (SL: 342).[12] When later she asks Dennis to dance, she turns to Anne and asks: '"You're not angry with me, madame?"', as if she were now Anne's possession. In the cloakroom shortly before Anne's departure, Josephine kisses her 'on the mouth, and Anne was glad to be kissed' (SL: 352). Afterwards, exhausted from her vacillating feelings, Anne tells Maurice she is returning to the hotel and asks him '"to give Dennis fifty francs to give to the girl from her"' (SL: 352). This curious gesture links her erotically with both Dennis and the prostitute (as well as to Maurice, who is to convey the payment).

The sight of the two women dancing together had provoked Dennis into thinking about his confusing relations with women, and his thoughts reveal the fragility of the hold 'civilizing' convention makes on a male psyche shaped by patriarchal ideologies of dominance and control. He realised that he desired the young woman, as he 'desired all women', and he 'needed her, not for the satisfaction of desire, which passed easily and unregrettably away, but to arrest his fluctuant self'. Furthermore, 'in her he could assert himself against the tumult of instinct and impulse which beset him'. He feels he would 'justify himself' in the eyes of Anne, and also, 'more strangely in the tremulous sneering lips of Miss Etheredge', if he could conquer Josephine: 'To go away with her, to treat her as any one of the thousand men he saw and detested in their traffic with women' (SL: 341):

The purpose hardened within him as his eyes firmly followed their dance. The girl was Anne's now; but she would have to come with him, have to come into the power of his money. It was the idea of compulsion and brutality upon which he fastened. He would rather she came against her will than liking him. The more she seemed to lose herself in the dreamy intoxication of her dance with Anne, the more the joy of his secret determination glowed beneath him. He followed her every movement. His glance passed from her slender yellow arms to the head which she pillowed as though in sleep on

Anne's breast. He felt her little body shrink under his touch; he saw her eyes open in a childish stare of horror. (SL: 341)

Within the context of the lesbian subtext, Dennis's realisation that it would be his *money* that would take Josephine away from Anne (not his masculine sexual power as Lawrence might have explained it), is particularly revealing.[13] It allows Murry to diminish Dennis's sexual prowess at the same time as he allows it to be enacted. Maurice's retreat from pursuit of Josephine (or, one could his say, his rejection by her, for after all she chooses Dennis for her sexual favours) is thereby counteracted. The tension of the unspoken competition between the two men remains yet without resolution. All of this conforms nicely with Luce Irigaray's observation that 'heterosexuality has been up to now just an alibi for the smooth workings of man's relations with himself, of relations among men' (Irigaray 1985: 172).

Maurice seems bewildered during his drive back to the hotel in a cab with Anne. He senses that 'the last bond that held him to a being who loved him was broken. He was perilously and terribly alone'. And he is confused about what has happened to them all in the café. He finds it strange that 'Dennis would stay behind with that girl', and he cannot grasp the meaning of Dennis's abstruse conversation with him while the women were dancing: '"I didn't understand it all. I couldn't listen. But he has an idea of symbolic regeneration"' (SL: 353). Considering Dennis's sadistic fantasies about the young prostitute, with their undertone of physical brutality and domination, it is tempting to invert Katherine Mansfield's statement, which I quoted earlier, that mysticism is 'perverted sexuality'. Dennis's 'idea of symbolic regeneration' then, could be called 'perverted mysticism'.

Notes

1. In his journal, on 17 January 1914, Murry questions the implications of realism and comments: 'There is only one kind of realism which worth more than a tinker's curse, and that is psychological realism, and there it's not the realism but the psychology which matters' (MSX 4147: 25).
2. Originally published in *The Blue Review* in July 1913.
3. Although Murry does not mention in *Between Two Worlds* that Goodyear went along with them to Paris, he states in an editorial note to the first edition of Mansfield's *Journal* that Goodyear 'accompanied us to Paris on our unfortunate expedition in the winter of 1913' (Mansfield 1927: 60). For an interesting fictional portrait of Frederick Goodyear, see C. K. Stead, *Mansfield* (Stead 2004: 87–101).
4. It is no surprise that a triangular paradigm provides the central plot device

for *Still Life*, for not only is it the most common narrative convention, according to René Girard in *Deceit, Desire, and the Novel* (1965), but it also fits the pattern of Murry's own love affairs. Even his romance with Marguéritte involved a triangular complexity. Joyce Cary's biographer describes Cary's 'proposed ménage à trois with Marguéritte and Murry' (Bishop 1988: 78).

5. This replicates the situation of Murry and Mansfield when he first moved in with her as her 'boarder' in 1912, and it took some time before they actually became lovers.

6. Frederick Goodyear was also writing an autobiographical novel. See Alpers (1980: 163). Sadly, Goodyear would never be able to realise himself as a novelist: he was killed in the war on 23 May 1917.

7. See Sedgwick (1985: 21) on Girard's theory about the intensity of the bond between male rivals. This is particularly relevant to the situation between Maurice and Dennis.

8. For a useful discussion of the prevalence of 'lesbian exoticism' in the work of nineteenth-century French writers such as Gautier, Balzac and, especially, Baudelaire, see Lillian Faderman (1981: 254–76).

9. Some of these passages are included in Murry's 'definitive' edition of the *Journal of Katherine Mansfield*, published in 1954 (Mansfield 1954).

10. A caricature of Katherine Mansfield by 'Georges' Banks appears in the October 1912 issue of *Rhythm*.

11. On Mansfield's relationship with Carco, see Gerri Kimber (2008: 63–76), and Christiane Mortelier (1994: 137–57).

12. There may be a link between the dancing scene and Mansfield's letter from Paris to Murry on 22 March 1915, where she mentions dancing with a young woman at a party at Beatrice Hastings's flat (KMCL 1: 164).

13. Murry's reference to 'the power of his money' might be a belated jab at Gordon Campbell over his sudden rejection. By the time Murry wrote this section of the novel – after the breakdown of his friendship with Campbell – he belittled Campbell in his journal for being too focused on making money.

Chapter 2

Still Life and *Women in Love*

I

According to Murry, he only sought from Lawrence 'the warmth and security of personal affection' when he visited Greatham in February 1915. He later recognised that Lawrence's response to his need was more complex: 'What his consciousness required was an impersonal bond between us: that we should be servants of the same purpose, disciples of the same ideal' (BTW: 332). Murry was confused by that because 'ideas and purposes meant nothing to me. Persons were everything . . . But when, as now, we were intimately together, I felt that Lawrence was making a personal appeal to me to follow him impersonally' (BTW: 332). Murry admitted that he had not been completely honest in professing to accept Lawrence's ideas, but was more 'like a woman instinctively humouring her husband by accepting his argument and principles, although in fact they are quite indifferent to her' (BTW: 333). He was 'uneasy' about his own willingness to go along with Lawrence in this way, which, as his awkward simile suggests, placed him in the 'feminine' role in their relationship. During that conversation on 21 February, Lawrence was to make a statement that would have significant long-range implications in the relations between the two men. Murry writes that Lawrence 'was sad, for he was a forerunner, like John the Baptist before the Christ, whose place it was to give up & surrender' (BTW: 336). Lawrence saw his own purpose as 'preaching the revolution of the conditions of life', and said that he felt 'clumsier' than Murry. Murry responded modestly by saying: 'My lack of clumsiness . . . was largely nervelessness'. Lawrence continued to reverse Murry's self-deprecation by turning each remark into something positive:

'Yes, there is a lot of inertia in you, but that is valuable. Your effort somehow seems to be purer than mine'.

'You have more strength'.

'Yes, of a certain kind; but less, again, than you of another kind'. (BTW: 336)

The very young Murry appears out of his depth during this conversation. Although he does not argue with Lawrence's assumption that he 'was somehow to succeed him', and that the two of them 'made a real combination from which something . . . must come', he admits to himself that he cannot really grasp the implications of these words from 'the only man I had met whom I felt to be definitely older than I'. Murry listens to Lawrence saying 'a few words about the revolution as to means – nationalisation of land, industry, railways' (BTW: 336–7), but admits, in the section of this journal entry not included in *Between Two Worlds*, that 'part of the time I was thinking of the remainder of my novel', and then continues with new thoughts about *Still Life*, apparently stimulated by Lawrence's larger vision:

> Anne must speculate in her mind about existence & the community, her end & what she has achieved; and the conclusion must have a glimpse of something more even than the common vision of Dennis and herself. The activity beyond the pinnacle of community; that is a moment, and there must be the glimpse of something more permanent. (MSX 4143)

Murry's rather convoluted prose here is an indication that he really had not grasped the essence of Lawrence's social vision. It is no wonder that he is stymied when he tries to work on the novel the following day: 'Whatever I write down here seems to be strangely unreal-false even while I write it, though afterwards it may seem tolerable.' Nonetheless, he could still shift his thoughts back to Lawrence and recognise that his friend 'is sad with some idea of the approaching sacrifice of his personality for his revolution. I like him so' (MSX 4143).

The influence of Lawrence's revolutionary ideas must have dissipated while Murry continued on with his novel; its conclusion is anything but visionary. It reveals instead a typically modernist fracturing of any notion of 'community'. Its characters remain self-enclosed, in self-imposed isolation. Anne's decision to travel to Avignon with Dennis at the novel's close is a spontaneous gesture, a going-along-with rather than a coming-together, an acceptance of mutuality rather than unison. Would it have been different had Murry remained longer with Lawrence, allowing their bond to deepen and mature? I think not. Murry, like Anne, Dennis, and Maurice in his novel, was a person whose emotions were extraordinarily contingent on immediate influences, and his enthusiasms rose and fell in waves of momentary attractions and fearful withdrawals. Murry recognised this trait in himself and specifically gave it to Maurice, his alter ego, whose 'whole life seemed to be histrionic, broken by one only impulse to throw himself into another's keeping, and thus be rid of the unending necessity of choosing and acting the part he chose' (SL: 8–9).

Much would change between Murry and Lawrence after their days of closeness at Greatham. Their friendship began to unravel, largely due to the disaster of their experiment in communal living in Cornwall in the spring of 1916, where he and Mansfield would witness scenes of violence between Lawrence and Frieda and realise the extent of Lawrence's escalating anger and despair.[1] Lawrence's mood after the couple moved away in June continued to darken, and his letters reveal increasing disappointment and rage. Perhaps not coincidentally, Katherine Mansfield was also experiencing extraordinary bouts of raging depression. She wrote to Ottoline Morrell on 27 October that she was 'just living on a kind of quaking crust with blackness underneath' (KMCL 1: 283).

Despite Murry's later recollection that during the autumn of 1916 he 'was on the verge of a sort of insanity' (RDHL: 82), the last weeks of the year might not have been as bleak for him as for Lawrence and Mansfield. He was finally experiencing some success as an author. *Still Life* was to be published in December, and the book he had written in Bandol shortly before the Cornwall venture, *Fyodor Dostoevsky: A Critical Study*, had appeared in August.[2] Lawrence disagreed with Murry's work on Dostoevsky and his correspondence uses his complaints about it as a springboard for personal attacks on Murry, such as the one to Koteliansky I quoted at the beginning of the first chapter in which he called *Still Life* a 'kind of wriggling self-abuse', but now situate in its temporal context. In that letter, written on 15 December 1916, Lawrence derides Murry for not being 'an artist, but only a little ego', and calls him 'a little muckspout'. He recollects how he had read *Still Life* in manuscript, but found it 'merely words, words' (LDHL 3: 53).

Lawrence's reaction to *Still Life* suggests a disturbance deeper than simply a recognition of the novel's obvious aesthetic flaws. His memories of the manuscript, which he had read nearly two years earlier, must have been shaky. He no longer remembered that he once had praised it to Ottoline Morrell.[3] It must have maddened Lawrence to see that it was to be published at all. That fact alone, after his disastrous experience with *The Rainbow* the previous year, seemed to have elicited his envious antagonism, especially because he feared that his new novel, *Women in Love*, would meet the same fate. And he was right to be worried, for his fears proved accurate. The book would not be published for another four years.

It is suggestive that Lawrence's complaint that *Still Life* is 'wriggling self-abuse' was made less than two weeks before he had the manuscript of the first version of *Women in Love* sent to Ottoline Morrell.[4] He would not send it to her because of good feelings or the desire to earn her praise, but to fend off what eventually actually happened: Ottoline's outrage, her threatened lawsuit, the end of their friendship. He already must have suspected that Murry was mixed up with it all; it might very well have been Murry who told Ottoline that she was 'the villainess of the new book' (LDHL 3: 41). The immediate and pressing problem for Lawrence was how to protect himself from Ottoline's reaction to his characterisation of Hermione. For instance, on 2 December he insisted in a letter to Catherine Carswell that Hermione is not Ottoline 'really at all – only suggested by her' and that 'it is probable she will think Hermione has nothing to do with her' (LDHL 3: 44).

Yet Lawrence did not feel it necessary to worry about Murry's reaction to his characterisation of Gerald Crich. It simply did not enter his head to think that Murry would see himself as Gerald, and nowhere in his letters does he suggest otherwise. Lawrence had already created the character of Gerald when he wrote the first version of the novel, *The Sisters*, before he had even met Murry.[5] It was actually Murry who was responsible for the widespread assumption that Gerald was based on himself. In his *Reminiscences of D. H. Lawrence* (1933), Murry said the following:

> the nature of my ignorance is shown by the fact that I did not, even in 1921, regard that crucial novel as having any special reference to *me*, and I had no suspicion that it had been written in 1916, or that the real core of it was precisely that abortive struggle between a conscious Lawrence and an unconscious Murry at Higher Tregerthen. (RDHL: 10)

Part of this is completely disingenuous. Of course Murry knew the novel had been written in 1916; everyone in Lady Ottoline's circle knew about it. The other part is more suggestive, and Murry developed it much further two years later in *Between Two Worlds*. He remarks that the 'theme, or at least the germ of it, was the relation and the situation between the four of us', and that years later he was 'really astonished when . . . Frieda told me that I was Gerald Crich' (BTW: 411). When he had read the novel after its publication in 1920, and wrote a hostile review of it, he did not recognise any of this. Suggestively, Murry quotes the passage where Birkin refers to his belief in 'the additional perfect relationship between man and man – additional to marriage', as an example of a detail taken from his conversations with Lawrence:

> This is more or less what Lawrence said to me, and no doubt the queer wrestling-match between the two is more or less what he meant by the 'blood-sacrament' between us at which he hinted. But I, being a little scared

and more than a little naïve, envisaged it rather as some sort of ceremony of black magic to be performed amid the great stones of the eerie Cornish moors. (BTW: 412)

Kinkead-Weekes believes that Murry 'was wholly mistaken in thinking that Gerald was meant as a portrait of him and the relationship with Gudrun as a treatment of his with Katherine' (Kinkead-Weekes 1995: 534), but he may not have given Murry enough credit for recognising an *interior* congruence.[6]The great difference between the rich, physically powerful, 'manly' Gerald, 'the Industrial Magnate', and the impoverished, 'boyish', itinerant intellectual Murry shields, but does not eliminate, many of the traces of the Murry/Lawrence relationship. Murry's statement that 'the real core' of *Women in Love* is 'that abortive struggle between a conscious Lawrence and an unconscious Murry at Higher Tregerthen' is not a negligible recognition. Neither is his belief that 'the theme, or at least the germ of it, was the relation and the situation between the four of us'. That Murry did not perceive this internal 'theme' at first is not surprising, as it is not presented with the flamboyantly obvious external details which had so outraged Ottoline Morrell about the portrayal of Hermione, and which, despite Lawrence's half-hearted protest to the contrary, were recognisable to every one of her circle who read the manuscript.

Lawrence knew that there would always be repercussions from his use of friends and family as subject matter for his fiction. He expected them to be as willing as he was to undergo the peculiar transformations his creative process brought about, and to realise how surface details were derived from many sources, often a number of individuals and differing histories. Just as he could distinguish himself from Paul Morel or Rupert Birkin, he expected Ottoline to do so with Hermione. If a transformation was successful, a new and unique being emerged, bearing only traces of its origins. Thus his objection on 20 November to Gilbert Cannan's novel *Mendel*: 'It is, as Gertler says, journalism: statement, without creation. This is very sickening. If Gilbert had taken Gertler's story and *re-created* it into art, *good*. But to set down all these statements is a vulgarising of life itself' (LDHL 3: 35).[7]

Yet Lawrence's hostility to *Still Life* was of a different order. Part of it might have stemmed from his recognition that Murry had intruded into his own territory, but Lawrence was most disturbed by the novel's self-reflexivity. It was not that it was autobiographical, but that it was so *transparently* a self-portrait that it embarrassed him by its level of self-criticism: its 'wriggling self-abuse'. It may not be entirely coincidental that Lawrence uses nearly the same image for Gerald close to the end of the first version of *Women in Love* (the one that Ottoline Morrell had read). He writes of the dead Gerald: 'Poor Gerald. Yet he had tried. But had he? – or had he only wriggled?' (Lawrence 1978: 442).

II

Murry's insistence that he never read *Women in Love* until after it was published in 1920 makes it futile to argue that *Still Life* was influenced by *Women in Love*. The reverse argument, that *Still Life* influenced *Women in Love*, would also be an insupportable contention. Nonetheless, an intertextual reading can bring forth the changing emotional valences of the Murry/Lawrence relationship, as well as some of the ideological and aesthetic issues behind each novel's representations. The novels each pursue a similar interrogation of the modern sensibility: its disillusionment and corruption; its awareness of the conflict between inherited notions of 'civilised' behaviour and subconscious and suppressed motivations. In reading *Women in Love* in tandem with *Still Life* one discovers a number of points of interpenetration, revealing a parallel responsiveness to a world their authors inhabited – at least partially – together. In this way biographical elements also work intertextually: if Gudrun Brangwen bears traces of Katherine Mansfield, so does Anne Cradock; if Gerald Crich bears traces of Murry, so does Maurice Temple. But it is more complicated than that. There are also traces of Murry in Birkin. And even more interestingly, traces of Gordon Campbell in Gerald. Or, I could say, traces of Dennis Beauchamp in Gerald.

Murry exposed in his protagonist, Maurice Temple, many of the same character flaws that Lawrence had so often criticised in Murry. Lawrence had berated Murry at the Cannan's Christmas party in 1914 for revealing his weakness before the crowd; now Murry was revealing it in print. Lawrence believed in saving face. He might allow for self-criticism in his depiction of his own alter ego, Birkin, in *Women in Love*, but he would not let it be the motivating power of the novel. Gudrun may criticise Birkin: '"He can't hear what anybody else has to say – he cannot hear . . . He cannot allow that there is any other mind than his own"' (WL: 263), but she prefaces her complaint with words of admiration: 'There is an extraordinary rich spring of life in him, really amazing, the way he can give himself to things' (WL: 262). Lawrence is able to show how Birkin comes to terms with his emotional limitations and does so largely through depicting the intense debates he has with Ursula, who dishes out criticism and reveals his self-delusions. Lawrence insists on Birkin emerging finally as the leader, the stronger personality able to take control because he has triumphed over his earlier debilitating despair.

The Birkin/Crick dyad seems to have absorbed a great deal of the emotional conflict, subliminal sexual desires and intellectual concerns of both the Cornwall and the earlier Rose Tree Cottage periods. Birkin's spiritual crisis, for instance, is quite reminiscent of Murry's 'intellectual mysticism' (BTW: 268) as Lawrence had observed it. Of course it corresponds with elements of Lawrence's own self-division as well, but it is cast in the same terms that he had often used to criticise Murry, revealing how much he served as Lawrence's 'other': the man on whom he could project his own psychological conflicts. So, here is Birkin in a low moment: 'He knew that his spirituality was concomitant of a process of depravity, a sort of pleasure in self-destruction. There really *was* a certain stimulant in self-destruction, for him – especially when it was translated spiritually' (WL: 309). Those long, pseudo-mystical discussions between Murry, Lawrence and Campbell are brought back into focus here – the 'stimulant' of 'self-destruction', the 'pleasure' in it which even Murry recognised as a 'vice' (BTW: 269). As we have already seen, that same passionate will-to-self-destruction permeates Murry's depiction of Maurice Temple in *Still Life*. Birkin's nihilism in the 'Prologue' Lawrence was writing while Murry and Mansfield lived next door reflects Birkin's sense that 'the whole world's constructive activity was a fiction, a lie, to hide the great process of decomposition, which had set in' (WL: 496). Like Maurice, whose sense of 'physical loneliness' made him feel that 'he was only trembling upon the brink of a void into which he never would be plunged' (SL: 402), Birkin is tormented by the question of 'how escape this phosphorescent passage into the tomb', and his nihilism is related to an 'incapacity to love, the incapacity to desire any woman, positively, with body and soul' (WL: 497).

But this negative 'spiritual' energy shifts from Birkin to Gerald as *Women in Love* proceeds. The description of Gerald after the death of his father is highly reminiscent of Murry's experience of the 'void' at Rose Tree Cottage: Gerald is 'like a man hung in chains over the edge of an abyss . . . Whatever he thought of, was the abyss – whether it were friends or strangers, or work or play, it all showed him only the same bottomless void in which his heart swung perishing' (WL: 337). Lawrence uses expressions such as 'the bottomless pit of nothingness', 'the ultimate experience of his own nothingness' (WL: 337) with repetitive force to finally propel Gerald out into the darkness 'through the wood, stumbling and feeling his way, to the Mill'. Gerald's first impulse, though mindless, is to run to Birkin, just as Murry had run, distraught and raging with fever, over the fields to Lawrence at Greatham. But Gerald discovers that Birkin is not at home, and continues to run – with equal mindlessness – onwards to Gudrun's house and his attempted resurrection through sexual love in 'the great bath of life' (WL: 344).

This phrase is reminiscent of Murry's in his description of Anne Cradock's effect on Maurice Temple: 'She had bathed him in herself' (SL: 119). Although Lawrence treats the initial sexual encounter between Gerald and Gudrun with his characteristic awareness of its implicit violence – for example, Gerald's 'starched linen . . . seemed to snap like pistol-shots' and Gudrun feels how 'the terrible frictional violence of death filled her' (WL: 344) – he resembles Murry in emphasising an essential maternalism in the woman's role in the sexual act. Murry had depicted Maurice crying with his head in Anne's lap, and her kissing him and saying 'You hurt like a child' (SL: 93). Lawrence writes: 'Mother and substance of all life she was. And he, child and man, received of her and was made whole' (WL: 344). Lawrence emphasises this image of child at its mother's breast by repeating it again and again: 'Like a child at the breast, he cleaved intensely to her . . . as an infant is at its mother's breast' (WL: 345) until Gerald 'was glad and grateful like a delirium, as he felt his own wholeness come over him again, as he felt the full, unutterable sleep coming over him, the sleep of complete exhaustion and restoration' (WL: 345).

The parallel with *Still Life* is most acute when Lawrence describes Gudrun's state of mind after this sexual encounter, how she 'lay wide awake, destroyed into perfect consciousness'. Gudrun is 'left with all the anguish of consciousness, whilst [Gerald] was sunk deep into the other element of mindless, remote, living shadow-gleam'. Aware of 'this awful, inhuman distance which would always be interposed between her and the other being', Gudrun realises that 'there was nothing to do but to lie still and endure'. She resents that and feels 'a dark understirring of jealous hatred that he should lie so perfect and immune, in an underworld, whilst she was tormented with violent wakefulness, cast out in outer darkness' (WL: 346). She feels exhausted, but 'must continue in this state of violent active superconsciousness . . . conscious of everything – her childhood, her girlhood, all the forgotten incidents'. She imagines that 'she must haul and haul at the rope of glittering conscious, pull it out phosphorescent from the endless depths of the unconsciousness, till she was weary . . . fit to break, and yet she had not done' (WL: 346). Similarly, Anne Cradock lies awake after her first sexual intercourse with Maurice: 'Even now the trace of a shudder passed through her as she recollected the agony with which she had, so vainly, prayed for unconsciousness' and she remembered 'how he had rested his head upon her breast and gone to sleep, while she had watched her own poignant unhappiness fade away' (SL: 177).

Another similarity is the reaction of each woman on the morning afterwards. Like Anne, who feels 'very old' after she 'passed back into herself' (SL: 178), Gudrun too feels 'old, old' in relation to her lover, whose 'face was so warm-looking, wide-eyed and full of newness, so perfect' (WL: 348). The two men's responses are also quite similar. Maurice, who that morning is moving 'quickly forward over the fields' and is 'happy in the steady harmonious march of his body', is much like Gerald, whose 'mind was beautifully still and thoughtless, like a still pool, and his body full and warm and rich' (WL: 349). Murry describes Maurice as putting out

> tendrils of being with nervous care, which slowly wound about the joy of health and active happiness. Gradually, more and more of himself seemed to work out of depression and insecurity into carelessness, out of a past where he was uncertain of himself into a future where he simply lived. (SL: 179)

The contrast then between 'a still pool' and 'a rope of glittering consciousness' is evident in both novels, and suggests an assumed dichotomy between women's weariness and men's post-coitus renewal of energy.

Obviously, this parallel between the two couples could simply be attributed to the fairly common sexual conundrum of premature male release and female dissatisfaction. But both Murry and Lawrence suggest more. The women, cast into the maternal role, remain guarded – like mothers watching over their children – and cannot lose consciousness. They carry the burden of the relationship, the responsibility. In keeping with his far greater understanding of the dynamics of sexuality, Lawrence is able to articulate the deeper manifestations of the problem better than Murry. The maternal impulse later becomes distorted, a function of a sexual struggle that is really a power struggle, a fight to the death:

> 'Ah, I don't want to torture you,' she said pityingly, as if she were comforting a child. The impertinence made his veins go cold, he was insensible. She held her arms round his neck, in a triumph of pity. And her pity for him was as cold as stone, its deepest motive was hate of him, and fear of his power over her, which she must always counterfoil. (WL: 443)

Gudrun's 'senses were entirely apart from him' when she asked Gerald to tell her he loved her: 'It was her overbearing *will* that insisted' (WL: 443). And Gerald felt such 'frightened rage and despair' that he thought '"If only I could kill her . . . I should be free". It seemed to him that death was the only severing of this Gordian knot' (WL: 442).

Murry's treatment of Maurice and Anne's sexuality emphasises instead Maurice's relative inexperience, his fruitless nostalgia for an even more 'innocent' lovemaking with his abandoned Madeleine. In *Still Life*, the will-to-violence in sexuality is not demonstrated by Maurice, but by Dennis Beauchamp, the friend and rival who plays a role in relation to him similar to that of Gerald to Birkin. Dennis pursues an instrumental sexuality reminiscent of Gerald's before his involvement with Gudrun, when 'after a debauch with some desperate woman he went on quite easy and forgetful' (WL: 233). Dennis considers his attraction to the young prostitute Josephine:

> 'I wonder now why I'm going home with this woman . . . It's not because I want her. I've wanted hundreds of women before – women of the same kind. I can't tell whether it's just vanity – the will to power. There's a good deal in that idea of the will to power'. (SL: 347)

Dennis later says that he '"was horrified at this cruelty that seemed to have taken shape inside"' him when he went home with the woman: '"I saw she was frightened of me; and when I saw that I wanted to be more and more cruel to her, so cruel . . . that she should not cry at all, but just stare at me – stare' (SL: 455). Lawrence describes Gerald's attraction to 'Pussum' in *Women in Love* in very similar terms:

> He felt an awful, enjoyable power over her, an instinctive cherishing very near to cruelty. For she was a victim. He felt that she was in his power, and he was generous. The electricity was turgid and voluptuously rich, in his limbs. He would be able to destroy her utterly in the strength of the discharge. (WL: 65)

Dennis and Gerald also share other traits, which suggest how the development of both characters might have been influenced by the friendships of their authors with Gordon Campbell. Dennis and Gerald are depicted as men of the world, powerful in arenas of consequence to society: medicine and industry. Yet each of them becomes disaffected by his socially approved functionality and is drawn towards the lure of escape into the bohemian milieu; each man is attracted to women involved in the arts; and each man becomes aroused at the sight of women dancing with other women: Anne and Josephine in *Still Life* (SL: 339–41), Gudrun and Ursula in *Women in Love* (WL: 91–2).

III

The structural frame of the internal conflicts in each novel reveals its submerged erotics. Lawrence constructs a foursome: two heterosexual couples; Murry constructs the more conventional triangle: two men and one woman. The triangle is energised by the element of homosocial desire – the rivalry of the men in relation to the woman. Lawrence eliminates that conventional rivalry by including two women; but he does not eliminate the desire. If anything, it is even more explicit because it does not have the excuse of homosocial rivalry to shield it. In both novels then, male/male relationships are of central importance.

Lawrence wrote the now notorious discarded 'Prologue' to *Women in Love* during April 1916, just at the time when Murry and Mansfield began their stay at Higher Tregerthen. By 1 May, Lawrence was already concerned that 'it is already beyond all hope of ever being published, because of the things it says' (LDHL 2: 602). There is disagreement amongst biographers about the likelihood of Lawrence's sexual attraction to Murry during this period. Janet Byrne describes a Lawrence 'struggling with a powerful attraction to [Murry]' and believes that the prologue 'was a forthright confession of Lawrence's newly activated love for Murry' (Byrne 1995: 201, 203). Kinkead-Weekes, on the other hand, may be too quick to dismiss any homosexual attraction of Lawrence towards Murry, by insisting that Murry was not one of Lawrence's two 'types' (and here Kinkead-Weekes uses Birkin's two types as synonymous with Lawrence's). This ignores the way homophobia operates to disguise original sources of desire. The differences between Murry and Gerald need not eliminate a subliminal erotic charge between Lawrence and Murry. That Murry was not one of Birkin's two types is true, but Lawrence's description of the two types of men who aroused Birkin – 'white-skinned, keen-limbed men with eyes like blue-flashing ice and hair like crystals of winter sunshine' and 'men with dark eyes that one can enter and plunge into . . . dark-skinned, supple, night-smelling men, who are the living substance of the viscous, universal, heavy darkness' (WL: 513–14) – is already highly aestheticised and need not correspond with Lawrence's own desires. Its schema involves artistic patterning of symbolic constructs of considerable complexity, where light and dark, north and south, mind and body culminate in Gerald's death by ice.

Kinkead-Weekes points out that Murry 'was intellectual and soulful, and it was *that* which made him lovable to Lawrence and drew Frieda's wrath' (KW: 330). Moreover, '"Little" Murry had the dark eyes of the other type, but certainly not the physical aura'. Somehow, to me this argument almost feels like 'wriggling'. Why should Kinkead-Weekes, who has already described the manner in which Lawrence's characters are often vastly altered versions of their supposed real-life models, be so hesitant here and anxious to disavow such an attraction? (Even the remark that Murry did not have the 'physical aura' is questionable in light of Murry's sexual appeal to so many people throughout his life.)[8]

Given that both Frieda Lawrence[9] and Katherine Mansfield felt threatened by Lawrence's intense focus on Murry during the Cornwall episode, I suspect that Murry was not quite as innocent as Kinkead-Weekes suggests when he remarks that 'Murry did not suppose blood-brotherhood involved homosexual relationship, though he could never see what it did involve' (KW: 331). When Murry first wrote about Lawrence's proposed blood-brotherhood sacrament in *Reminiscences*, soon after Lawrence's death, any published allusion to possible homo-sexuality would have been socially unthinkable. That does not mean that Murry himself would have been unable to think it. And Murry might have had at least a partial recognition of the submerged meaning behind Lawrence's words. If we look at Murry's own words here in the following passage, we can see how their ambiguity forces a reader to fill in the gaps. He describes how Lawrence's rages terrified him and Mansfield. How he heard Lawrence 'crying out from his bedroom next door: "Jack is killing me"' (RDHL: 72). He feared Lawrence's 'lapse into the mindless world':

> Half he wanted to resist it, half he desired to succumb. The real function of Katherine and myself was to help him resist it, but at other moments he wanted me to go with him. And all this was never formulated, never openly expressed between us. He wanted me to swear to be his 'blood-brother,' and there was to be some sort of sacrament between us. I said, perhaps rather childishly but with perfect sincerity, that I thought I was his 'blood-brother,' and I did not see the need of any sacrament. 'If I love you, and you know I love you, isn't that enough?' No, it was not enough: there ought to be some mingling of our blood, so that neither of us *could* go back on it. For some cause or other, I was half-frightened, half-repelled, and I suppose my shrink-ing away was manifest. He suddenly turned on me with fury: 'I hate your love, I *hate* it. You're an obscene bug, sucking my life away.' The vindictive-ness with which he said it made me almost physically sick. But the words were burnt into my brain. (RDHL: 73)

Murry's attempt to re-create this scene after fifteen years must have been hampered by a combination of editorial discretion, the need to construct his own self-image as an innocent, and his typical unwillingness to bring to consciousness his own subliminal motivations. Yet his selection of particular words and details is highly suggestive. Why, for example, does he not question what there was about himself that Lawrence might have believed was 'killing' him? What was this 'mindless world' and what would Murry's entry into it with him entail? If 'the real function' of *Katherine* and Murry 'was to help him resist it', why then was it only

Murry whom 'he wanted . . . to go with him' into it? Murry insists that 'all this was never formulated, never openly expressed between us'. It is not openly expressed between Murry and the reader either. The vagueness of his interpretation of this 'lapse into the mindless world' to which Lawrence 'half . . . wanted to resist' and 'half . . . desired to succumb' should make the reader of Murry's words aware of the libidinous quality of this interaction. Murry's ambivalence too is strengthened by his repetition of 'half' four times in the paragraph: Murry is only '*half*-frightened, *half*-repelled'.

In his later account in *Between Two Worlds*, Murry emphasises the timing of this episode. He says that as he 'began to withdraw towards Katherine', Lawrence 'felt my withdrawal' and 'became more urgent to bind me to him', now talking about blood-brotherhood: 'the need of some inviolable sacrament between us – some pre-Christian blood-rite in keeping with the primeval rocks about us' (BTW: 409). In this version of the episode Murry only comments: 'Timidly, I withdrew only the more'. It seems that Murry allowed this later interpretation to resemble the situation in *Women in Love*. He suggests that Lawrence's 'relation with Frieda left room, and perhaps need, for a relation with a man of something of the kind and quality of my relation with Katherine; and he wanted this relation with me' (BTW: 409). This is itself an odd sentence. Does he mean that Lawrence needed a relation with a man who would respond to Lawrence as he did with a woman? Murry's discomfort with that conclusion is revealed in the clumsiness and ambiguity of his sentence. His phrasing is reminiscent of that in his own suppressed letter to Gordon Campbell: 'I can hear Lawrence say that it would only have been possible between a man and a woman. I don't think so. It would have been possible for us, had you been other than you are' (Glenavy 1964: 65).

Lawrence's treatment of Gerald's reaction to Birkin's proposal of *Blutbruderschaft* suggests he understood more of Murry's reaction to his own proposal than Murry had. He describes Gerald as 'so deeply bondaged in fascinated attraction, that he was mistrustful, resenting the bondage, hating the attraction' (WL: 207). And when 'Birkin sought hard to express himself', 'Gerald hardly listened. His face shone with a certain luminous pleasure' yet 'he kept his reserve. He held himself back'. Gerald's response when Birkin puts out his hand to him was 'just' to touch it, 'as if withheld and afraid': '"We'll leave it till I understand it better," he said, in a voice of excuse.' Birkin feels 'a little sharp disappointment, perhaps a touch of contempt came into his heart'. Interestingly, only a 'touch of contempt' here, not the furious outburst of rage as in Murry's account.

But in the earlier version of *Women in Love*, the version of 1916, closer to the event which inspired this scene, Gerald 'convulsively . . . clasped Birkin's hand in both his'. Lawrence here depicts a Gerald who seems to long for Birkin's love, who asks him 'with hot eyes and a pleading voice: "I often wonder . . . what you think of me – whether you care for me – well, at all – any more than you do for any man you meet in the streets"' (Lawrence 1998: 190–1). *This* Gerald is the one who has the passion:

> He wanted the other man to put his arms round him, and hold him. He could not look at Birkin's dark, steadfast eyes any more, he turned aside, panting slightly, because he so much wanted the other man to take him in his arms and hold him close in peace and love. Yet it was so impossible.
>
> 'A Blutbruderschaft,' said Birkin, wearily, reassuring, as if to comfort the other. (Lawrence 1998: 191)

In this earlier version, Birkin seems surprised by Gerald's intense interest in him. The erotic charge comes from Gerald; Birkin in *response* feels 'a hot pang of love for him, and a deep pity, a deep sorrow. Then finally a cold weariness'. Lawrence has not as yet made the thematic relevance of this scene explicit, which he does in the final version of the novel:

> the problem of love and eternal conjunction between two men. Of course this was necessary – it had been a necessity inside himself all his life – to love a man purely and fully. Of course he had been loving Gerald all along – and all along denying it. (WL: 206)

Lawrence concludes the episode with Birkin's recognition of Gerald's limitations, of 'the man himself, complete, and as if fated, doomed, limited'. He sees in him a man 'limited to one form of existence, one knowledge, one activity' and – in a phrase curiously appropriate to Murry's own usage – 'a sort of fatal *halfness*, which to himself seemed wholeness' (my emphasis).

Earlier in the novel, Lawrence had described 'a pause of strange enmity between the two men, that was very near to love', 'a strange, perilous intimacy which was either hate or love, or both':

> They parted with apparent inconcern, as if their going apart were a trivial occurrence. And they really kept it to the level of trivial occurrence. Yet the heart of each burned from the other. They burned with each other, inwardly. This they would never admit. They intended to keep their relationship a casual free-and-easy friendship, they were not going to be so unmanly and unnatural as to allow any heart-burning between them. They had not the faintest belief in deep relationship between man and man, and their disbelief prevented any development of their powerful but suppressed friendliness. (WL: 33–4)

Lawrence here emphasises the subliminal nature of the erotic attraction, the avoidance of the 'unmanly' and the 'unnatural'. As the novel progresses, Gerald's resistance to Birkin demonstrates how he is unable to go further than affectionate camaraderie:

> Gerald was held unconsciously by the other man. He wanted to be near him, he wanted to be within his sphere of influence. There was something very congenial to him in Birkin. But yet, beyond this, he did not take much notice . . . It was the quick-changing warmth and versatility and brilliant warm utterance he loved in his friend. It was the rich play of words and quick interchange of feelings he enjoyed. The real content of the words he never really considered: he himself knew better.
>
> Birkin knew this. He knew that Gerald wanted to be *fond* of him without taking him seriously. And this made him go hard and cold. (WL: 59)[10]

This passage resembles Murry's recollection that he had only wanted from Lawrence 'the warmth and security of personal affection'; but here it seems clear that Lawrence recognised Murry's resistance to becoming 'disciples of the same idea' (BTW: 332).

Lawrence immediately juxtaposes his analysis of Gerald's inability to understand Birkin with Birkin's accompanying thoughts about the end of 'Humanity'. It is perfectly appropriate that in this context of repressed desire Birkin considers 'if our race is destroyed like Sodom' (WL: 59), alluding to the 'sin' that Lawrence had suppressed by eliminating his overtly homosexual 'Prologue'. Sodom is enacted in both *Women in Love* and *Still Life* through depictions of degenerate Bohemias: Lawrence's in London; Murry's in Paris. These are the sanctuaries for the 'painters, musicians, writers – hangers-on, models, advanced young people, anybody who is openly at outs with the conventions, and belongs to nowhere particularly' (WL: 69). In one instance, Lawrence draws details from exactly the same Bohemian party that Murry had used in *Still Life*, which takes place in Ramsay's studio where Anne and Dennis first meet Miss Etheredge. Gudrun's description of the '"*fine* party one night in Fanny Rath's studio"' (WL: 393) evokes the one Mansfield and Murry had attended during their trip to Paris in December 1912, which predated their acquaintance with Lawrence, who evidently heard about it later from Gordon Campbell.[11] It also bears a connection with the Cannan's Christmas party of 1914, with its 'atmosphere – very like a Dostoievsky novel' (MSX 4147: 52).

Despite Lawrence's defensive explanation to Gertler about Loerke's origins, there is still enough in the portrait to link it with Gertler: the Jewish background, childhood poverty, 'the black look of inorganic misery, which lay behind all his small buffoonery' (WL: 422). Some of the details may recall also Francis Carco, who was the intended lover

Gertler was standing in for in the dramatisation at the Cannan's party, although this could only be Carco as Lawrence might have imagined him, as they had never met. The suggestions of bisexuality, 'the figure of a boy, almost of a street arab', the 'strange, dumb, depraved look of knowledge' (WL: 422), are details similar to those in Mansfield's version of Carco in 'Je ne parle pas français', which I will discuss in Chapter 4.

Lawrence is said to have incorporated features of Mark Gertler's great painting *Merry-Go-Round* (1916) in the granite frieze Loerke had designed for a factory in Germany:[12]

> It was a representation of a fair, with peasants and artizans in an orgy of enjoyment, drunk and absurd in their modern dress, whirling ridiculously in roundabouts, gaping at shows, kissing and staggering and rolling in knots, swinging in swing-boats and firing down shooting galleries, a frenzy of chaotic motion. (WL: 423)

Yet Lawrence's description here, though it contains the roundabouts and the modern dress, resembles less Gertler's rigidly mechanical figures in his painting and more Murry's Parisian street fair in *Still Life*. Murry's description of the street fair emphasises its 'frenzy of chaotic motion'; its climax is the ride on the roundabout, a juxtaposition of Murry's cast of bored, intellectual sophisticates and the machine of childhood pleasures:

> The man in the white shoes came forward to the top of the steps and shouted out that it was the last turn but one . . . The whole crowd seemed to surge forward on to the steps. Into the swans, on the horses, swarmed pairs. Into the motor-cars crowded fours. It took a long while for the men to collect the money. The machine revolved more slowly under the new weight. Even the organ seemed to groan painfully. (SL: 415)

The ludicrous combination of swans, horses and miniature motorcars – a mixture of unrelated components both organic and mechanical – suggests an ironic take on modernism. This is no Futurist revelling in the beauty of modern technology. As in *Women in Love*, the pleasure-seeking in *Still Life* masks a descent into deeper levels of despair. The street fair scene is preceded by a disjointed discussion in a restaurant where Maurice and Anne desultorily admit when they are questioned about their plans that they have '"[n]o more idea than we had yesterday"' and that '"it doesn't matter very much"' (SL: 397). Maurice feels disconnected from everyone, even his mentor, the Fauvist painter Ramsay, who now seems to him 'remote and trivial'.

Discussions of the significance of art to the current crisis of modern civilisation are features of both *Women in Love* and *Still Life*. By this late moment in Murry's novel, the whole subject of art itself is no longer

even a possible source of meaning for Maurice, who responds 'mechani-
cally' to a discussion of one artist's new painting: 'He was nearly
impelled to tell them that he would never see any pictures any more.
They had for him neither use nor meaning' (SL: 398–9). Then he lashes
out at the artists around him while he

> recoiled from the sight of his own disintegration. 'But I don't see how you
> can expect to be primitives in 1913. The world-consciousness or whatever
> you call it, won't allow it; or if it does allow, it's no more than a protest, like
> throwing a brick through a plate-glass window. You talk about moderns –
> but really, there hasn't been a modern painter since Rembrandt. And even
> now he's a hundred years ahead of you . . . But you know you haven't suc-
> ceeded in being a bit more modern than the people who began your move-
> ment. You've only made a theory out of their work that they never had
> themselves. (SL: 399)

Maurice's friend counters with '"Oh, you're an impossible reactionary"', perhaps a reminder of Murry's own ambivalent stance towards
avant-garde modernism, a subject to which I will return in subsequent
chapters.

Implicit in Maurice's 'reactionary' position here is his old ideal of
'harmony in the soul', which I discussed in Chapter 1. In fact, this conversation about modern art – after Maurice's disillusioning involvement
with Anne – reveals that he has not moved from the position he held
before his affair began. At the dinner party where he had met Anne, he
argued with one of the fashionable guests about the function of art in
relation to modern civilisation. He was unimpressed with her comment:
'"We're effete. The only thing to do is to go back to the primitive,
uncontrolled people. They're splendid, unconscious"' (SL: 23). Maurice
countered with his preference for Greek sculpture with its '"repose, or
calm, or dignity"' (SL: 33). That emphasis on 'harmony', which we have
seen was at the centre of Murry's youthful aesthetics and philosophy,
must have seemed particularly simplistic and suspicious to Lawrence. It
cannot be accidental that Lawrence gives Gerald a similar ideal:

> he had come to the conclusion that the essential secret of life was harmony.
> He did not define to himself at all clearly what harmony was. The word
> pleased him, he felt he had come to his own conclusions. And he proceeded to
> put his philosophy into practice by forcing order into the established world,
> translating the mystic word harmony into the practical word organisation.
> (WL: 227)[13]

Despite Lawrence's disappointment with Murry and his statement of
7 November that he was through with him, by 22 January 1917, he was
tentatively asking Gordon Campbell: 'have you heard of Murry lately?'

(LDHL 3: 81). The emotions of Birkin in the first version of the novel seem closer to Lawrence's sense of loss over Murry's defection than in the final, more schematic ending of the published *Women in Love*:

> 'Never mind,' he whispered to his dead friend. 'Never mind, perhaps it had to be this way – But I had hoped–' the hot tears of anguish surged up from his heart again – 'I had hoped we might all be happy together, Gerald'.
> Birkin cried in a paroxysm of pain beside the dead body.
> 'And it's failed,' he murmured, in a poignancy of pain, 'you're dead'.
> (Lawrence 1998: 443)

Notes

1. See Alpers (1980: 200–14), Tomalin (1988: 145–53), and Kinkead-Weekes (KW: 311–28) for descriptions of the Cornwall debacle.
2. Murry also wrote introductions for two translations that he had worked on with Koteliansky: Dostoevsky's *Pages From the Journal of an Author*, and Lev Shestov's *Anton Tchekhov, and Other Essays*, which were published in December, the same month as a *Still Life*.
3. On 22 February 1915, Lawrence told Ottoline Morrell that Murry 'is just finishing his novel – his first – *very* good' (LDHL 2: 292).
4. The manuscript had already been seen by several other friends of Lawrence, including the poet H. D. (Hilda Doolittle). Apparently, it was she who forwarded it to Ottoline according to Lawrence's instructions. For a full account of the fate of this early manuscript, see the introduction to *The First 'Women in Love'* (Lawrence 1998: xix–lv).
5. Kinkead-Weekes, in his 'Appendix' to the Penguin edition of *Women in Love* (Kinkead-Weekes 1995: 534), mentions other models for Gerald, such as Thomas Philip Barber, who had modernised his mines near Eastwood.
6. Kinkead-Weekes sees similarities between Gudrun and Mansfield, however, such as their 'sharpness of tongue and liking to pin people down in a phrase' (KW 1995: 533).
7. Frieda Lawrence was more sanguine than Ottoline about seeing herself in *Mendel*. She remarked: 'I suppose I am the murdered woman. We live and learn, I never recognized myself! . . . I was sorry that Gilbert made me quite so horrid, so vulgar. But there' (F. Lawrence 1982: 218).
8. Claire Tomalin remarks that 'some attraction drew both men and women to him like flies to honey' (Tomalin 1988: 97).
9. In Murry's journal of 12 August 1956, he copied a recent letter from Frieda in which she remarked: 'I think my nose was a bit out of joint when you stayed with us and L. was more interested in you than in me' (MSX 4160: 167).
10. See Lawrence's letter of 15 August 1915: 'Murry says that the spirit matters, but that an idea is bad. He says he believes in what I say, because he believes in me . . . He says the whole thing is personal: that between him and me it is a case of Lawrence and Murry, not of any union in an idea' (LDHL 2: 380).

11. Frieda Lawrence mentioned 'just a bit of a party where Campbell was in Paris at Ann Estelle Rice', in a letter to Koteliansky on 6 February 1917 (F. Lawrence 1982: 219).
12. See KW, 343, for a discussion of how Lawrence 'would proceed to alter the whole nature of Loerke's frieze' after seeing a photograph of Gertler's painting.
13. There might be an ironic subtext here of Lawrence's annoyance with Murry's increasing involvement with the establishment. By the time he published *Women in Love*, Murry was editor of the *Athenaeum*.

Chapter 3

From *Still Life* to 'Bliss'

I

The gradual shift from the influence of Lawrence to that of Bloomsbury marks a significant turning point in Murry's and Mansfield's positioning within British modernism. Their tentative, still awkward entry into the circle around Lady Ottoline Morrell at Garsington in the summer of 1916 would lead them in new directions, with profound consequences. It would not take long, however, for the same configurations of erotic desire and displaced sexual energy that lurked behind Murry's writing of *Still Life* to surface under the pressures of a new, if painfully familiar, triangular situation. This time Mansfield's jealousy would not be aroused by Murry's intimacy with another man – as it had been with Campbell and Lawrence – but another woman: Ottoline Morrell. It may well be that the events I describe in this chapter form the emotional background of one of Mansfield's most famous stories, 'Bliss' (1918). C. A. Hankin goes so far as to assert that 'the germ' of Mansfield's 'central idea in "Bliss" . . . seems to have been her own and Murry's relationship with Ottoline Morrell' (Hankin 1983: 142).

Beyond that 'germ', however, is the strong relationship between numerous elements of the story with Murry's *Still Life*. Its central character, Bertha Young, resembles Anne Cradock. Both are women around thirty, married, financially secure, their social lives centred in a world of fashionable people, artists and writers, up to date on the latest craze. Both women are hostesses, interested in bringing together the producers and consumers of 'art'. At the Cradocks', 'art' is represented by the young writer Maurice as well as by Anne's husband, Jim Cradock, a drama critic, at the Youngs' by 'the Norman Knights – a very sound couple – he was about to start a theatre, and she was awfully keen on interior decoration', as well as a young poet, Eddie Warren, 'whom everybody was asking to dine' (KMCS: 95). Both women shield, through surface gaiety, an unacknowledged dissatisfaction with the outward perfection of their lives. Characteristically, Mansfield begins with Bertha's 'bliss' and then proceeds to demolish it through the revelation of her husband's infidelity with the very woman Bertha also desired. The feeling of 'bliss' corresponds with awakening sexual desire in a woman who has been frigid with her husband in a marriage where they considered themselves to be 'such good pals'. No such frigidity bothers Anne Cradock, however. She seems comfortable with her husband: 'The atmosphere of his big physical perfections enveloped all her wilfulness and contrariety in a subtle security' (SL: 69), but she knows that he does not take her seriously. Whenever 'she had attempted to tell the truth about herself, he had been distracted, comprehending nothing, sure that he was deeply understanding when he had stroked her hair and had dismissed the attempted exposure as fanciful' (SL: 70).

The moment of 'bliss' occurs to both women while they are out walking: Bertha before her dinner party, Anne the morning afterwards. Mansfield's story begins: 'Although Bertha Young was thirty she still had moments like this when she wanted to run instead of walk, to take dancing steps on and off the pavement, to bowl a hoop, to throw something up in the air . . .' (KMCS: 91). Murry also juxtaposes Anne's longing for the abandon of childhood pleasures with a recognition of her age. Before she leaves the house she studies herself in the mirror and remarks: '"I'm young enough"' (SL: 48), and during her walk 'the omnibuses were toy omnibuses, the motor-cars were toy motor-cars, and the people were for all the world tin soldiers or their brothers; everything seemed to be going very fast, while she looked upon it all from an immense distance above, as though it were a wonderful game spread out for delight' (SL: 51).

Murry, however, cannot convey Anne's 'bliss' with the immediacy of Mansfield's absorption in it. Anne tells herself: '"I feel very happy. I never believe Spring can do it, until it does"', but then catches herself with '"Oh! What nonsense. What was it I wanted? . . . oh, my bag . . . I've left it about somewhere"' (SL: 48). In contrast, Mansfield lets the reader enter directly into Bertha's consciousness:

> What can you do if you are thirty and, turning the corner of your own street, you are overcome, suddenly, by a feeling of bliss – absolute bliss! – as though you'd suddenly swallowed a bright piece of that late afternoon sun and it burned in your bosom, sending out a little shower of sparks into every particle, into every finger and toe? (KMCS: 91–2)

Aside from the vast difference in their skills in exposition, Murry's and Mansfield's presentations of the state of 'bliss' diverge in the matter of distance from the sensuous details each character perceives. Anne is a voyeur. She *watches*. Her stimuli are all visual. Bertha's very body is *entered* by the piece of sun that she has 'swallowed', and she feels its shower of sparks in 'every particle' of her body. She realises immediately the wide gulf between her honest acceptance of her body's pleasure and society's strictures against admitting that pleasure: '"Oh is there no way you can express it without being 'drunk and disorderly'? How idiotic civilisation is! Why be given a body if you have to keep it shut up in a case like a rare, rare fiddle?"' (KMCS: 92).

Similar sentiments occur to Anne Cradock, but Murry constructs the opposition between desire and 'civilisation' both more narrowly and more concretely. As Anne continues her walk, she is 'compelled to ask the policeman which was the way to the Marble Arch, although she knew it perfectly well . . . She felt she had been found out, and hurried away, until she reached a seat where the policeman could see her no more' (SL: 50). Anne's guilty pleasure in her increasing desire must therefore be tested by her momentary contact with authority. Once she's out of sight of the policeman, she can sink back into her self-absorption:

> Immediately she was tired with the intoxication of the spring air, and far too lazy to think, she said to herself. [Bertha Young also feels 'quite dizzy, quite drunk. It must have been the spring. Yes, it was the spring. Now she was so tired she could not drag herself upstairs to dress' (SL: 97).] And she sat still for a long time with her eyes closed, drowsily happy to feel that the blood was hurrying about in her veins and conscious only of her eager bodily existence. Even she clasped her hands together, knowing that they were already too hot, in order that she might feel the goodness of her own flesh. And she wondered why it should be improper for her to pass her hands down her legs and delight herself in the sense that they were firm and hard. (SL: 50–1)

Murry's description tends to make Anne's desire narcissistic. There is an implied mirror here, an imposition of a male gaze to which the self-pleasuring is directed. By focusing specifically on the hotness of her flesh and on her legs – objects of male sexual desire – Murry's understanding of Anne's behaviour seems conventionally masculine. Although he tries to imagine – and sympathetically convey – Anne's awakening desire, he perceives it primarily as *visually* stimulated and finally, mental, as Anne futilely proceeds to analyse her feelings of excitement: 'all her thinking was not doing very much good, although she had spent a very long time over it' (SL: 51). This is all very much like what Lawrence called 'sex in the head'. Bertha Young's body consciousness throughout 'Bliss' is instead conveyed by imagery of internal flowering, of women's *hidden* sexual intensities: 'this blissful treasure that burned in their bosoms and dropped, in silver flowers, from their hair and hands' (KMCS: 102).

Anne's excitement seems not to have a conscious object for its fulfilment. She does not acknowledge to herself that it began following a
conversation with her husband at breakfast about the immature young
man, Maurice Temple, who spoke so much at their party the previous
evening. Anne was 'exhilarated by the conversation and the morning'
and though she began to be self-critical when she looked at herself in
the mirror, she decided 'it would be silly to go on thinking, because the
excitement was too good to be destroyed, nor could she have subdued
it' (SL: 47). She does not think about Maurice throughout her walk, and
when it ends, she is surprised to find herself at the British Museum, 'tin-
gling with an involuntary excitement', wondering whether her direction
was accidental or whether 'the idea had been at the back of [her] mind
all day' (SL: 53). Of course she is drawn there by Maurice's conversation
about 'the Greek heads' the night before. The coincidence of him turning
up as she sits looking at *The Three Fates* is simply a conventional plot
device.

That conventional plotting here relies on the equally conventional
assumption that a reader will know what is behind Anne's excitement
before she does. But Mansfield's story upsets such conventions. Bertha
Young is equally unaware of the cause of her excitement, but unlike
Anne Cradock's, which is a relatively straightforward attraction to
a younger man, Bertha's 'bliss' is ambiguous, involving suppressed
desires and forbidden sexuality. Its intensity seems directed towards
another woman, Pearl Fulton, whom Mansfield describes as 'a "find"'
of Bertha's. 'They had met at the club and Bertha had fallen in love
with her, as she always did fall in love with beautiful women who
had something strange about them' (KMCS: 95). This is not just an
enthusiastic appreciation for a woman friend, equivalent to Bertha's
other enthusiasms: 'this absolutely satisfactory house and garden. And
friends – modern, thrilling friends, writers and painters and poets or
people keen on social questions' (KMCS: 96). Pearl's very presence
causes Bertha to ask herself: 'What was there in the touch of that cool
arm that could fan – fan – start blazing – blazing – the fire of bliss that
Bertha did not know what to do with?' (KMCS: 99). It is Pearl Fulton
with whom she stands looking at the pear tree in blossom: 'caught
in that circle of unearthly light, understanding each other perfectly'
(KMCS: 102).

It is only when Bertha tries to imagine explaining to her husband
when they 'are in bed to-night', what she and Pearl 'have shared', that
her 'bliss' becomes intermixed with anxiety: 'something strange and
almost terrifying darted into Bertha's mind. And this something blind
and smiling whispered to her: "Soon these people will go . . . And you

and he will be alone together in the dark room – the warm bed . . .'". The very thought leads her to run over to the piano, to exclaim twice incongruously, '"What a pity someone does not play!"' She suddenly recognises, overtly, her sexual desire: 'For the first time in her life Bertha Young desired her husband'. Her libido is thus transferred from the forbidden lesbian desire to an acceptable heterosexual resolution: 'But now – ardently! ardently! The word ached in her ardent body! Was this what that feeling of bliss had been leading up to? But then then –' (KMCS: 103–4).

But notice how Bertha still questions. What does her new awareness portend? And why does it still produce in her more anxiety, which is expressed in the way she behaves when her guests begin to depart: '"Good night, good-bye" she cried from the top step, feeling that this self of hers was taking leave of them forever' (KMCS: 103)? Shortly she will discover her husband making an assignation with Pearl: her two newly revealed objects of desire are secretly involved with each other. How quickly is her newly found 'bliss' deflated! Mansfield gives neither Bertha nor the reader any opening for escape. The rules of polite 'civilisation' are maintained: Miss Fulton thanks Bertha and reminds her of '"your lovely pear tree"'; Harry Young remains 'extravagantly cool and collected'. Bertha's final question, '"Oh, what is going to happen now?"', is unanswered: 'But the pear tree was as lovely as ever and as full of flower and as still' (KMCS: 105).

It may be that Mansfield has cut off the possibility of Bertha's awakening bearing fruit because she knows that Bertha does not have the *power* to let that 'self of hers . . . [take] leave of them forever'. From the beginning of the story, she depicts Bertha with a combination of sympathy and a nearly cruel satirical thrust of criticism. Each momentary rise of elation in Bertha is rapidly deflated by a revelation of how little power she really has in her household. Her baby is in the care of a nurse who does not want her interfering: 'How absurd it was, why have a baby if it has to be kept – not in a case like a rare, rare fiddle – but in another woman's arms?' (KMCS: 94). (These last words provide a clever bit of foreshadowing.)

In her relations with her husband, Bertha is clearly dominated by his strong personality. Moreover, he is the one who has made possible 'this absolutely satisfactory house and garden', as well as the books and music and travel and the 'new cook' who 'made the most superb omelettes' (KMCS: 96). This implicit *economic* power has much to do with Bertha's childishness, her need to embellish her body in beautiful clothing and her house with artistic arrangements of fruit for the dinner table. While on the surface she appears to have the autonomy to direct her life's course, she actually remains fixed in her passivity, as 'still' as the tree she yearns towards.

The power dynamics in *Still Life* are completely inverted. Anne Cradock is the powerful partner. *She* seeks out Maurice. *She* decides to run away with him. *She* is the actor, Maurice the acted upon (at least during the first part of the novel). Anne's assertiveness grows from a central core of self-assurance unknown to Bertha Young, based on Anne's economic autonomy. Anne is able to leave her husband because she has her own income. That income, in fact, makes it possible for her to take Maurice to Paris, buy him elegant clothes and expensive cuff-links, and encourage him to stop scrounging for journalistic writing assignments and concentrate on serious writing. Consequently, Maurice's dependence is an important subtext of the novel. In a very revealing passage, Maurice realises that if he left Anne, he would have to find a way to make a living again:

> The idea flickered into a half-reality and faded away. It came back contorted, revealing a sordid depth in himself that he could not believe. Without Anne he would have no money: he would have to go too – go to Cradock again. (SL: 403)

The irony here, emphasised by the repetition at the end, is that while Anne need not be dependent upon her husband, Cradock, for financial support, her lover might have to turn back to him for an income. (Cradock had been providing Maurice with writing assignments for his paper.) Maurice's guilt over the 'sordid depth in himself' causes him to try to push these thoughts away and resurrect his feelings for Anne:

> God alone knew what he would have to do. He could not think about that; but to be without Anne was real to him, now that it meant to be without money. That he could see and feel. 'My god,' he moaned to himself, striving to thrust the thought away, loathing the very mechanism of his mind that had brought it before him. It dissolved away. His mind and his body were one in passionate hunger to be enfolded in Anne's arms again. (SL: 403)

At the heart of Maurice's situation is his growing awareness of his emotional impotence, his inability to escape from an existential meaninglessness. His need for Anne remains always infantile: he is the child seeking wholeness through symbiosis with the maternal: 'He could not look into the void without her, it was too close and too terrible. It was in him now. His mouth opened. He looked upwards suddenly, as one who sees a horror and cannot trust that the world is real' (SL: 401). Since the maternal so thoroughly determines his relations with Anne, it is not surprising to find that the erotic charge of her presence for him is not strong. Whenever Murry describes Maurice longing for Anne, he emphasises the need to be held in her arms, to be comforted, to be made to feel complete. It is almost embarrassing to reiterate the now commonplace interpretation of the psychological dynamics here. Nearly a century's worth of Freudian theorising makes Maurice's oedipal problem obvious to a contemporary reader. For of course Maurice's diminishing sexual ardour for Anne is a function of his cultural inheritance of the virgin/whore dichotomy that a patriarchal society has constructed as a corollary of the oedipal paradigm. Although Anne would be considered a free woman sexually (after all, she is engaged in what society calls an adulterous affair), which ordinarily would place her in the 'whore' category, she is experienced by Maurice as a representative of the other half of the dichotomy. In fact, Murry actually conveys her as such at one point in the novel through Dennis, who describes her as '"bewilderingly virgin" . . . a certain naiveness in what he knew was the perfection of her movement, recalled to his mind unsophisticated pictures, always of the Virgin, and always pictures' (SL: 321).

The incest taboo operates to undermine any attempt on Maurice's part to explore a more convulsive, wilder sexuality. Even taking into account Murry's sense of novelistic decorum – he was writing *Still Life* years before *Lady Chatterley's Lover* – the erotic temperature of the novel is low. Curiously, there is more sexual tension when Maurice remembers Miss Etheredge's 'massive body' and how he had wanted 'to kiss' her, thus eliciting the rise of colour to his cheeks and an 'excited shortness' to his breath, than in most of the passages describing Maurice's attraction to Anne.

Maurice's repressions are loosened somewhat by the stimuli of the urban scene. The Paris streets, the lively cafés, the music and dancing provide momentary release. Shortly after Maurice's realisation that he might lose Anne (and her money), when he resolves his self-disgust through a sense that 'his mind and his body were one in passionate hunger to be enfolded in Anne's arms again' (SL: 403), he is drawn to the sight of the street fair. A definite shift in mood takes place here, and Murry describes how 'the triumphant steam organ magnified a whistled tune into an orgy of music, that poured out with the flooding light'. It is hard to resist making a comment about the obvious phallic connotations of this passage, one of a number in the novel where one feels that Murry *must* have been aware of their sexual nature. For my purposes here, it is probably better to imagine that Murry was not aware of the image's Freudian implications, for by not becoming self-conscious and eliminating it, he reveals the underlying libidinal rhythm in the novel's structure that relates to its most frustrating aesthetic problem. As a novel without a satisfying 'climax', its title becomes perfectly appropriate.

The meaning and effect of 'stillness' resonate differently in *Still Life* and 'Bliss'. Both narratives conclude with their protagonists set adrift, their futures uncertain. Maurice, when challenged by Miss Etheredge to respond to her attack – '"You think you're the hell of a fine fellow because you've made a muck of everything – quite proud of it"' – chooses not to argue: 'Inwardly he asked himself if it were true. The answer seemed to tremble like the needle of a balance, and be trembling still, while he said, holding out his hand: "Well, good-bye"' (SL: 463). Although the trope suggests a slight modicum of motion, it is only the motion of stasis – a 'trembling' of the suppressed. The needle must always return to the still point of the balance. The miniaturisation of the phallic figure suggests simultaneously the infantile and the impotent. The novel's narrative energy is depleted, reminding us of Murry's later recognition that with *Still Life* he was 'analyzing [his] own inward life to immobility' (BTW: 397).

'Bliss' also ends in stasis: 'the pear tree was as lovely as ever and as still'. Yet the stasis at the end of 'Bliss' is not that of enervation, nor is it the inability to allow submerged desires to surface and be realised. Despite Bertha's entrapment in the trivialities of social existence, despite her ignorance of the libidinal sources of her bliss, there is yet a courage in her leap of hope, her desire to believe in the possibility of communion with another, and to be willing to look at Pearl Fulton and feel 'as if the longest, most intimate look had passed between them – as if they had said to each other: "You, too?" – that Pearl Fulton . . . was feeling just what she was feeling' (KMCS: 100).

Of course, such willingness to believe makes Bertha a fool – as all lovers are, by definition, fools. But that sudden opening to ecstatic possibility is what turns Mansfield's story from satire to tragedy. Bertha is far more than the socialite still gently teased by Mansfield's reference to 'the beautiful red soup in the grey plate' (a reminder of the limitations of Bertha's aesthetic impulses). Through the rhythm and imagery of Mansfield's prose, we sense the depths of feelings beyond Bertha's powers of articulation: the 'ardent' 'ardent' passions 'burning' in the luminous night. Although Bertha's epiphanic moment is brutally destroyed afterwards in the knowledge of her husband's and Pearl's duplicity, the symbol of its creative fertility retains its potency: still, but in flower.

II

While Murry and Mansfield lived in Rose Tree Cottage during the early months of the war, their social milieu had been dominated by Lawrence's powerful presence. Lawrence was the central intellectual force within the group of artists and writers who mingled at the Cannans' windmill, which 'became for a time a poor man's Garsington' (Farr 1978: 108). It was Gilbert Cannan who provided Murry's initial connection with Lady Ottoline Morrell by introducing Lawrence to her in 1914 (KW 131). She began visiting Lawrence while he lived at Greatham in the early months of 1915, and one of her visits, on 23 February, occurred while Murry was staying there. Only the day before, Lawrence had prepared her for meeting Murry with high praise for his friend, calling him 'one of the men of the future', and telling her that his novel in progress is '*very* good': 'At present he is my partner – the only man who quite simply is with me – One day he'll be ahead of me. Because he'll build up the temple if I carve out the way' (LDHL 2: 291).

Little did Lawrence know that Murry was seething with envy during Ottoline's visit. She only noticed that when they 'climbed to the top of the Downs to look at the view towards Arundel and the sea – a view by which [Lawrence] said he tested the character of his friends . . . Murry lagged with a melancholy air behind us as we climbed' (Morrell 1964: 276). Murry's journal entry for that day reveals the reason for that 'melancholy air'. He writes that he 'felt painfully that L. was the centre of attraction' and that made him feel 'unreal & self-conscious'. Moreover, he 'was jealous and sad' when Lawrence talked with Ottoline about E. M. Forster and Bertrand Russell, and felt excluded because he did not know them. Overwhelmed with a sense of inadequacy, Murry then tried to overcome it by making himself the centre of attention:

> I told about my past, strangely exaggerated – and then having told resented L's laughter at it and Banks. I felt that I may laugh not he . . . Why in God's name should I be anxious to impress O. M. because L. was there. Comparatively I feel empty. Am I really empty or full with future things? (MSX 4143)

We do not know what story Murry told about George Banks, whether it emphasised her violence or her lesbianism. That he told it to puff himself up in Ottoline's eyes is intriguing, partly because it intrudes a possible lesbian subtext into his relationship with her at its very beginning.

Fantasy and deception were predominant features of both Mansfield's and Murry's relations with Ottoline. They each felt threatened and inconsequential in her presence. Murry's exaggeration about his past in the story he told her about George Banks is paralleled by Mansfield's behaviour when she had first visited the Morrell's Bloomsbury house, only a couple of weeks earlier than Murry's encounter at Greatham, where, according to Beatrice Campbell, she and Mansfield wandered through 'the large drawing-room examining pictures and furniture, and she said softly to me, "Do you feel that we are two prostitutes and that this is the first time we have ever been in a decent house?"' (Glenavy 1964: 88). Ironically, Ottoline's memory of this same occasion reveals that *she* 'felt shy and lost' and wondered 'how on earth I should entertain them' when she saw 'these great figures [Lawrence, Mansfield, Koteliansky, and the Campbells] trooping in' (Morrell 1964: 284).

Lawrence was responsible for the invitation Murry received from Ottoline Morrell to spend Christmas at Garsington in 1915. Mansfield remained in Bandol, where she and Murry had relocated soon after her brother's death in October. Murry had found Mansfield's self-absorption in her grief so hard to bear that he returned to London on 7 December, using as his excuse that he wanted to help Lawrence with *The Signature*, the short-lived magazine they had started during the summer.[1] That visit to Garsington gave Murry his first full exposure to the atmosphere of Bloomsbury, and as he remarked to Mansfield in his letter on 26 December, it made him feel as if he had 'been knocked suddenly tumbling into a different world'. He was finding it 'so strange to go for long walks with people like Lytton Strachey & Clive Bell, and spend the whole time talking about everything under the sun, just for the sake of talking' (LJMM: 88). This letter reveals much about Murry's youth and social immaturity, evidenced by his surprise that people actually liked him and that they 'seem to be rather deferential' to what he says. Since Murry must have known that Mansfield felt abandoned in Bandol while he was enjoying these new social encounters, he tried to assuage her resentment by suggesting that she plays an important role in his success at Garsington. He claims that he carries about with him the aura of 'that incredible thing called a *grande passion*', which impresses the others:

> But perhaps it's because I'm so conscious of you that I don't care a rap whether they like me or not, and my indifference is enough to make them more eager to get hold of me. In any case, though they are rather a close corporation – most of them have known each other for ten years or more, they are a fairly decent lot, fantastic and fin de siècle, perhaps, but pretty good underneath. (LJMM: 88)

Murry's wary first visit to Garsington thus marks the beginning of a position of defensive outsidership that will come to define his and Mansfield's stance towards Bloomsbury. However, Murry's social insecurities were already apparent even in his relations with close friends. Only ten days earlier he had remarked to Mansfield that 'All our friends hurt me; Kot very deeply – Campbell insufferably; Lawrence least of all

– but all of them hurt. I wonder are we, am I, as selfish and hard as they are?' (LJMM: 71).

It is hard to take seriously Murry's insistence in the same letter that he and Mansfield

> belong to our own kingdom, which truly is when we stand hand in hand, even when we are cross together like two little boys. Somehow we were born again in each other, tiny children, pure and shining, with large sad eyes and shocked hair, each to be the other's doll. (LJMM: 71)

Yet, it was all part of the love-play between them, infantilising and deceptively sentimental as it was. Mansfield enjoyed the game as much as Murry did. Her previous letter to him undoubtedly inspired his imagery with its description of her fantasy of attending a circus, dressed like Colette and sitting next to her and eating 'tiny little jujubes out of a much too big bag', while they talked about their childhoods (KMCL 1: 213). Her reference to Colette, in a letter where she actually is angry with Murry for leaving her in France, allows her to use a veiled allusion to lesbian identity as both a playful threat and device for shifting her feelings from anger to a condescending love for him. The conclusion of her letter offers conciliation when she tells him she loves him, but infantilises him at the same time when she refers to his 'blessed little head against [her] breast'.

It almost seems as if Murry unconsciously reverses the lesbian undertone of Mansfield's letter to a male homosexual one by duplicating her image of likeness: 'two little boys' now. Mansfield picks up the new image when she responds to him a few days later: 'How I love you – we are two little boys walking with our arms (which won't quite reach) round each others shoulders & telling each other secrets and stopping to look at things' (KMCL 1: 220).

Although some critics have been hard on both Mansfield and Murry over this child-play in passages like these in their correspondence, I prefer to take an oppositional stance here, to emphasise instead the transgressive – and potentially more radical – aspects of their mutual straining towards likeness. Their use of these images of children suggests the instability of gender boundaries in their relationship, their attempts – both playful and serious – to transcend gender itself by insisting on an essential likeness, a core identity not shaped by socially sanctioned rules of 'adult' standards of appropriate gendered behaviour. Such transitory moments of likeness – although they cannot be sustained and are continually overpowered by the pressures of their actual lives as social beings – provide the bursts of energy that fuel their increasingly endangered relationship and allow it to survive.

However, despite Mansfield's ecstatic tone in her letters to Murry during his Christmas visit to Garsington, she worried that he was attracted to other women there. On Christmas Day she wrote: 'I hope you don't kiss anybody at Lady Ottoline's' (KMCL 1: 230). Apparently he behaved himself at the party, but after he returned to Bandol, something about his enthusiastic description of Ottoline Morrell stirred Mansfield to desire a special relationship with the woman as well. The first letter she would write to her, on 21 January 1916, reveals how she was already working up a romantic context for this new friendship:

> I have been wanting to write to you for nearly three weeks – I *have* been writing to you ever since the day when Murry came and said: 'there's a perfectly wonderful woman in England and told me about you. Since then I have wanted to send you things, too – some anemones, purple and crimson lake and a rich, lovely white, some blue irises that I found growing in the grass, too frail to gather, certain places in the woods where I imagine you would like to be – and certain hours like this hour of bright moonlight, when the flowering almond tree hangs over our white stone verandah a blue shadow with long tassels. (KMCL 1: 244–5)

On the surface the letter could be read as a painfully obvious attempt to ingratiate herself with a potential patron. Not a shred of Mansfield's earlier role-playing as a prostitute in Lady Ottoline's grand house remains, instead the role she now plays is wholesome: a happy young 'wife' in love with her husband. Although the letter could be seen as only a ploy to abort a possible flirtation between Ottoline and Murry, it also could suggest a genuine longing for a special intimacy with that same woman, as Bertha felt for Pearl in 'Bliss'. Here too, the symbol of a flowering tree centres that longing, even if at this point in Mansfield's relationship with Lady Ottoline, the 'flowering almond tree' is primarily a motif in a carefully manoeuvred social courtship.

Mansfield's epistolary relationship with Ottoline continued throughout the following months, and after she and Murry had joined the Lawrences at Higher Tregerthen, her letters served to intensify a growing rift between Ottoline and the Lawrences. Although she continually emphasised in them that: 'Murry and I are so happy together – its like a miracle' (KMCL 1: 268), by the time that they had left the Lawrences and moved to Mylor, their relationship was falling apart. Once they were in London again, Murry began working at the War Office, and it was during that War Office phase that the subliminally triangular relationship with Ottoline Morrell reached its embarrassing conclusion.

Murry, who was feeling that he had 'become an automaton' in his work translating German at the War Office, had started writing private letters to Ottoline. Alpers quotes from one of them, written on 22 September 1916:

> I have at times a queer suspicion that I must be in love with you. I don't know. It's very hard to get at what I feel: so rarely do I feel towards persons any emotion more intimate than amusement or blank terror. But when I try to find a name for my feeling towards you, – then it is that I begin to suspect that I am in love with you. (Alpers 1980: 219)

By early December, the correspondence between Murry and Ottoline had become a topic of Bloomsbury gossip. Clive Bell mentioned to Vanessa that Ottoline 'writes to him and he leaves her letters about' and that 'Ottoline is trying to get up an affair with Murry' (Alpers 1980: 219).[2] Apparently, Mansfield was still unaware of Murry's duplicity.

Christmas at Garsington in 1916 recycled both the one of 1914 at the Cannans', with its self-revealing play-acting, and that of 1915, with Mansfield's fear that Murry might kiss someone at the party. Again, a 'play' was the main entertainment, this time written by Mansfield, who had become a significant participant in the group, rather than the absent – but romantic – lover of the previous year. (Murry was given the part of a Dostoevsky-like character named Ivan Tchek.)[3] Mansfield's anxiety about Murry's propensity to flirt with other women would have been justified this year, had she known that on the day before Christmas he had written to Ottoline, referring to 'our love, I will not call it by another name' (Alpers 1980: 226). The long Christmas festivities at Garsington drew to a calamitous close this year, however. On 27 December, Ottoline received the manuscript of *Women in Love*. Furious, hurt, outraged, she recognised immediately the caricature of herself in Hemione Roddice. What seemed to her most unforgivable was that he had made Hermione 'a corrupt Sapphist' and depicted her making 'indecent advances to the Heroine, who was a glorified Frieda' (Morrell 1974: 128).

Since Murry and Mansfield did not read the manuscript, their concern was only with Ottoline's distress, their anger only with Lawrence's apparent treachery towards his devoted patron. In this situation it appears as if they were at one and aligned with Ottoline *together*. The furore over Lawrence's manuscript allowed for an intensification of Mansfield's friendship with Ottoline Morrell, and the 'Bliss' motif appears in several letters, beginning with her remark on 2 January 1917: 'It is so lovely here that just to be alive is a kind of bliss almost too great to be borne' (KMCL 1: 289). Later that month, her description of 'a perfect day' comes close to the emotional valences of 'Bliss':

Such air – full of little lilac flowers and new grass and the first butterflies –
What can one do with this intolerable love of almost sensational life – of the
outsides of houses half moonlight and half black shadow – of the sounds of
music and the shapes of people standing in those round pools of light that the
street lamps shed. (KMCL 1: 295)

Mansfield's phrasing: 'What can one do with this intolerable love of
almost sensational life' resembles that of 'What can you do if you are
thirty and, turning the corner of your own street, you are overcome, suddenly, but a feeling of bliss – absolute bliss!' (KMCS: 91).

The climax to the mutual – and, alternatively, separate – wooing of
Ottoline by Mansfield and Murry apparently occurred following the
weekend of 21–3 July 1917, after Mansfield returned to London while
Murry remained at Garsington. According to Ottoline, one evening
Murry asked 'if he might "come into my heart", and went on to say that
it was so wonderful to him and Katherine to have found anyone that
they could love and trust'. She says she 'was quite unprepared for any
emotional intimacy with him':

After we had said good night I felt, as I often did, that I must slip out into the
garden to look at the flowers by moonlight, and think over all he had been
talking of. The night seemed as if it was held in a magic spell. After wandering
about for some time I couldn't resist calling up to Murry in his room, as I saw
that his light was still burning, 'You must come down, Murry. It is wicked
to miss this lovely night.' Directly I had done it I was sorry and wished I had
not; but soon, however, he came down, and we walked round and round the
flower garden, looking at the beautiful old grey house lit up by the moon,
which gave it such great intensity and beauty. We talked very openly, very
intimately, 'not of love but of life'. (Morrell 1974: 190)

Ottoline Morrell's memoirs tell one side of the story. She insists that
it was Murry who made the approach and that following this incident
Mansfield's letters became cold and distant. Their friendship only
resumed after they finally spoke together and uncovered the 'facts'.
Apparently Murry had told Mansfield that Ottoline had 'fallen deeply
and passionately in love with him', and Mansfield believed that 'this
woman, whom she felt she could love and trust', was 'just as bad and
treacherous as everyone else and at the first opportunity tried to steal
Murry from her' (Morrell 1974: 190).

Mansfield's reaction to Murry's version of his encounter with Ottoline
elicited a letter to her on 11 August that reveals the intensity of her
disillusionment and conveys it in a tone quite similar to that of 'Bliss':

Quite suddenly, just after you had been so near, so thrilling and so enchanting
– for no reason that I can explain away – it was if the light changed, and you

vanished from me . . . The strangest part was that my memory of the days we had just spent together was as perfect as ever – as bright as untroubled. I still saw the blue spears of lavender – the trays of fading, scented leaves, you in your room, and your bed with the big white pillow – and you coming down in the garden swinging the gay lantern – But between these lovely memories and me there opened a deep dark chasm – it *trembled* open as if by an earthquake – and now it is shut again and no trace of it remains. (KMCL 1: 323)

Attempting to assure Ottoline that her friendship for her could never end, 'whatever may happen', she tells her she 'longs' to see her again. Then she includes the following:

Murry came to see me this evening. He showed me a handkerchief you had given him. I took it in my hands and the scent of it shook my heart – Yes, just as if I had been a young person profoundly in love with you. (KMCL 1: 323)

Mansfield's recognition that the beauty that preceded her hard knowledge – the 'deep dark chasm', 'was as perfect as ever – as bright as untroubled' is the same recognition that Bertha Young experiences after she sees her husband kissing Pearl Fulton: 'But the pear tree was as lovely as ever and as full of flower and as still' (KMCS: 105). The reference to the handkerchief in the letter, which smells of Ottoline yet is taken from Murry's hand, serves as a conduit for the desires which – she hopes – still bind the three of them together.

Notes

1. Only three issues of *The Signature* ever appeared, two in October and one in November 1915.
2. Ottoline Morrell's biographer, Miranda Seymour, comments that 'it is inconceivable that Ottoline was writing [Murry] passionate letters at a time when every page of her journal was dominated by her love for Sassoon' (Seymour 1992: 275).
3. See KMN (2: 76–9) for the script of the play, entitled *The Laurels*. In addition to Murry and Mansfield, the other actors were Lytton Strachey, [Dora] Carrington, Aldous Huxley and Maria Nys.

Chapter 4

'A Furious Bliss'

I

There is a moment in *Women in Love* when Birkin at last concedes to Ursula's demand and admits that he loves her, saying: '"Yes, I do. I love you, and I know it's final. It is final, so why say any more about it"' (WL: 251). He then embraces her and suddenly feels

> such peace and heavenly freedom, just to fold her and kiss her gently, and not to have any thoughts or any desires or any will, just to be *still* with her, to be perfectly *still* and together, in a peace that was not sleep, but content in *bliss*. To be content in *bliss*, without desire or insistence anywhere, this was heaven: to be together in happy *stillness*. [my emphases] (WL: 252)

The words 'still' and 'bliss' should remind us of the titles of the two works of fiction by Murry and Mansfield which have occupied our attention so far in this book. If Murry – who could not stop talking – envisioned what is *still* as lifeless, and Mansfield a *bliss* that was deflected hysteria, Lawrence – seemingly without effort – momentarily penetrates to the essence of these words. True, he describes a moment that will not last, as is the nature of all epiphanic experience. But linked with his emphasis on *finality*, it is a moment that should endure underneath the struggles yet to come. And when, soon after, Birkin questions whether Gerald was doomed to the 'mystery of ice-destructive knowledge, snow-abstract annihilation', and 'fated to pass away in this knowledge, this one process of frost knowledge, death by perfect cold' (WL: 254), he draws back from these fearful thoughts by formulating a theory of the true relationship:

> There was another way, the way of freedom. There was the Paradisal entry into pure, single being, the individual soul taking precedence over love and desire for union, stronger than any pangs of emotion, a lovely state of free proud singleness, which accepts the obligation of the permanent connection

with others, and with the other, submits to the yoke and leash of love, but never forfeits its own proud individual singleness even while it loves and yields. (WL: 254)

No matter the irony of the contrast between this ideal and the embattled relationship between Lawrence and Frieda as witnessed by Murry and Mansfield. Lawrence's creative energy allows him to envision a kind of relationship beyond the imagination of Murry, who seemed to him to be a man locked into the 'mystery of ice-destructive knowledge'.

Mansfield, however, was as devoted as Lawrence to discovering how to convey epiphanic moments in her own fiction. For example, there is a scene in an unfinished play, written before 'Bliss', probably in April 1917, in which a young man – patterned after her dead brother, Leslie Beauchamp – describes to his mother '"a feeling of such terrific happiness that it's almost unbearable . . . if you don't give it to somebody or get rid of it somehow – tear it out of yourself – you'll simply die – of – bliss"' (KMN 2: 108). The 'bliss' here is ecstatic, even violent, rather than 'a peace that was not sleep'. Most significantly, it is not related to the conjunction of one lover with another, although its passion resembles the longing for sexual release. In this instance, the speaker attempts to describe it to another person, unlike in 'Bliss', where Bertha's feelings remain unsaid.[1] More typically, such 'moments' are experienced by characters who are *alone*. In fact, the epiphany itself uncovers their frightening isolation and reveals the destruction of the illusion of unity with another, as in 'Bliss' when Bertha's 'moment' of oneness at the pear tree with Pearl Fulton proves deceptive.

While Lawrence's aim was directed towards 'the obligation of the permanent connection with others', it depended upon an ego strong enough to maintain its 'state of free proud singleness' without being overcome by the power of the other. Mansfield's sense of the multiplicity of the self made it more difficult for her to grasp a 'singleness that might both love and yield and yet remain whole'.[2] (Murry gave that sense of multiplicity to Anne in *Still Life* when he referred to 'one of her own possible selves' [SL: 376].) Katherine Mansfield's experience as a woman would have made her as suspicious as Ursula of the power imbalance implicit in Lawrence's notion of 'an equilibrium, a pure balance of two single beings – as the stars balance each other' (WL: 148). Like Ursula, she would have been quick to see the female in this equation as 'A Satellite' (WL: 150) to the overpowering male. Murry's use of a complementary image suggests that he understood how a woman could be suspicious of figurative attributions of equality. He astutely provides Anne with a more realistic trope for her relations with Maurice: 'They were like two circles that had been important in her algebra, she thought, one wholly containing the other' (SL: 123). Coincidentally, Murry also uses an image more similar to Lawrence's: 'They might have been two planets on their courses, meeting for a moment in eternity' (SL: 377). Aside from the conventionality of Murry's use of this image, it does suggest a totally different paradigm for love, however. In this case, he uses the trope to suggest contingency: the accidental meeting of Anne and Dennis on the street in a prelude to their eventual conjoining. Yes, there is an inevitability to their coming together, but no sense at all of any *finality* to it. It is a momentary conjunction, not a 'permanent connection'.

From its inception, Mansfield's relationship with Murry had relied on a delicate balance dependent upon her maintenance of individual freedom. Murry later wrote about his disinclination 'to urge any claim' on her. He declared that he 'always was, and always would be, man enough to ask nothing of a woman but what of her own motion she could not help giving' (BTW: 320). This concept of personal freedom had first been tested in 1915, during Mansfield's brief romance with Francis Carco, and again, late in 1916, when both she and Murry were swept into the intrigues and gossip of Garsington. Murry was then preoccupied with his work at the War Office and with his attraction to Lady Ottoline Morrell, while Mansfield was unsettled, unfocused and longing to be alone. She too seemed to need an outlet for her emotions and an epistolary flirtation with Bertrand Russell – who had been Ottoline's lover – appears to have briefly served that purpose.

Mansfield's letters to Russell during November and December of 1916 are filled with exultant exclamations about the art of writing, but she actually had not been able to do much of it during those months while she and Murry were living in London, at 'The Ark', along with Dorothy Brett and Carrington, in John Maynard Keynes's house on Gower Street. She wrote to Russell on 1 December about 'so many interruptions. Life seemed to rush in and out of my door like the teller of the tale in a Dostoievsky novel' (KMCL 1: 285). Those interruptions must have included Murry, who also intrudes – at least subconsciously – in her allusion to Dostoevsky, for Murry's book on him had just been published. In fact, Mansfield had not been able to detach herself from her personal life enough to devote herself to her writing ever since the failure of the experiment in communal living with the Lawrences in Cornwall earlier that year. Since then, everything she wrote remained sketchy or unfinished.

She hoped to remedy that problem by taking a studio in Chelsea. By February 1917, she and Murry had moved out of 'The Ark', and were living separately, she in her studio and he in rooms not far from it, but they saw each other every evening for supper. To complicate matters, L. M. (Ida Baker), back from a two-year stay in Rhodesia, was now working as 'a tool setter in an aeroplane factory' (Baker 1972: 100), and had moved into Mansfield's studio, where she slept behind a screen. What this peculiar arrangement meant to the sexual life of Mansfield and Murry is not precisely known, but it can be surmised.[3]

During this period, Murry felt he had been condemned to 'hack-work', yet longed to elevate the status of criticism. He published *thirty* unsigned reviews of French literature for *TLS* in 1917.[4] These demanded an enormous amount of reading, and all this work was additional to his full-time job at the War Office, where he was translating German news-papers. Murry later said that he was 'near the verge of madness' (BTW: 429), and insisted that 'every faculty of mine was now strained upon the war. I was not' (BTW: 432). But read against his journal entries, these later statements are questionable. The clarity of his journal comments on the art of writing, his gossipy interest in L. M.'s behaviour in Mansfield's studio, and his astute observations about the war do not suggest a man on the 'verge of madness'. They also suggest that he might not have been miserable *all* the time. An entry written on 9 April 1917 provides an antidote: 'This has been one of those strange things that I must call "a happy day"'. He then writes a description of himself and Mansfield waking up, 'sleepy and warm in each other's arms'. In the afternoon they go to the National Gallery and look closely 'only at the pictures we wanted to look at'. Clarifying their artistic preferences, Murry exclaims: 'We wouldn't have Rembrandt's "Saskia as Flora", because we didn't like her, even though she was Rembrandt's woman & Rembrandt did her. We basked in the clear light of Poussin's grave and deliberate masterpieces because we loved them' (MSX 4147: 64).[5]

The return of spring appears to have remained true to its traditional associations with love and romance in the relationship between Murry and Mansfield. Murry's pleasure in waking with Mansfield in his arms is paralleled by a love letter Mansfield wrote to him in his 'private book' on 19 May 1917:

> Last night, there was a moment before you got into bed. You stood, quite naked, bending forward a little – talking. It was only for an instant. I saw you – I loved you so – loved your body with such tenderness – Ah my dear – And I am not thinking now of 'passion'. No, of that other thing that makes me feel that every inch of you is so precious to me.

She describes then his 'creamy warm skin', his 'ears, cold like shells are cold', his 'thin young back' and her hopes that the two of them 'shall do very great things'. But at the end of the letter Mansfield makes this claim:

'I want nobody but you for my lover and my friend and to nobody but you shall I be *faithful*' (KMCL 1: 307–8), which sounds very much like a disavowal of the 'freedom' she was accustomed to claim. Yet it might well have been a ploy in her continuing wariness of the threat posed by Garsington. An editorial footnote to this letter to Murry points out that he was on his way to spend the weekend at Garsington just at the moment Mansfield was writing it (KMCL 1: 308).

Ambiguous motivations notwithstanding, the sensual blossoming of the spring was accompanied by a creative blossoming as well for Mansfield, who was now energetically writing – and publishing – stories and 'Fragments' in *The New Age*. While she appears to have been basking in the pleasure of this renewed creativity and the enticements of new social possibilities, Murry was slowly sinking into depression. His only relief from his work at the War Office and his unrelenting journalism was, as he put it, 'an intensity of speculation – using the word in Keats' sense – far more consuming than ordinary work could ever be' (BTW: 443). This completely mental activity at first shielded him from realising the onset of a breakdown, both physical and emotional. The doctor who examined him feared he might develop tuberculosis and wanted him to take a recuperative rest in the country. His condition was serious enough for the War Office to give him sick leave and continue his salary.

A far more socially conscientious Murry of the 1930s remarked that this was his 'one authentic taste of the condition of a future society in which there is economic security for all' (BTW: 444). Yet there is quite a bit of irony in the fact that Murry would spend that sick leave at Garsington, under the care not of a beneficent welfare state, but of an aristocratic patron. Regardless of Lady Ottoline's disappointment with Murry, she nonetheless quite graciously invited him to stay at Garsington after Mansfield begged her to do so.

A much darker irony, of course, is that Murry recovered and Mansfield fell ill during this – retrospectively ominous – Garsington sojourn. She was chilled on the way from the station to visit him there and when she returned to London the chill developed into fever – perhaps, as the doctor diagnosed at first, an attack of pleurisy. And then shortly afterwards, he discovered a spot on her right lung.

On 13 December, Mansfield had written to Murry: 'I cant sleep for a nut. I lie in a kind of *furious bliss*!' (KMCL 1: 344). And Murry later remarked that 'the fury of the bliss would suddenly change into a fury of irritation' (BTW: 449). He began to see in her 'a quite unfamiliar note of exasperation'. Whether Murry really experienced then 'the grim sense of foreboding' that he describes in *Between Two Worlds* is not possible to know, but it dramatically enhances his construction of his life's tragedy:

> I was engulfed in a black wave of unfaith. And such was the state of mind which lay in wait for me that the sudden reversal of our roles – my illness as it were in a moment transferred to her – was sinister with destiny. That possibility had never entered my mind; but now that it was a reality, it seemed to be self-evident. That was precisely how Necessity – the Beauty of Necessity – would reveal itself in us! (BTW: 450)

Murry's reference to 'Necessity' also suggests a new paradigm for his interpretation of experience. For Murry, Garsington at the end of 1917 had provided his own symbolic *intellectual* turning point. It was during his stay there that he read Sidney Colvin's *Life of Keats*, and 'began to read the poetry with a new understanding' (BTW: 446). The shift from the influence of Dostoevsky to that of Keats would have significant consequences for Murry's career as a literary critic. But more personally, it demarcates a point beyond which everything would be dominated by the subject of tuberculosis. Murry sensed that its intrusion had 'suddenly' made Mansfield 'become a different person. Her "furious bliss" and her furious exasperation belonged to another Katherine than [he] had known' (BTW: 450).

II

Mansfield's exhausting journey to Bandol, where she had been so happy with Murry in 1916, only weakened her further and intensified her emotional volatility. She wrote to Murry on 11 January 1918 that she felt 'like a fly who has been dropped into the milk jug & fished out again but is still too milky & drowned to start cleaning up yet' (KMCL 2: 8). Although her doctor had discovered tuberculosis in her right lung, she complained to Murry on 18 January that now she had pain in her left lung too. She definitely was not improving. She began writing 'Je ne parle pas français' on 29 January, a day when she was upset that she had not received any letters from Murry and was not ready to believe that hers were being delayed in the mail. She did not yet realise how much the intensification of the war had affected the delivery of mail, nor did she know until the next day that the Germans had bombed London, killing forty-seven people on the night of the 28th. Did this momentary disruption in the frantic pace of the couple's intense letter writing elicit intimations of duplicity again? Despite her constant expressions of love for him in her correspondence, even on the *same* day that she began writing 'Je ne parle pas français', she must have felt an undertow pulling her towards submerged resentments and suspicions. Only two days earlier, in a letter to Murry full of depressed anger, she referred to Ottoline Morrell as '*corrupt – corrupt*' (KMCL 2: 42).[6]

When she tried to explain the origin of the story to Murry, she suggested that it 'is of course taken from – Carco & Gertler & God knows who' (KMCL 2: 214). Her lonely return to France seems to have brought back the memory of that earlier escapade there with Francis Carco in 1915. Now, he would be added to her growing list of the 'corrupt' and her new story could not repeat the pattern of her affair with him, for that would have situated *her* as the duplicitous partner to Murry. Instead it harks back to Murry's initial friendship with Carco in 1911, and also to her own first meeting with him in 1912 when she supposedly said: 'Je ne parle pas français'.[7] (There was also her second encounter with Carco in the winter of 1913–14, when he took Murry 'on a strange journey into the underworld' (BTW: 276) to sell their furniture in the brothels of Paris.)

But why does she also mention Mark Gertler here? Mansfield's imaginative linking of the two men, who never knew each other, appears to date back to that famous Christmas Eve party of 1914 at Gilbert Cannan's windmill, when Mansfield performed the skit in which she left Murry for Gertler, who represented Carco. There is an entry in Murry's journal on 29 December 1914 that suggests an additional reason Mansfield might have mentioned Gertler. Murry describes a conversation he had with him soon after the Cannan's party, in which Gertler recounted his sexual history. Murry seems amazed by the details Gertler revealed, such as the fact that by the age of eight he had become completely developed physically and sexually active. Murry also writes down some of Gertler's anecdotes, including one about a sexual encounter with a girl of only fourteen, and then compares his own naivety with Gertler's sexual sophistication (MSX 4147: 52–4).

Given their mutual delight in gossip, it is likely that Murry went over the details of this conversation with Mansfield, and now, three years later, she found herself combining Gertler's precocious and promiscuous sexuality with that of Carco, to bolster her now seemingly obsessive focus on 'corruption'. Her letter to Murry about the story's origin continues with:

> I read the fair copy just now and couldn't think where the devil I had got the bloody thing from – I cant even now. Its a mystery. Theres so much less taken from life than anybody would credit. The african laundress I had a bone of – but only a bone – Dick Harmon of course is partly is (KMCL 2: 56)

(The reference to the 'african laundress' who seduced the ten-year-old Duquette seems to be derived from an incident in Carco's childhood.) Yet, Mansfield's paragraph drops off here unfinished. Dick Harmon, the man who brings his lover, 'Mouse', to Paris and then abandons her there, is, obviously, 'partly' Murry.

The 'plot' of the story, as Alpers suggests, links Mouse 'partly' with 'the Marguéritte whom [Murry] deserted in 1911 and allowed to think his mother was to blame' (Alpers 1980: 273). Mansfield would have known about Murry's love affair with Marguéritte because he had told her about it at the very beginning of their relationship, when they used to talk for hours about his troubled past. Whether he confessed his lingering guilt then, or whether he even told Mansfield that he had *abandoned* Marguéritte is uncertain. Nonetheless, she would have more recently discovered the persistence of Murry's unresolved feelings through reading *Still Life*. There, his fictional reconstruction of the situation sets it firmly within the context of its protagonist's *current* relationship with a woman very similar to herself. In her now vulnerable condition, alone and very sick, did she begin to worry about Murry abandoning her?

The parallels with the Murry/Marguéritte situation, however, need to be put into perspective by considering some more recent history: the pattern of triangular relationships that had affected Mansfield's feelings for Murry over the past few years. In this way, 'Je ne parle pas français' is a counterpart to 'Bliss', which she would write only two weeks later. In 'Bliss' the triangle is composed of two women and one man; the erotic energy of the story is bisexual. In 'Je ne parle pas français' the triangle is composed of two men and one woman, and again, bisexuality infiltrates the story's emotional core.[8] Both stories reveal betrayal and disillusionment, but the latter depicts rejection and abandonment as well. If 'Bliss' draws some of its emotional complexity from the triangular relationship between Murry, Ottoline Morrell and Mansfield, 'Je ne parle pas français' reprises the homosocial triangle of Murry, Lawrence and Mansfield (or the earlier one of Murry, Gordon Campbell and Mansfield).

In Murry's *Still Life*, there are two interlocking romantic triangles. The first consists of Maurice Temple, Dennis Beauchamp and Anne Cradock. The second, more submerged triangle, is that of Maurice, Anne and the *memory* of the French woman, Madeleine. That memory, and the guilt it elicits from Maurice, undermines – and eventually destroys – his relationship with Anne, who turns to Dennis and leaves with him at the novel's end. Additionally, the novel actually duplicates two subtexts of 'Je ne parle pas français'. The first is Maurice's use of his mother as an excuse for abandoning Madeleine, which is reprised in

Dick Harman's abandonment of Mouse for the same reason. The second is the intensity of the male friendships, which in both stories position the Murry-like characters in the passive role.

Along these lines it may be useful to read some details intertextually. There is, for example, the letter Dick Harmon leaves for 'MOUSE, MY LITTLE MOUSE':

> 'It's no good. It's impossible. I can't see it through. Oh, I do love you. I do love you, Mouse, but I can't hurt her. People have been hurting her all her life. I simply dare not give her this final blow . . . It would kill her – kill her, Mouse. And, oh God, I can't kill my mother! Not even for you. Not even for us.' (KMCS: 87)

The letter almost seems like a commentary on Murry's own use of a letter from Maurice's mother, to suggest her role in destroying his love affair with Madeleine:

> 'You promised me that you would never write to her again . . . But I can't see that it would matter now when you don't even care enough for me to let me know where you are living . . . I don't even know if you are alive. If you only knew what I have had to suffer in the nights thinking of you.' (SL: 239)

In the same envelope, Maurice's mother encloses another letter, a painful one from the abandoned Madeleine, who bemoans his long silence, and melodramatically tells him she will not write again: 'Je serais morte' (SL: 240–1). Madeleine's final desperate attempt to contact Maurice through his mother will not be Mouse's response to Dick, however. When Dick begs her at the end of his letter: '"And don't write. I should not have the courage to answer your letters and the sight of your spidery handwriting – "' (KMCS: 88), her response to his desertion is far more stoical than Madeleine's. When Duquette asks if she would try to see Harmon again: '"What an extraordinary idea!" she said, more coldly than ever. "Of course I shall not dream of seeing him. As for going back – that is quite out of the question. I can't go back"' (KMCS: 89).

Dick Harmon's letter, with its emphasis on 'hurting' and its equivocation, is highly reminiscent of Maurice's self-excoriation in *Still Life*:

> Here I am twenty-four, absolutely tortured by the thought of all the people there are roaming about the world whom I've hurt in some way or in another . . . The funniest part of it is that the reason why I hurt all these people is that I haven't got the courage not to. If I'd just told them I was – well, just what I am – quite early on, it would have been all right . . . I can see myself telling my mother that I knew I was going to make a mess of everything. (SL: 327)

These words of Maurice's are said to Dennis in reference to his problems with Anne, as well as alluding to his past mistreatment of Madeleine.

But the significance of the conversation is in its revelation of the intensity of Maurice's feelings for *Dennis*, as when Maurice says:

> 'If I once begin to think about myself really, I can't see where my sentimentality stops. It's mixed up with everything I do, somehow. It's not only that I can't end anything, but I can't even believe that anything is going to end . . . For instance, when you go away again. You'll have to sometimes, I suppose? I simply can't face the idea of saying good-bye to you, and yet I can't get it out of the back of my mind. That a thing should be over and done with for ever – it almost makes me freeze with horror.' (SL: 327)

Although Maurice slides the discussion back to Anne, more safely maintaining the aura of homosocial rivalry, the strongest emotion in the conversation is his fear of Dennis's leaving. But that fear is in itself ambivalent, for his unconscious rivalry over Anne is what makes the idea of that departure almost a wish that it happen. It is the same kind of ambivalence that marks Raoul's reaction to Dick Harmon's letter to Mouse. Although he had been imagining that Dick had 'shot himself', he recovers quickly from his fantasy after reading Dick's letter: 'My relief at his not having shot himself was mixed with a wonderful sense of elation. I was even – more than even with my "that's very curious and interesting" Englishman' (KMCS: 88). That Mouse, the rejected woman – whom Dick rather hysterically asks at the end of his letter to 'forgive' him: '"Don't love me any more. Yes. Love me. Love me"' – is used primarily as the locus for two men's relations with each other might well be Mansfield's point.

Dick Harmon appears to be the passive partner in his friendship with Duquette despite Duquette's claim that 'Even with Dick. It was he who made the first advances' (KMCS: 70). Since Duquette's first-person narration never (except in the case of Dick's letter) allows the reader to penetrate the thoughts of other characters, Dick's feelings for Duquette remain unclear. It is Duquette who describes his own pleasure in being invited to dinner by Dick: 'I was so deeply, deeply flattered that I had to leave him then and there to preen and preen myself before the cubist sofas. What a catch! An Englishman, reserved, serious, making a special study of French literature . . .' (KMCS: 71).

When Duquette catches a glimpse of a photograph of Dick's mother, he imagines her saying to him: '"Out of my sight, you little perfumed fox-terrier of a Frenchman"' (KMCS: 72). And the fox terrier image thus becomes an extended metaphor for Duquette's sense of his role with regard to Dick. When Dick suddenly decides to return to England, Raoul 'stood on the shore alone, more like a little fox-terrier than ever', and thinks how 'after all it was you who whistled to me, you who asked me to come! What a spectacle I've cut wagging my tail and leaping round you, only to be left like this while the boat sails off in its slow dreamy way'. His romantic feelings change rapidly to anger:

> 'Curse these English! No, this is too insolent altogether. Who do you imagine I am? A little paid guide to the night pleasures of Paris? . . . No, monsieur. I am a young writer, very serious, and extremely interested in modern English literature. And I have been insulted – insulted.' (KMCS: 73–4)

Mansfield captures here a not atypical reaction of people to Murry, who himself recognised that 'time and time again, both men and women, whom I thought to be my friends, have made it a capital charge against me that I possess some mysterious "personal charm": to which they succumb, and then cherish resentment against me for my behaviour to them' (BTW: 209).

Murry's response to 'Je ne parle pas français' was – not surprisingly – complex and ambiguous. He had no idea at first that any hostility towards himself might have contributed to Mansfield's 'furious' creative energy during its composition. When she had told him she was working on it and believed that it was 'the real thing' (KMCL 2: 51), he responded with genuine enthusiasm and respect for her creative powers. She had only sent him the first 'chapter' of the story on 4 February, however, and suggested – perhaps as a way to adjust his reading of it – its connection to 'Carco & Gertler & God knows who'. That letter reveals how anxious she was that Murry read the story in the right way: 'Oh God – is it good? I am frightened . . . Tell me – dont spare me. Is it the long breathe as I feel to my soul it is – or is it a false alarm?' (KMCL 2: 56). Mansfield here seems to appeal to Murry for a *diagnosis*. Her reference to 'the long breathe' and the 'false alarm' belongs to the discourse of medicine, a reminder of the predominant issue of her life now.

Murry's response on 8 February was everything she could have wished for: 'not only first rate; it's overwhelming. The description, no, not description, creation, of that café is extraordinary' (LJMM: 114). He did not simply offer praise, however, he analysed his impressions as seriously as he would do in one of his literary critiques. Making a significant observation about the story's echoing of Dostoevsky's *Letters from the Underworld,* he told her that it affected him in a way no other writing has 'except D's'. He was intrigued by the character of Raoul Duquette, and remarked that Duquette

> isn't what he would be if it were either Dostoevsky (or me) writing, for then he would be Dostoevsky thinking aloud. But instead of this, you have got this strange person, who's strange, not, as D's man would be, because he has

thought everything to a standstill, but because he is conscious of a piece out of him . . . Yes, he's conscious of having no roots. He sees a person like Dick who has roots and he realises the difference. But what it is he hasn't got, he doesn't know. Nor do I. (LJMM: 115)

Murry's analysis here is characteristically self-reflexive. There is his linking of himself and Dostoevsky, most obviously, especially his reference to thinking 'everything to a standstill'. There is also his initial identification with Dick – 'who has roots' – and that puffs him up considerably. But Duquette's awareness of 'a piece out of him' is one of Murry's continuing fears about himself.

At this stage of his reading then, Murry was definitely perplexed: 'What you are going to do with them I haven't the faintest idea. But I am ravenous to know.' He struggled to define what it was about the story that distinguished it from her others:

This is the only writing of yours I know that seems to be *dangerous*. Do you understand what I mean – by the adjective? Its *dangerous* to stop the world for a timeless moment.
    To put it another way. Here you seem to have begun to drag the depths of your *consciousness*. (LJMM: 114–15)

Of course Mansfield was delighted with Murry's response, but she must have felt uneasy by the time she received it, since she had, by then, shown that Dick's 'roots' were in very thin soil indeed: 'I read it & I wept with joy. How can you so marvellously understand – and so receive my love offering. Ah, it will take all of the longest life I can live to repay you.' Yet despite her pleasure in his response, she adds: 'But Christ! A devil about the size of a flea nips in my ear "suppose he's disappointed with the 2nd half?"' (KMCL 2: 68). Mansfield's light-hearted concession to doubt ('the size of a flea') belies her anxiety. She must have known that as astute a reader as Murry would recognise the animus mixed into the ingredients of her brew. And she was not finished working through it either. She closes her letter with a brief remark: 'My new story is signalled'. That story would be 'Bliss'.

It took Murry a while to react to the second half. When he received it on 15 February, he telegraphed her and then wrote that he 'wasn't prepared for the tragic turn of *Je ne parle pas*, and it upset me – I'm an awful child' (LJMM: 121). His letter reveals his ambivalence, although he tries to cover it up by praising Mansfield's artistic delineation of 'Mouse'. He then quickly veers to the other story she had sent him at the same time, 'Sun and Moon', which clearly seemed to garner his emotional energies more fully by allowing him an unambiguous avenue for identification. Its central character, the little boy, 'Sun', evokes the image of the sensitive child-self that Murry liked to believe he still held inside himself.

It would not be until 23 February, after Mansfield had written to express her concern that he was dissatisfied with her story and asked him to explain his reactions, that Murry finally tried to analyse his feelings about it. He insisted that he was not 'disappointed' with it, but rather 'utterly bowled out by it', that he was 'so passionately fond of the Mouse' that he was devastated by what happened to her:

> Look here, you must see that what you call my disappointment . . . was just my confession that you had done it – done it absolutely. My disappointment as a child was my satisfaction as an artist . . . 'Sun & Moon' were really tinies. His tragedy would be put right. But Mouse & Dick, they were too much like us. If they had been exactly like it wouldn't have upset me because I know we're alright. But they were different, our brothers & sisters spiritually. (LJMM: 127)

III

Murry cannot admit to his recognition of the attack on his relationship with Mansfield hidden within 'Je ne parle pas français'. He has to insist that he knows *they* are 'alright'. To go any further would damage the love story they were carefully constructing in their letters during these months of separation. That separation, although it made them miserable, was having a remarkably energising effect on their writing. In fact, their entire correspondence until Mansfield's return on 11 April 1918 might well be read as a collaborative text in which each participant engages in the construction of a writing self. That text has a narrative structure – teleological from its inception – in which the story it depicts is the heroic struggle of two lovers separated by fate in the forms of war and illness. The story's climax is the bombardment of Paris, and its denouement will be the wedding of its two lovers.

Murry's theme in this collaborative epistolary text is clearly outlined in his journal entry of 15 January 1918:

> It seems as though, because we are more in love than any other man & woman in the world, we must go through a perpetual torment of absence and illness – and, most awful of all to bear – illness in absence. I do not believe that any one has ever had more than we, the sense of the vastness and inhumanity of the world and of our own frailness & smallness. (BTW: 454–5)

His letter to Mansfield the next day retains this sense of victimisation, but tones down – if it does not avoid – its embarrassingly hubristic sense of exceptionality. It also draws attention to one of his favourite rhetorical strategies: irony, here used self-reflexively, to emphasise the disjunction between Mansfield's suffering and the tedium of his work at the War Office, translating German newspapers:

> When you say the word *malade*, the sky falls on my head. Parceque je suis tellement malade: it has gone echoing through my brain all day long. That and the eternal click of my typewriter. My God, talk about irony. Was ever an irony ever conceived like this which sends my fingers racing over the typewriter, my brain careering through the German papers, and parceque je suis tellement malade thrusting up every now and then and tearing my soul? (LJMM: 104)

From the long view of retrospection, a contemporary reader is aware of a further irony in the letters of late January: Murry's construction of his writing self as poet. Unfortunately, as with his similar desire to be a novelist, he would fail to make this self-projection coincide with his talents. Despite Murry's immersion in the avant-garde of artists and writers during his editorship of *Rhythm*, despite his knowledge of modern French poetry and his interest in Baudelaire, despite his knowing about Eliot's 'Prufrock' from Mansfield who had read the poem aloud at Garsington on 3 June 1917, Murry's imagination remained trapped in a late Victorian kind of formalism. Mansfield, on the other hand, had much earlier already incorporated the influence of French symbolism into her prose fiction.[9]

It did not help matters that Mansfield kept propping up Murry's poetic aspirations by giving him unrealistic praise, as for example, when his poem 'To My Dead Friends' appeared in the *Nation* on 19 January: 'Great God! To think that this lovely voice still sings in England – that you're alive, twenty-eight years old – and that youre to be – who could doubt it for one instant after this poem – the Great Poet of our time' (KMCL 2: 39). Although before her illness she used to criticise Murry's hyperbolic style, now she seemed to need to believe that *both* of them would become famous as creative writers, that their creativity was a function of their inseparability as lovers. She wanted to assure him – and herself – that they were engaged in the same endeavour. In her letter of 11 February, which was accompanied by the second part of 'Je ne parle pas français', she refers to the piece as 'the rest of our story', and mentions 'this fusion of our minds. You talk of love poetry – all I write or ever ever will write will be the fruit of our love – love prose –' (KMCL 2: 66). How much of this straining for likeness is genuine and how much is self-protective? (After all, 'Je ne parle pas français' – with all its elements of anger, disappointment and alienation – is difficult to read as 'love prose'.)

The increasing intensity of Mansfield's and Murry's interest in poetry (or poetic prose) during this period of separation is closely related to their mutual fascination with the Romantics, which was occurring at the same time. Given the general orientation of modernist poetry, this devotion to the Romantics feels retrogressive if considered through the critical lenses of T. S. Eliot and his followers, but it is important to underscore the fact that Murry and Mansfield were identifying themselves with the Romantics as *people*, not only with their poetics and aesthetic theories. Mansfield's tuberculosis made her identification with Keats a new pivot for her self-reflection. That identification was reinforced when she had her first haemorrhage on 19 February. In her letter to Murry that day, she tries to protect him by moving tentatively towards revealing it: 'I want to tell you some things which are a bit awful – so hold me hard'. She insists that 'this is NOT serious does NOT keep me in bed is absolutely easily curable, but I have been spitting a bit of blood'. In telling him not to worry, she reminds him that 'after all Lawrence often used to . . .'. But as the letter proceeds she cuts deeper: 'Now Im confiding . . . its not serious. But when I saw the bright arterial blood I nearly had a fit' (KMCL 2: 79–80). Her use of the phrase 'bright arterial blood' would have immediately alerted Murry, who was familiar with Keats's famous outcry: 'I know the colour of that blood; it is arterial blood. I cannot be deceived in that colour. That drop of blood is my death warrant'.[10]

During the weeks following Mansfield's haemorrhage, the references to the Romantics in their letters became both more frequent and more personal. Four days after the bleeding episode, Mansfield would complain that Yeats was a 'pompous ass' because he called Keats '"The coarse-bred son of a livery-stable keeper"'. Later in the same letter she objects to 'a review of Coleridge in the Times – so bad so ill-informed' and declares: 'But then of course I feel I have rather a corner in Coleridge and his circle. In fact you and I are the only two people who can write and think and whose opinion is worth while –' (KMCL 2: 88).

Murry was reading Coleridge's *Lectures on Shakespeare* on 1 March and was also contemplating a purchase of Charles Lamb's letters. He enthusiastically acclaimed to Mansfield:

> What wonderful days those were. We belong to these people. And just as Keats, Lamb, Coleridge, Shelley, Wordsworth fed themselves on the Elizabethans, we must feed on them both . . . And then to think that you & I are the direct inheritors of all this, fellow-heirs. My God! And then to think of those mingy, bingy Frenchmen! (LJMM: 131–2)

Murry's taking up sides here – the Romantics (and the Elizabethans) versus the French – was prompted by his sympathy with Mansfield's plight. It also might have been compounded by his feeling of satiation after an overdose of French literature in his work as reviewer for *TLS*. Surely he must have resented having to read so many volumes not of his own choosing when he longed to spend his free time writing poetry. His slam against 'those mingy bingy Frenchmen' ignores his continuing interest in and appreciation for a number of French wartime poets and writers.[11] Murry's remark here also suggests that he was already beginning to formulate the distinctions between romanticism and classicism that he would later debate with T. S. Eliot, including his insistence that the 'true' genealogy of English literature reveals an unbroken connection between the Elizabethans and the Romantics. His intellectual evolution into the defender of romanticism can be said to have its emotional origins here, developing like many belief systems out of a personal matrix. In this case, an important element is that Murry's and Mansfield's identification with the Romantics allows them to have a literary coterie of their own. Accordingly, Mansfield calls them 'our "special" set' and 'the people with whom I want to live' (KMCL 2: 107–8). They had once had a 'set' composed of the Lawrences, Koteliansky and Gordon Campbell, but that grouping had splintered. Murry and Mansfield were now poised at the edge of Bloomsbury, wary of Virginia Woolf and having only a deteriorating connection with Lady Ottoline's group at Garsington.

The dream of 'The Heron' is their counterpoint to Bloomsbury and Garsington. Not only would they live 'somewhere deep in the country', Murry writes on 11 February, but that he wants 'to be able to live only for you and for poetry' there. To make it all seem more realistic, he adds to the dream cottage his wish for a printing press, which might actually provide them with an income once he no longer had his good salary from the War Office. Yet as his letter continues, his vehemence against his dependence upon the Bloomsbury establishment surfaces: 'I can't ask people any more. I hate them. Really, the blackness of my hatred of people like O. M. staggers even myself' (LJMM: 118–19).

Mansfield echoes Murry's sentiments about Ottoline, referring to her as a 'witch' in her letter of 22 February. Yet on that very same day, she finds herself writing a letter to her, falsely jocular in tone, telling Ottoline that she wishes she were there. Such duplicitous behaviour is symptomatic of Mansfield's continuing ambivalence, and it also suggests a certain amount of self-disgust, because she knew that they *needed* Lady Ottoline (thus Murry's own outburst of 'hate') and kept taking from her. It may well be that the upsurge in hostility towards Ottoline and Bloomsbury at this moment is largely scapegoating, deflecting Murry and Mansfield's more immediate worries about the war. They so encourage each other's beliefs in their unique experience of suffering that they seem to be unaware that the ones they 'hate' and envy are affected by the war as well: that only two months earlier Leonard Woolf's brother Cecil was killed and another brother, Philip, badly wounded by the same shell;[12] or, that on 29 January, Virginia Woolf was writing to her sister: 'Well, you almost lost me. Nine bombs on Kew; 7 people killed in one house, a hotel crushed' (LVW 2: 214).

Mansfield, however, soon had an even closer scapegoat at hand. Ida Baker (L. M.), though uninvited, had joined her in Bandol on 12 February, just at the moment she was beginning to write 'Bliss'. She reacted to her as a devious intruder into her privacy rather than as a devoted friend who had gone through considerable trouble to get leave from her factory job, fight for a passport and permit to travel during wartime, and who had taken a 'nightmare' journey to reach her.[13] Mansfield now had an outlet for the furious fits of anger which overcame her in the weeks to follow, anger triggered by L. M.'s seemingly inoffensive, if inappropriate, behaviour: unrelated remarks, too much interest in food, ordinary clumsiness. She complained to Murry on 23 February: 'It is impossible to describe to you my curious hatred and antagonism to her', which she compared to what 'Lawrence must have felt with Frieda', and then exclaimed: 'You remember the feeling Lawrence had (before he was so mad) that Frieda wanted to destroy him; I have oh – just that!!!' (KMCL 2: 89). This sudden identification with Lawrence, with whom neither Mansfield nor Murry had had contact for some time, reveals perhaps an unconscious understanding of *Lawrence*'s own illness, which had not yet been definitely diagnosed as tuberculosis.[14] It also might signal a recognition of her *creative* identification with Lawrence now, in opposition to her troubled relations with Bloomsbury, a declaration, perhaps, that he was, after all, still part of their own 'set', along with Keats and Coleridge.

IV

Murry added a new member to their special 'set' when he described on 10 March – in a singularly remarkable letter – the subject of his current review, Jean-Jacques Rousseau, as 'of the same kind as us':

> What I have written about him seems to be luminously simple; but it is *all new*. No-one has had the faintest idea of what I have discovered about him before. And I feel certain that we shall find, in just the same way, the secret of all the great men we love. No-one else can understand them except us – no one else at all. And when we go away from the world to the Heron we

shall discover the secret of them all, have them dwelling with us like friends. (LJMM: 136)

Murry's essay 'The Religion of Rousseau' was published in the *Times Literary Supplement* on 21 March 1918 as a review of *La formation religieuse de Jean-Jacques Rousseau* by Pierre-Maurice Masson, who had been killed in the war 'before the book to which he had devoted ten years of his life was published. He had prepared it for the press in the leisure hours of the trenches' (A: 15). That 'one of the most distinguished of the younger generation of French scholar-critics' should meet 'a soldier's death' was a perfect opportunity for Murry to put into critical prose the sentiments expressed in his journal entry two months earlier on 16 January: 'Talk of irony! The Mind that imagined this conjuncture of soul & body had a conception of irony that would freeze the mind alive if it could but grasp it' (BTW: 455).

The Rousseau essay's reflective, measured tone is in striking contrast to the building manic excitement of Murry's letter of 10 March, written the morning after he finished the review. Although the letter begins with a practical and detailed critique of Mansfield's use of 'inverted commas' in 'Bliss', it gathers force when he takes up the notion of his 'fusion' with Mansfield, that they 'are manifestations of the same being' (LJMM: 136). The letter swerves once the concept of their exceptionality enters the discourse: the references to 'no-one else' being able to understand what he has discovered, or to 'the secret of all the great men we love'. He is still aware that if he 'were to say this to anyone else but you they would think me raving'. Despite his protests to the contrary, as the letter continues there are even more disturbing implications about his mental state:

> Sometimes now I begin to think tremulously *high* thoughts, thoughts that make me dizzy. Suddenly, I seem to know the secret of the universe. And this at least I know, beyond all doubt, that I know the way to the secret and that my life will be spent in trying to make the pathway clear. I know this, too, that you are I are *geniuses*. I didn't know it before the real meaning of the Heron began to dawn upon me as it has lately done. (LJMM: 136)

The delusional exhilaration of this outburst continues while he tells her he 'want[s] to keep a record' of the 'coincidences' in their letters, such as Mansfield's sending him 'a collection of pictures of the place that really made Rousseau what he was'. But it shifts quickly to a more 'normal' tone as it winds down. Immediately following his discussion of 'coincidences', Murry suddenly writes from a more typically pragmatic viewpoint: 'Another thing, if any of my letters are alive still, will you keep them? I have all yours – and I think they may be important to us one day?'[15] This shift in tone is indicative of how easily Murry could demarcate the different sides of himself. He ends his letter with a few quotidian details: he is sending Mansfield a cheque for £5, he refers to the weather, and finally, reassures her that he has prepared his 'casseroles' for supper.

Nonetheless, this extraordinary letter, with its near-crazed rhapsodic tenor, its manic pursuit of oneness and its overriding egomania shows how close to breakdown he must have been. He later would recall that he felt so distraught at times that he walked the streets during the air raids 'in the superstitious hope that a merciful bomb would drop near me. That we were marked down by destiny was plain to my sick and apprehensive soul, and I was weary of waiting for the issue' (BTW: 469). Murry realised that he could not completely confide 'the strange adventures of my soul' to Mansfield, although if she had been able to read his letters more perceptively, she might have recognised his growing derangement. Her response to this one shows no evidence of such a perception. She responds primarily to Murry's critique of 'Bliss', which had preceded the manic part of his letter. Of course she would not have wanted to recognise fully Murry's state of mind, because as a very sick, desperate person herself, she was similarly self-enclosed. When she did respond with anxiety over his condition, it was to his physical self she referred – was he eating properly, in particular, thus Murry's comment about the casseroles.

To admit to full consciousness that Murry's emotional state was disordered would indict her own; she needed and contributed to the grandiosity of their mutual admiration society. She needed The Heron and the Romantics and an imaginary 'uncorrupted' country of the mind. And Murry sensed and later knew how much he conspired with her. During the worst period of all, the three weeks before 10 April when Mansfield was trapped in Paris during the bombardment, Murry let it slip in one of his letters that: 'In other words, being parted from you, I used literature as a drug, and now, at the crisis, I feel I've taken too many tabloids. A sense of emptiness hangs over me' (LJMM: 144). Mansfield's emotions were far more volatile during that 'crisis' (or, in the teleological narrative of their mutual epistolary text, the 'climax' of the story). More than a 'sense of emptiness' afflicted her; she was filled with a nihilistic loathing:

> An old dead sad wretched self blows about – whirls about in my feverish brain – & I sit here in this café – -drinking & looking at the mirrors & smoking and thinking how utterly corrupt life is – how hideous human beings are. (KMCL 2: 129)

The crisis was initiated by Mansfield's decision to leave Bandol earlier than her permit allowed, forcing her to seek official permission, and that involved an exhaustive trip to Marseilles, dealing with unsympathetic bureaucrats, and an unscrupulous doctor she hoped would give her a medical excuse. Her frantic efforts only served to get her to Paris in time for the bombardment, and she was trapped there, prevented from crossing the Channel. When Murry realised what had happened to her, he immediately grasped its tragic irony:

> I am in that state of mind, not seldom with me now, when I can see symbols in everything. Your having gone to Paris on the day when the great German attack began now seems to me as inevitable as all our correspondences. (quoted in L: 62)

She arrived on 22 March after a feverish train trip, unduly complicated by the loss of L. M.'s baggage. Murry, not yet aware of Mansfield's dreadful situation, was blithely writing to her that same day to tell her that he had just purchased a letter press. Perhaps his impulse to do so was hastened by having spent the past Sunday evening at the Woolfs, which brought to mind the Hogarth Press.[16] Virginia Woolf wrote in her diary afterwards:

> Poor Murry snarled & scowled with the misery of his lot. He works all day, & writes when he comes home. Worst of all, K. M. has been very ill with haemorrhage from the lungs, out in France, & has to be brought home, wh. is difficult, in order to see how bad she is. But I thought him very much more of a person & a brain than I had thought him before. (DVW 1: 129)

Woolf adds that '[h]e will never write another novel, he says. Poetry is a short cut & "life seems to me now very precarious"'. This was one of the rare occasions when Woolf seemed to have sympathy for Murry, even telling Lytton Strachey: 'Katherine Mansfield has been dangerously ill, and is still pretty bad, so that Murry was sunk in the depths, what with that and overwork, poor wretch' (LVW 2: 224).

Mansfield's letters in the days following show clearly how the whole experience was destroying any possible recuperation of her health. Whatever improvement she might have gained during her weeks of rest in Bandol was lost. She suffered from the extreme unseasonable cold, from her exhausting daily trips to Cooks in hopes of letters from Murry (which were not reaching her because of the closing of the Channel), and most of all, from the horror of the shelling itself. It is painful to imagine how hard it must have been for such a sick woman to have to go down into the 'caves' [cellars] at one o'clock in the morning, as she explained to Murry on 25 March, and sit 'in a heap of coal on an old upturned box' (KMCL 2: 139).

The Germans were shelling Paris with a 'super Kanon', a long-range gun, and many people were being killed; in one instance, when a nearby church was bombed, eighty died and ninety were wounded. Mansfield mentioned that to Murry, on 30 March, and also that she had been close to where the explosions occurred and in danger of being killed. Then she continued with an almost casual remark that if it were not for him she would not really care if she were killed or not, which suggests how deeply her nihilism had taken hold.

A few days later she described coming up from the cellars and finding the 'whole top of a house as it were bitten out' and in the broken trees which 'had just come into their new green'

> strange bits of clothes and paper hung. A nightdress – a chemise – a tie – they looked extraordinarily pitiful dangling in the sunny light. One thing which confirms me again in my dreadful feeling that I live wherever I am in another Sodom & Gomorrah – This. Two workmen arrived to clear away the debris. One found, under the dust, a woman's silk petticoat. He put it on & danced a step or two for the laughing crowd – That filled me with such horror that I'll never never get out of my mind the fling of his feet & his grin and the broken trees and the broken house. (KMCL 2: 150)

Mansfield's reference here to 'Sodom & Gomorrah' intensifies her growing preoccupation with 'corruption', but enlarges it from its earlier connotation of sexual exploitation in 'Je ne parle pas français' to a more universal sense of human depravity. It is 'hideous Humanity' she finds packed into the cellars: 'So hideous indeed that one felt a bomb on them wouldn't perhaps be as cruel after all.'

Murry's critical energies during the weeks of Mansfield's enforced stay in Paris were engaged in a new project, an introduction to the catalogue for an exhibition of J. D. Fergusson's paintings. The essay that he produced, 'The Daughter of Necessity', is one of his most convincing written during the war.[17] His biographer goes so far as to suggest that it 'is the key to nearly all Murry's work' (L: 61). This essay finally gave Murry the chance to formulate theories about the purposes of art – especially the relation between art and suffering – which had grown out of his and Mansfield's painful experiences of the past few months.

By defining art in its relation to necessity, Murry combines two precepts common to Romantic aesthetic theory: the disregard for conventions which inhibit the visionary power of the artist, and the role of the artist as a sacrificial victim whose 'destiny' is 'to know . . . the truth towards whose beauty he is inevitably driven' (E: 54–5). Murry's indebtedness to Keats is obvious when he refers to 'Art' as 'the pinnacle of the soul's exercise', which

> seeks no purpose, demands no glorious destiny, shrinks from no evil, is not chilled by the death of the universe; no despair can cast it down, neither can joy lift it out of the sight of the things that are; it does not cry that pain shall

be called good or seek a path to salvation by suffering. Experience holds nothing that it will deny. The beauty of true art is identical with truth. It is more than this; it is the only statement of the truth. (E: 52)

More significantly, Murry's discussion is also informed by the dichotomy Mansfield had made between 'joy' and 'a cry against corruption' in her letter to him on 3 February 1918 (KMCL 2: 52). When Murry had responded on 8 February that 'Je ne parle pas français' was 'dangerous', that '[i]ts dangerous to stop the world for a timeless moment' (LJMM: 115), his insight would later emerge in a new formulation in 'The Daughter of Necessity', where he now recognised the relationship between Mansfield's refusal to 'deny' the extremity of experience her writing expressed and 'the beauty of true art':

> Art is . . . at once the most human and the most inhuman thing we know. It is the most inhuman because its beauty is indifferent. It annihilates all standards and all aspirations but its own (and it may be that in the last encounter it annihilates even them). (E: 54)

Murry's high rhetoric in this essay contrasts greatly with the level of diction appropriate to the daily traumas of these last days of separation. Mansfield's ability to achieve what Murry in his essay calls 'that sudden plenary vision to which alone the inevitable unity of discrepant and hostile particulars is plain' (E: 51) is beautifully apparent in her rendering of the workman in the woman's petticoat dancing before the crowd and her recurring memory of 'the fling of his feet & his grin and the broken trees and the broken house' (KMCL 2: 150). The epistolary text contains more than enough evidence of 'Art'.

Mansfield's last letter to Murry from France, on 9 April 1918, written while she frantically readied herself for the journey home, manages to convey a fusion of discordant elements: terror ('I keep on writing – you know why – & now of course its in case the boat is submarined'), practicality ('I have bought 2 quarts of butter – and am going to try to bring them'), and optimism ('I too am terribly timidly just beginning to think of a bud of hope. Ever so tiny a one'). And she 'artfully', despite her haste, pulls it all together with a resonant symbol: 'My courage is just about mouse high'. She signs her letter: 'Mouse –' (KMCL 2: 159).

Notes

1. A much later example of such an attempt to communicate the ineffable is in 'The Garden Party' (1921), when Laura tries to explain what she means by 'life' to her brother.

2. See Kaplan (1991: 169–87) for a discussion of Mansfield's awareness of the multiplicity of the self and its relation to her aesthetics.
3. See Alpers (1980: 240–2) for a vivid description of the complex situation between Mansfield and L. M. in the small studio. He quotes a passage from Murry's journal describing L. M. standing naked in front of Mansfield's door, hoping for her admiration.
4. See David Bradshaw (1991), 'John Middleton Murry and the "Times Literary Supplement"' for the listing of all Murry's unsigned pieces in *TLS*.
5. In her letter to Ottoline Morrell on 24 April Mansfield noted the 'little Poussin cherubs climbing up & down the budding tree outside my window' (KMCL 1: 305).
6. On 29 January, Woolf remarked about Ottoline to Vanessa Bell: 'But she's got Murry back' (LVW 2: 214).
7. The evidence for this is not certain, since it is only recorded in Carco's memoir of 1940, *Bohème d'artiste*, and could have been constructed out of his reading of her story.
8. In a formal analysis, W. H. New draws attention to 'the triangular pattern' of the story, 'one that is conventionally associated with a corrupted love'. The pattern involves more than one triangle: the first consists of Duquette, Dick and Mouse; the second of Dick, Mouse and Dick's mother; yet another of 'Raoul, Dick, and their sexual ambivalence'(New 1999: 93).
9. For an extensive discussion of the influence of French symbolism on Mansfield's writing see Gerri Kimber (2008), *Katherine Mansfield: The View from France*.
10. Murry refers to Keats's statement in reference to Mansfield's comment in *Between Two Worlds* (BTW: 468).
11. In 'The Discovery of Pain', *TLS* (7 June 1917), Murry had written of the strength of recent French writing:

> The strange and splendid honesty of soul which seemed once to be the prerogative of Russia alone is descending upon France also. Within a few short months Barbusse, Benjamin, Romains, and Duhamel, young men of letters whom before the war we knew were not unlike their similars in England, have now with a common impulse of the spirit passed beyond them into another world. In them the war has cauterised the lie in the soul. (E: 270)

12. Editor's note in *The Letters of Virginia Woolf* (LVW 2: 209).
13. See L. M.'s painful account of Mansfield's cold reception, when she asked her 'What *have* you come for?' (Baker 1972: 107).
14. Claire Tomalin suggests that Mansfield might have caught the disease from Lawrence during their time of 'close proximity': 'This may have been the real *Blutbruderschaft* more sinister than Lawrence had ever intended' (Tomalin 1988: 163).
15. Mansfield responded to this request on 14 March: 'I have, of course, kept all of your letters ever since my arrival here, knowing that they will be of use to us one day' (KMCL 2: 122).
16. The Woolfs were in the process of printing Mansfield's 'Prelude', which would finally be published in July 1918.

17. 'The Daughter of Necessity', written for the May 1918 exhibition of Fergusson's paintings, is reprinted in Murry's *The Evolution of an Intellectual* (Murry 1920).

Chapter 5

'With Cannonballs for Eyes'

I

A happy ending to their epistolary story remained only in the realm of the imagination for Murry and Mansfield. The linear movement of a teleological narrative suggests some form of apocalyptic transformation: the timeless 'bliss' of The Heron. But Mansfield's return to London on 11 April 1918 is only the beginning of another story, a return to a cyclical rather than a teleological pattern. It is a return to dissatisfaction with Murry, to Bloomsbury social politics, to the competition and opportunism of the literary life, a narrative pattern far more in keeping with the flavour of modernist disjunction, disillusionment and deconstruction. This is not to say that the teleological Romance is completely destroyed, however. It continues to haunt their relations with each other. But for Mansfield now, the only certain resolution of it is her dying. And for Murry, as we shall see, it will remain both a motivating force and an explanatory tool for his life's trajectory, in which a variety of utopian plans and schemes continue to collide with cyclical encounters with what he called 'Necessity'. These collisions exemplify his enduring propensity both to repeat and to escape from the defining moments of his life.

Instead of the longed-for 'Heron', Mansfield had returned to live with Murry in his dreary rooms on the Redcliffe Road. They were finally married on 3 May 1918 with Brett and J. D. Fergusson as their witnesses. In her diary, Virginia Woolf describes Mansfield, only six days afterwards, as 'marmoreal, as usual, just married to Murry, & liking to pretend it a matter of convenience. She looked ghastly ill' (DVW 1: 150).

It had been one thing for Murry to read about Mansfield's coughing fits and her haemorrhage in her letters. It was another thing entirely to live with them. Murry was, after all, only twenty-eight years old, and totally unprepared for his new role as caretaker.[1] In his autobiography he explains how Mansfield wanted him to behave as if she were healthy, but he could not. Her 'cough seemed to jar on [his] spine' and he was anguished to see her looking 'a gaunt and bright-eyed shadow of what she had been four months before'. He admits that he had moments when he felt exasperated and trapped in an untenable situation: 'to have my anxiety for her interpreted as a desire to be rid of her was too much' (BTW: 481).

Mansfield's stay in London was to be short-lived, however, and she soon reluctantly agreed to a recuperative rest in Looe, Cornwall. This separation from Murry after only six weeks together must have been especially disheartening, destroying those desperate delusions of unity that had sustained both of them during her months in France. Murry does not reveal in his autobiography what must have been the devastating effect on their sexual life of Mansfield's illness. He only comments – in a phrase that sounds Lawrentian – that her illness 'made an end for ever of the instinctive carelessness of natural living for which she pined' (BTW: 489). Mansfield turned to her writing to express her bitter disappointment, for example her letter of 27 May: 'Our marriage – You cannot imagine what that was to have meant to me. Its fantastic – I suppose. It was to have shone – apart from all else in my life – And it really was only part of the nightmare, after all. You never once held me in your arms & called me your wife' (KMCL 2: 198).

At the end of May, Murry sent Mansfield *Civilisation 1914–1917*, a book he had just reviewed, by the French writer Georges Duhamel.[2] He drew her attention to one of the stories in it about a man so grievously wounded that he is at the point of death, but who regains the will to live when his wife suddenly appears by his bedside. Mansfield was so impressed with Duhamel's writing that within a few days she began to incorporate him into her domestic pantheon. She recounts to Murry in a letter on 8 June, her fantasy of inviting Duhamel and his child to stay with them at The Heron (KMCL 2: 228). As was the case with Murry's reading of Rousseau, it seems as if Duhamel would be joining their 'special set'. (It is suggestive that as she develops her fantasy further, she decides not to include Duhamel's wife in this imagined visit. After all, Mansfield liked triangles, but – as we have seen in the situation with the Lawrences – not quartets.)

In his correspondence with Mansfield, Murry also uses Duhamel as an imagined source of personal connection. When he feels sucked into a vortex of depression over his writing, he tells her that only she and 'perhaps Duhamel' could understand what he was trying to say (LJMM: 169). His review of Duhamel's book contains no sign of this kind of personal identification, but it appears to be yet another chapter in that larger 'text' in which Mansfield's illness and the war are fused. Murry heads directly to such a fusion by quoting from Duhamel's earlier *La vie des martyrs*: '"A human being . . . suffers always in his flesh alone, and that is why war is possible"' (E: 60). From *Civilisation*, Murry quotes Duhamel's comment that '"one cannot lend imagination to those who have it not"', and this conforms well with his and Mansfield's long-standing belief in their own exceptionality:

> One broods and broods, but there is no escape. Over a pale and fevered few the curse of understanding hangs like a thundercloud that will never move so long as they live. It is not true that all men have understanding, and that they steel their hearts to the suffering of a struggle for a greater good. (E: 61)

Murry's figurative language – such as 'pale and fevered' and his trope for civilisation's decline: 'The splendid flower of the sensitive plant is too heavy for the stem, for the sap runs elsewhere now and is turned to viler uses' (E: 62–3) – allows him to absorb Mansfield's illness and his own sense of himself as a 'divided' man into this larger social context. 'Consciousness has outrun life', he writes, an observation dating back to his debates with Lawrence and to his self-criticism in *Still Life*. But 'civilisation', that 'long process which has culminated in the consciousness which can imagine and suffer and find intolerable the pain of another', has yet 'created the means and the possibility to inflict pain of a kind and extent undreamed of. Therefore what has been called the bankruptcy of civilization is, more exactly, the failure of a mode of consciousness' (E: 62).

Murry recognises that Duhamel's method works to temper that 'failure' by engaging readers in a process which should bring them – if successful – to that same difficult but necessary understanding experienced by the 'pale and fevered few'. He senses that for Duhamel:

> the present is an hallucination . . . It has the exact and unmistakable quality of a dream, for the mind in the same moment accepts and refuses it as real. And this effect is more terrible because [Duhamel] does not deliberately aim at achieving it. The life of suffering is spread before us, full of familiar things. We can touch the walls of the hospital with our fingers if we would, and look out of its windows with our bodily eyes. But in this concrete scene which unfolds before us there are tiny, almost invisible, chasms, which are the souls of men in pain suddenly gathered up into an unforgettable phrase. Often we pass over the chasms from one firm rock to another and do not look down; only at a later moment does it flash into our minds that if we had looked down we should have seen things unspeakable. While we are still doubting, the moment comes when the suffering soul seems to utter a word that is and is not. A phrase looms up whose meaning is out of all relation to its actual words, ridiculous and terrible, and we are engulfed and lost in an abyss of pain. (E: 63–4)

Murry concentrates here on the impact upon the reader of Duhamel's technique. In trying to explain how the author achieves his effects, Murry's own values become readily apparent: 'the simple honesty which is the final perfection of art' is foremost. But the gaps – the 'chasms' – between the surface details and the hidden pain are what allow for the epiphanic experience which might permanently alter the reader's resistance. In focusing on the disjunction between the familiar and the 'unspeakable' in Duhamel's writing, Murry might also be describing Mansfield's technique, as in her letter of 2 April 1918, discussed in the last chapter, which describes the after-effects of a bombing with bits of clothing hanging from the trees and a workman dancing in a woman's petticoat pulled from the wreckage. Such a technique depends upon the proper use of irony and an astute awareness of its impact on a reader. Murry's paragraph ends appropriately enough with such a reader's epiphany: the unexpected phrase that shatters his resistance and forces him out of complacency into an 'abyss of pain'.

Murry's appreciation for Duhamel's method undoubtedly influenced his reaction to the next book he took up for review, one also based on wartime experiences, Siegfried Sassoon's *Counter-attack and Other Poems*.[3] Since both books contain 'unspeakable' things, it is understandable that Murry would compare them:

> We have read, for instance, in the pages of M. Duhamel, far more terrible things than any Mr. Sassoon has to tell, but they were made terrible by the calm of the recording mind. Mr. Sassoon's mind is a chaos. It is as though he had no memory, and the thing itself returned as it was. That is why the fact, or the spectacle of Mr. Sassoon is so much more impressive than his verses. (E: 78–9)

Murry recognises that Sassoon's 'verses – they are not poetry' depict 'realistic pictures of battle experience', but their 'language is over-wrought, dense and turgid, as a man's mind must be under the stress and obsession of a chaos beyond all comprehension' (E: 71). He finds here not 'true art, which is the evidence of a man's triumph over his experience, that something has after all been saved from disaster, but that everything is irremediably and intolerably wrong'. Murry's critical approach accords with his typical reliance on the concept of harmony (he also does not miss the opportunity to use Wordsworth as a touchstone):

> There is a value in the direct transcription of plain, unvarnished fact; but there is another truth more valuable still. One may convey the chaos of immediate sensation by a chaotic expression, as does Mr. Sassoon. But the unforgettable horror of an inhuman experience can only be rightly rendered by rendering

also its relation to the harmony and calm of the soul which it shatters. In this context alone can it appear with that sudden shock to the imagination which is overwhelming. The faintest discord in a harmony has within it an infinity of disaster, which no confusion of notes, however wild and various and loud, can possibly suggest. It is on this that the wise saying that poetry is emotion recollected in tranquillity is so firmly based, for the quality of an experience can only be given by reference to the ideal condition of the human consciousness which it disturbs with pleasure or with pain. But in Mr. Sassoon's verses it is we who are left to create for ourselves the harmony of which he gives us only the moment of its annihilation. It is we who must be the poets and the artists if anything enduring is to be made of his work. He gives us only the data. (E: 73–4)

The following excerpt offers a preview of Murry's position in relation to the question of artistic impersonality, which will become a more prominent issue as he develops as a critic. His objections to Sassoon's inability to separate himself from his experiences might seem paradoxical if considered in light of his own much later reputation as a 'confessional' writer:

The experiences of battle, awful, inhuman, and intolerable as they are, can be comprehended only by the mind which is capable of bringing their horror and their inhumanity home to the imagination of others. Without the perspective that comes from intellectual remoteness there can be no comprehension, no order and no art. Intellectual remoteness is not cold or callous; it is the condition in which a mind works as a mind, and a man is fully active as a man. Because this is wanting in Mr. Sassoon we are a prey to uneasiness when confronted with his work. We have a feeling of guilt, as though we were prying into secrets which were better hid. (E: 78)

Murry's language here suggests a subtext that might have little to do with the ostensible purpose of his critique. Why does he mention 'a feeling of guilt' and 'prying into secrets'? And why should such locutions follow from the phrase 'and a man is fully active as a man.'? Despite Murry's reasoned tone in the essay, it may well be that he was motivated less than he realised by the need to defend his aesthetic principles (such as his remark: 'There is danger that work such as his may pass current as poetry' [E: 74]) than by a suppressed competition between two males – a competition both professional (as poets) and personal. For unlike Murry's approach to Duhamel, in which an imagined sense of likeness energised his response, no such identification with Sassoon took place. Sassoon would never be considered for membership at The Heron. He was all too real, a man Murry actually knew (unlike Duhamel) and about whom he might have harboured jealousy. It was Sassoon, after all, who had been Ottoline Morrell's obsession at the same time in 1916 as Murry had written that he was falling in love with her. It was Ottoline

Morrell, in fact, who had asked Murry to write the review in the first place, soon after he had brought Mansfield back from Looe at the end of June.

Accordingly, Murry's resistance to considering that subtext might well have been a factor in the cause célèbre that the review's publication on 13 July 1918 set into motion, dividing Bloomsbury into pro- and anti-Murry factions. His attack on Sassoon would prove to be the first major debacle in his professional relations with Bloomsbury. (I am discounting for the moment Murry's earlier personal debacle with Ottoline herself.) Murry had been introduced to Sassoon a year earlier when Ottoline asked him and Bertrand Russell to advise Sassoon about publicising his objections to the war. Murry met with him a few days later – this time with Mansfield – on 11 June 1917, when he helped Sassoon edit his 'Declaration' as an officer in opposition to the continuation of the war. In recounting his memories of that evening with the Murrys, Sassoon noted that Murry's opinions matched his own even 'though he was at the time working in a government department of some sort' (Sassoon 1946: 78). Apparently, Murry had not divulged the nature of his war work, nor its importance. Here is another of those ironies Murry loved to explore: that he, a man who would soon be chief censor, was involved in a matter that could lead to a court martial.[4]

Given Sassoon's supposition that he and Murry thought along the same lines, it must have been particularly upsetting for him to read Murry's review. Although it had been published anonymously, everyone in Lady Ottoline's circle knew who had written it. Her husband, Philip Morrell, responded to it by sending an angry letter of protest to the *Nation*'s editor on 20 July, defending Sassoon as 'a gallant and distinguished author'. To exacerbate the controversy, Murry's review had appeared on exactly the same day as Sassoon was hospitalised for a severe bullet wound to the head, and Ottoline wrote to Murry to tell him that his review just might kill him (KMCL 2: 260 n1).

In a letter to Brett on 22 July, Mansfield expressed her worry that the Sassoon controversy would change her 'relation with Ottoline', but admitted that she was 'glad that this has happened':

> For one thing it shows what unfriendly country Murry had been repoging in
> – & it forces him to show his hand – to publicly draw apart from those who
> dont share his beliefs.
>   Hurrah! I am with him. We sit together and alone, an arrogant, hateful
> pair – with cannonballs for eyes – (KMCL 2: 257)

She was so pleased with her final remark that she repeated it with slight alterations the next day for Virginia Woolf's benefit: 'But it is only too plain from all this that Johnny Murry and I are arrogant outcasts with cannon balls for eyes' (KMCL 2: 257).

Their alliance now situated themselves in defiant opposition to anyone who might question their sense of moral integrity. The belief in their exceptionality that had shaped their epistolary romance and had linked them with an imaginary world of sympathetic compatriots would now be their bulwark against the fashionable intelligentsia. Nevertheless, Murry's review was making her own relations with members of that intelligentsia more difficult. Even if she resented them, she still needed their support for her creative efforts. Unlike Murry, who could at least rely on journalism to bring his ideas into print, Mansfield depended upon the acceptance of that smaller, more elite readership, dominated by Bloomsbury. Consequentially, within a few days after the publication of Murry's review, Mansfield was attempting to restore her relations with Ottoline Morrell by telling her of her longing for some 'exquisite, rare friendship' to offset the cruelty of life (KMCL 2: 254).

Mansfield casually mentions at the end of a letter to Ottoline on 3 August that 'Bliss' was appearing in that month's *English Review*, and she asked her to tell her what she thought of it (KMCL 2: 264). Although she must have recognised how remote the emotions of that story were from their present relationship, she might have feared not only the possible criticism of her story, but the revelation of its origins as well. Both of these factors might have been involved in Virginia Woolf's antagonistic reaction to the story. It is fortunate that Mansfield could not read Woolf's hostile comments in her diary entry of 7 August:

> I threw down Bliss with the exclamation, 'She's done for!' Indeed I dont see how much faith in her as woman or writer can survive that sort of story. I shall have to accept the fact, I'm afraid, that her mind is a very thin soil, laid an inch or two deep upon very barren rock. For Bliss is long enough to give her a chance of going deeper. Instead she is content with superficial smartness; & the whole conception is poor, cheap, not the vision, however imperfect, of an interesting mind. She writes badly too. And the effect was as I say, to give me an impression of her callousness & hardness as a human being. (DVW 1: 179)

Did Woolf recognise the story's associations with Ottoline Morrell and Murry? She was certainly aware of the gossip about them the previous year. But Woolf's reaction seems linked to something deeper than the details in her critique. She would remark to Vanessa Bell a couple of days later that was 'a little disturbed by a story of hers in the English Review. Its – well I wont say' (LVW 2: 266). The word 'disturbed' also suggests the uncovering of what has lain dormant. Was Woolf 'disturbed' about the story's intimations of lesbianism?

Mansfield entered a new phase in her life with Murry when they moved to Hampstead at the end of August 1918. She would now be living in a large, comfortable house, with servants and Ida Baker to care for her. Although her illness would prevent her and Murry from completing their dream of living at The Heron, Murry gave its name to the press he set up in the basement. There, perhaps in a silent competition with the Woolfs (who had published Mansfield's 'Prelude' on 11 July), he would proceed to publish both a book of his own poems and Mansfield's 'Je ne parle pas français'. On her birthday, 14 October, Mansfield turned thirty, and on that same day a specialist in tuberculosis told her that if she did not go to a sanatorium she would not survive. Rebelling against that advice, she decided she would stay at home, dedicating herself to her writing and to the renewing of her friendships.

Coincidentally, Lawrence would make a reappearance in her life that autumn. It happened that he and Frieda were visiting London and staying in Hampstead not far from the Murry's house on East Heath Road. She delighted in his 'passionate eagerness for life' when he visited her and his 'black self *was* not' (KMCL 2: 284). She remarked in her notebook, however, that 'Lawrence & Murry will never hit it off. They are both too proud & M. is too jealous. He is like a hawk over his possessions' (KMN 2: 139). Murry later remembered that when he saw Mansfield and Lawrence 'talking gaily together' he felt that he 'weighed on them like a lump of lead' (RDHL: 86).

For the first time since 1915, there would be no Christmas festivities at Garsington for either Mansfield or Murry. Mansfield would not have been strong enough to make the journey, in any case, but she also was determined to entertain her friends in her own home, perhaps in an attempt to restore the old grouping of that lively Christmas Eve of 1914 at the Lawrences. But the group had lost its centre: the Lawrences had by then left London, and only Koteliansky, Gertler and the Campbells were able to attend. Alpers suggests that the Murrys' party was a sad affair with its pathetic gestures of frivolity; it turned out to be Mansfield's 'last English Christmas' (Alpers 1980: 287).

Nearly a year earlier, Lawrence – foreseeing the problem confronting them all when the war was over – had written to Gertler about the end of 'the old way of life' and how they must all find a new way: 'a life based neither on work or love' (LDHL 3: 194). For Mansfield and Murry that would have seemed impossible. How could they ever create a new way of life if it were not to be based on work or love, their bulwarks against the insults of war and sickness? Those old utopian dreams were now even more remote: neither Lawrence's proposed ideal community, 'Rananim', nor 'The Heron' were in sight.

Nevertheless, Murry would have been in agreement with Lawrence that the 'old way of life' was finished. In a review in the *Nation* on 21 December 1918, he used the occasion of a book of letters and reminiscences by Frederick Keeling, a soldier killed in the war, to comment upon the failures of Keeling's – and by extension his own – generation, which 'had been emancipated from tradition and convention by the criticism of the generation immediately before it'. Murry thus describes this 'self-conscious generation', as 'irresponsible and egotistic', and yet 'prey to the consciousness of insecurity that comes from over-intellectualising experience', incapacitated by its 'indecision concerning what it was worth while to do' (E: 119–21).

Like Lawrence, Murry places sexuality at the centre of his analysis of this crisis of modernity, devoting much of his review to Keeling's description of the collapse of his marriage, his use of his wife 'as a concubine, or, in his own more modern language, as a breeder. To justify his own action, he proclaimed the theory of promiscuity as a social ideal' (E: 122). Murry suggests that before Keeling's self-transformation during the war, he acted as if 'the body politic and individual human beings had been vile bodies for experiment' (E: 131). There was in him 'a rigid line of division between his intellectual and his bodily appetites' (E: 130), and this made his political involvement as empty as his sexual relationships. In this way Keeling resembled the society in which he lived; he 'had lost contact with the human soul; he had suffered his conception of life and his fellow-men to be mechanised' (E: 124). Unlike Lawrence, however, Murry insists upon the need for *love* as the force behind the necessary transformation of society:

> [Keeling] had been slowly starving and approaching sterility because – let us say the word openly – he had no love. We are afraid, nowadays, to speak of love . . . And love alone can save the world, and raise humanity above the condition of beasts to whom civilisation has brought only a more various appetite for brutal satisfactions. (E: 131)

The desperation in Murry's tone may reflect his growing awareness that although 'love alone' might save the world, it was not enough to overcome the differences between himself and Mansfield. After their long separations, sustained by letters, their 'romance' was once again dissolving in the reality of day-to-day living.

II

Murry worried about how to support his expensive new household once his days at the War Office came to an end. Mansfield's allowance from her father and his own income from journalism would not be enough. Fortunately, a remarkable opportunity appeared for him after the turn of the new year when he was offered a yearly salary of £800 to become the editor of the *Athenaeum*, by its new owner, Arthur Rowntree.[5] During the next two years, Murry was to turn that old-fashioned, languishing periodical into a vehicle for the expression of a consolidating, Bloomsbury brand of modernism.[6] Here was a project that might finally overcome his and Mansfield's long-standing sense of dislocation and exclusion in relation to Bloomsbury. In contrast to their first collaborative efforts on the avant-garde journal *Rhythm* (1911–13), which had initiated their intimate yet deeply troubled relationship with the Lawrences, the *Athenaeum* would be a means to validate their position in the literary establishment.

Murry had only been 'given six hectic weeks to prepare the April number' (L: 65), his first as editor. He immediately needed to staff the paper and find writers for it, appointing his close friend J. W. N. Sullivan as assistant editor, and attempting to hire T. S. Eliot as second assistant editor (even convincing Rowntree to offer Eliot an annual salary of £500). It was a rather impulsive action on Murry's part as he had never even met Eliot before he offered him the position. After considering the offer, Eliot turned it down and Murry hired instead another denizen of Garsington, Aldous Huxley. Fortunately, Eliot agreed to write for the *Athenaeum* and his involvement with the paper would prove significant in his own development as a literary critic. As David Goldie observes, unlike the prose of Pound and Lewis, who 'appeared stuck in the strident, sometimes shrill forms of avant-garde coterie journalism, Eliot was able to craft a subtly polemical critical style entirely appropriate to Murry's popular, hybrid review' (Goldie 1998: 39).

Virginia Woolf's involvement in the *Athenaeum* reveals much about her ambivalent feelings about both Mansfield and Murry. It also reveals much about her insecurity over her positioning within the intelligentsia, something that people like the Murrys – on the borders of Bloomsbury – would have been surprised to learn. Apparently, Woolf felt hurt when she thought that she might not be asked to contribute to the *Athenaeum*, since Lytton Strachey and other friends had already been approached by Murry. In contrast, Murry relied on Mansfield to ask Woolf, and she did not do so until 20 February, wording her invitation in a manner more casual and off-hand than Murry's rather formal requests of others (KMCL 2: 302). The next day Woolf confided in her diary: 'I am asked to write for the Athenaeum, so that little scratch in my vanity is healed' (DVW 1: 243).

Woolf seemed to enter into the preparations enthusiastically despite that initial 'scratch', and eventually would contribute seventeen articles to the *Athenaeum* during Murry's editorship. Her diaries and letters contain the fullest and liveliest commentary available on Murry's activity during the initiation of the new periodical. Yet her alternating enthusiasm and resistance suggest an uneasiness about her contact with the 'underworld' of journalism altogether. Although she quickly took up Murry's editorship as a subject of entertaining gossip, she confided in her diary on 15 March that 'these little bits of literary gossip strike me as slightly discreditable. They point perhaps to one's becoming a professional, a hack of the type of Mrs W. K. Clifford, who used to know exactly what everyone was paid, & who wrote what, & all the rest of it' (DVW 1: 254–5).

Nonetheless, Woolf's 'little bits of literary gossip' allow us to see Murry's behaviour more clearly, as in her letter to Vanessa Bell on 19 March: 'Our chief amusement now is Murry and the Athenaeum. He is in a state of high exaltation, something like a Prime Minister, for everyone buzzes about asking for appointments' (LVW 2: 341). She is especially astute about his newly born self-assurance in her diary entry the same day:

> Success has already begun to do for Murry what I always said it would do. He is more freshly coloured, even in the cheeks than when we last met; & his mind has its high lights. Why, he chuckled like a schoolboy; his eyes shone; his silences were occupied with pleasant thoughts, I think; not that he would admit that to edit the Athenaeum was much more than preferable to a place in a government office . . . Murry is much of a small boy still . . . in spite of his tragic airs. I suspect his boast will come true; the Athenaeum will be the best literary paper in existence in 12 months. (DVW 1: 256)

Woolf uses the occasion of this visit with Murry to press for the inclusion of more of her friends – Desmond MacCarthy, for example – perhaps immediately perceiving what an opportune situation this might be for enhancing Bloomsbury cultural dominance. She also recounts how they 'went over all his names, & tried to think of others, but agreed that once our intimate friends were gone through the field was mown of its poppies'.

What most concerns Woolf, however, is finding out that Mansfield will be reviewing four novels each week: 'pray to God she don't do mine! I feel the acid in her once more' (DVW 1: 257). Her uneasiness about Mansfield will prove justified, as we shall see later, but she was able to put it aside for the moment and continue to preoccupy herself with her fascination with a woman who had such a similar love for 'our precious art. Though Katherine is now in the very heart of the professional world – 4 books on her table to review – she is, & will always be I fancy, not the least of a hack' (DVW 1: 258).

Murry's relations with Lawrence had never completely recovered from the Cornwall debacle, nonetheless, he still hoped to interest him in writing for the *Athenaeum*. Although Lawrence heard about Murry's appointment as editor in January, it took Murry until early March to ask him to contribute to the paper, suggesting his hesitancy over doing so. Lawrence's response was agreeable, if measured. Behind his politeness was the fact of his poverty. He really hoped for the chance to earn some money, therefore he would 'try to be pleasant and a bit old-fashioned', and even would be willing to use 'a nom de plume' (LDHL 3: 332). At this point, Lawrence was still able to separate his warm feelings for Mansfield from his distrust of Murry. His letters to her in February and March are filled with lovely descriptions of the snow-covered fields outside his window and references to mutually enjoyed books, but by the end of March that ended. It appears that there had been some kind of quarrel, a 'rumpus' as Frieda Lawrence apparently called it, perhaps – as O'Sullivan suggests – it 'had to do with KM's telling Frieda how she had been hurt by Lawrence' (KMCL 2: 310 n2). Soon afterwards, Lawrence was infuriated by Murry's rejection of some of the work he had sent him, and that closed off the possibility of his further involvement in the *Athenaeum*. Although the two men had once worked enthusiastically together on *The Blue Review* and *The Signature*, Murry was no longer in thrall to Lawrence. He had changed during the course of the war as much as, if differently from, Lawrence. The same self-assurance that Virginia Woolf noticed now made it possible for him to treat Lawrence as he might any other contributor. Or at least Murry believed that that was what he was doing. He was being *professional*. He was greatly concerned with establishing the right *tone* for his paper.[7]

Lawrence's defection was convenient for Murry, although he would have denied it. Without Lawrence's influence it would be easier for him to shape the *Athenaeum* more closely to his own emerging concerns; it could more likely fulfil its implicit role as the organ of Bloomsbury if Lawrence's critical voice were silenced. The stylistic and philosophical differences between Bloomsbury and Lawrence were deep-seated and had a difficult history, yet if Lawrence had become involved with the *Athenaeum*, perhaps some kind of reconciliation or cross-fertilisation might have been initiated by this new propinquity. Signs of the unlikelihood of this ever happening are visible in Virginia Woolf's response to the one piece by Lawrence published in the *Athenaeum*. In her diary on 17 April she remarks that she told Murry 'how [she] disliked Grantorto on whistling birds' (DVW 1: 265).[8] That she was unsympathetic to the essay without knowing its true authorship suggests a more essential difference than Lawrence's use of a nom de plume could erase.

Lawrence's essay appropriately complements Murry's editorial in the first issue of 4 April, which begins: 'Although as yet our heads ache too much from the bludgeoning of war for us to count our wounds, a menacing instinct warns us that we are somehow maimed; yet how we do not know' (E: 218). Lawrence more subtly suggests a similar dilemma: how to overcome the grave losses of the war and begin to reconstruct a culture in disarray. Although Lawrence's essay had been written before the war ended, in February 1917, its appearance in the *Athenaeum* more than two years later seems even more relevant to the situation at hand. He describes a landscape emerging from a great frost. Dead birds are everywhere, their bodies strewn across the fields and hedges, half-devoured by wild beasts. Suddenly as a warm wind begins the melting, everything seems startled into life by the sound of other birds. Lawrence here metaphorically evokes the present conundrum: 'How could they sing at once when the ground was thickly strewn with the torn carcasses of birds' (Lawrence 1972: 3). He reflects that 'it is no use any more to look at the torn remnants of birds that lie exposed' because 'under the surge of ruin, unmitigated winter, lies the silver potentiality of all blossom' (Lawrence 1972: 4). The essay's meditation on 'the utter incompatibility of death with life', the passing of 'winter' so quickly 'we cannot remember it', rises to an ecstatic assertion of 'life': 'The bird did not hang back. He did not cling to his death and his dead . . . Tossed into the chasm between two worlds, he lifted his wings in dread, and found himself carried on the impulse' (Lawrence 1972: 6).

Lawrence's heralding of 'a new world of spring' (Lawrence 1972: 3) finds its parallel in Katherine Mansfield's letter to Ottoline Morrell the following week, in which she too makes the change of the seasons an occasion for the contemplation of the possibility of psychic regeneration. Characteristically, she mentions to Ottoline that sometimes she 'is tired with *bliss*' and desires 'to feel it immediately shared – felt without [her] asking "do you feel it"?' (KMCL 2: 313). Sadly, she could not share that bliss with Murry. It was his inability to 'live passionately' that prompted her growing dissatisfaction. Her illness kept her largely imprisoned in her house, shut off from both the energies of the urban scene and nature's plenitude. Feeling ignored and isolated while Murry was away at the *Athenaeum* office or in his study for hours on end, she found some solace in recording her unhappiness in her notebook, complaining about Murry's behaviour, such as his bringing books home and not telling her about them:

He knows I can seldom go out, he knows I can *never* get to a bookshop, he knows how I *love* books . . . but all the same, he has never thought to share these finds with me – never for a moment. (KMN 2: 172)

From such facts she brings herself to a momentarily devastating conclusion:

All this hurts me horribly, but I like to face it and see all round it. He ought not to have married. There never was a creature less fitted by nature for life with *a woman*.

And the strange truth is I don't WANT him to change. I want to see him and then adjust my ways & go on alone & WORK.

Life without *work* – I would commit suicide therefore work is more important than life. (KMN 2: 172)

If work was to be her solace, it was also a reason for her pain. Murry's compulsive dedication to it was behind his emotional remoteness and exhaustion. Mansfield recognised a basic temperamental difference that seemed intractable.

III

With Lawrence absent from the *Athenaeum*, and seemingly removed from Mansfield's and Murry's personal lives as well, a new configuration of interpersonal energies began to emerge. This new configuration – a quartet composed of Mansfield and Woolf, Murry and Eliot – was primarily professional, without any kind of Lawrentian utopian plan or 'blood' bonding. That is not to say that it lacked emotional dimensions, however. If Woolf was initially flattered to be included among the contributors to the *Athenaeum*, she discovered quickly how deeply her involvement in it affected her tentative yet blossoming friendship with Mansfield, a friendship already vexed by the complexities of Bloomsbury gossip and the competitive pursuit of literary dominance. Yet the period of Murry's editorship culminated for both Woolf and Mansfield in a higher level of awareness of the possibilities and complexities of the prose medium. Woolf's centrally important essay, 'Modern Novels', and Mansfield's *Athenaeum* reviews of current fiction resonate with an implicit critical dialogue between the two women.[9] Woolf's and Mansfield's relationship was oddly paralleled by a similar set of interactions between Murry and Eliot, although the two men never approached the level of intimacy revealed in the correspondence of the women. The critical dialogue between Murry and Eliot centred more on the medium of poetry and eventually led to their famous, prolonged debates on classicism and romanticism during the 1920s, which I will consider briefly in Chapter 10.[10]

In retrospect, the *Athenaeum* years reveal the point of intersection of the talents of four writers who would emerge from them with their energies propelled towards their major intellectual and artistic contributions. During that short time of less than two years, literary modernism in England began to take on its predominant shapes and to articulate its recurrent obsessions with genius, form, tradition and modernity. In 1922, the year following that of Murry's resignation as editor, Eliot would publish *The Waste Land*; Woolf, her first experimental novel, *Jacob's Room*; Mansfield, the great stories of her maturity, *The Garden Party and Other Stories*; and Murry, his most influential book, *The Problem of Style*.

Although John Carswell remarks that 'the standards and the brow' of the *Athenaeum* 'were to be high to the point of ruthlessness' (J. Carswell 1978: 156), it might better be argued that Murry's achievement as editor was to advance modernist aesthetics and theory in a manner accessible to what Woolf called 'the common reader'. For instance, Eliot's critical writing reached a larger audience through the *Athenaeum* than it did through the *Egoist* (Ackroyd 1984: 96). The avant-garde journals (such as *Rhythm* and *Blast*) tended towards exclusivity, but the interdisciplinary character of the *Athenaeum*, which billed itself as a 'Journal of English & Foreign Literature, Science, the Fine Arts, Music & the Drama', would allow for new, broader conversations to take place amongst the educated middle class. These conversations would not be restricted to its general readers. The contributors to the *Athenaeum* influenced each other in numerous ways, which is not surprising, given the supposition that a writer is likely to read other articles in the same issue of a periodical in which she or he appears, especially if the periodical is a new venture, its editor a figure of interest (be that of envy, scorn or gossipy curiosity), and one's friends are also contributors. Although it might not be possible to *prove* that Woolf, for example, read a particular essay if she did not write about it in a letter or diary entry, yet one would be on fairly stable ground to suggest that she probably did read, say, Clive Bell's essay on Cézanne or Leonard Woolf's essay on writing history, and the review by E. M. Goodman of Alice Clark's *Working Life of Women in the Seventeenth Century*. And it is highly likely that she read J. W. N. Sullivan's articles on science. She certainly must have read all of Katherine Mansfield's reviews of current fiction, if only to compare them with her own reviews (or to wait in dread for the one about *Night and Day*).[11] T. S. Eliot might well have considered Edward Dent's argument about the change in attitude about rhythm in modern music, and as Michael Whitworth has convincingly argued, he seems to have been greatly influenced by Sullivan's articles on Einstein's theories (Whitworth 1996: 149–70).

Such intellectual intersections notwithstanding, a notable feature of the relationships amongst this quartet is professional competition, which takes place within a context of obsessive self-definition. Woolf would say of Eliot, for example: 'He is a consistent specimen of his type, which is opposed to ours' (DVW 2: 67), and Murry to Mansfield of Woolf: 'You see Virginia & (you & I) are fundamentally at cross purposes. We're right & she's wrong' (LJMM: 220). Woolf might bristle when she felt that Eliot 'completely neglected [her] claims to be a writer' (DVW 2: 67), but be heartened when Mansfield criticises Eliot's *Poems*, which is published by the Hogarth Press on the same day (12 May 1919) as Murry's long poem *The Critic in Judgement; or, Belshazzar of Baronscourt*, and Woolf's own *Kew Gardens* (KMCL 2: 318).[12] The simultaneous publication of the three small books would lead to further complexities in their authors' professional competition, evident in the peculiarly incestuous reviewing of these books in the *Athenaeum*: Mansfield reviewed *Kew Gardens* on 13 June, and the Woolfs jointly reviewed both *Critic in Judgement* and Eliot's *Poems* on 20 June.

During the first year of his editorship, Murry seemed preoccupied more with Mansfield's competition with Woolf than his own with Eliot, for that relationship continued to reflect the men's respect for each other and their shared sense of purpose. Murry wrote to Eliot: 'What a great pleasure it is to have you working with me. I only hope that the collaboration will not be interrupted until we have restored criticism' (Eliot 1988: 286). In contrast, he played a crucial role in abetting the competition between Woolf and Mansfield, as is apparent in his letter to Mansfield on 28 October 1919 referring to a conversation with Clive Bell:

> I told him that I considered you the only authentic writer of the present age. Of course, I said, I admired Virginia, thought her not only clever but the possessor of a delightful & rare fantasy; but that, I went on, is ultimately beside the mark. What Katherine has is the authentic writing gift, what Tolstoy had & Dostoevsky hadn't, something that can never come by taking thought. (LJMM: 198–9)

Murry's implied contrast between cleverness and authenticity reflects a central tenet of his emerging critical position, but here its genesis in the dynamics of personal interaction is most clearly visible. Such vexed interactions result from more than a social environment in which competition over status is pre-eminent. They reflect a deeper concern about the nature of artistic creativity itself, most apparent in the frequent recourse to the term 'genius' as a primary trope in their discourse, as it is in modernist discourse in general.[13] Murry's earlier, nearly hysterical exclamation to Mansfield while she was still in France: 'I know this, too, that you and I are *geniuses*' (LJMM: 136), was only a prelude to the heightened focus on the concept during the *Athenaeum* period. Now we find Murry telling Mansfield on 17 October 1919:

> How wonderful your descriptions are – 'like living inside a pearl'. No-one but you has the genius for these nowadays. Why the devil the whole literary world is not at your feet, I'll never understand. You are the only *genius* in the whole bunch of good ones among us (LJMM: 187)

and Mansfield responding to Murry's hyperbole on 22 October: 'Dont call me a genius – *you* are. It makes me embarrassed when you say it of me' (KMCL 3: 42). Woolf, more acidly remarks nearly six months later, that the *Athenaeum* has 'adopted Katherine as their writer of genius, which means, I'm afraid that poor Mrs. Woolf – but we writers are never jealous. Thank Heaven, I say to myself – that genius has arisen, though not in my particular headpiece' (LVW 2: 430). In her diary on 10 April 1920, Woolf fills out the context for her complaint: a review by Sullivan in the *Athenaeum* entitled 'The Story-Writing Genius', in which he compares Mansfield to Chekhov and Dostoevsky:

> I can wince outrageously to read K. M.'s praises in the Athenaeum. Four poets are chosen; she's one of them. Of course Murry makes the choice, & its Sullivan who rates her story a work of genius. Still, you see how well I remember all this – how eagerly I discount it. (DVW 2: 28)

Woolf's anxiety here – expressed through her self-consciousness about her envy of Mansfield – is related to a more substantive issue than professional competition, and it is directly related to the question of gender. Behind her use of the word 'genius' lies her awareness of the misogyny of a culture which did not recognise the possibility of female genius. Yet Woolf could easily see that Murry had been able to overcome that inherited ideology of bias against women enough to insist on that designation for Mansfield. Nonetheless, in a cultural economy so constricted in its willingness to offer inclusion to women, was it possible for more than *one* woman to be admitted to its pantheon of greatness?[14]

It was this concern which eventually led her to formulate the argument in *A Room of One's Own* that the emergence of genius is a function of historical process. She would then recognise that 'masterpieces are not single and solitary births; they are the outcome of many years of thinking in common, of thinking by the body of the people, so that the experience of the mass is behind the single voice' (Woolf 1963: 68–9). (Woolf tends to undercut this social-constructionist theory by her continuing use of the essentialist concept of 'genius' itself. Her fictional 'Shakespeare's sister' is *born* with a genius like that of her brother, even if it is silenced by her society.)

This question of genius would continue to preoccupy Murry in 'The Function of Criticism', which he published, unsigned, in *TLS* on 13 May 1920. In this article he considers the critic's role in discerning genius and enabling it: 'There is a sense that if . . . the writer of genius, were to appear, there ought to be a person or an organisation capable of recognising him" (A: 1). (Murry's definition of 'the writer of genius' here is decidedly male.) The difficulty of doing so reflects how 'in the world of letters everything is a little up in the air, volatile and uncrystallised . . . a strangely different world from that of half a dozen years ago'. Before the war, 'one had a tolerable certainty that the new star . . . would burst upon our vision in the shape of a novel. To-day we feel it might be anything . . . it has no predetermined form' (A: 1).

Murry holds fast here to an Arnoldian ideal. The critic, 'in regarding the work of art as a thing in itself . . . will never forget the hierarchy of comprehension, that the active ideal of art is indeed to see life steadily and see it whole, and that only he has a claim to the title of a great artist whose work manifests an incessant growth from a merely personal immediacy to a coherent and all-comprehending attitude to life' (A: 13–14). The ideal remains grand and austere, harking back to Murry's fondness for his old Platonic concept of an 'unchallengeable harmony in the spirit of man' (A: 13). Mansfield's implicit critical theory, expressed in a review of May Sinclair in the *Athenaeum* only a month later, posits a similar ideal: 'the great writers of the past have not been "entertainers". They have been seekers, explorers, thinkers. It has been their aim to reveal a little of the mystery of life. Can one think for one moment of the mystery of life when one is at the mercy of surface impressions?' (Mansfield 1930: 44).

Murry also strives to elevate the significance of the critic's role to bring it closer in its creative power to that of the artist, formulating the proposition: 'as art is the consciousness of life, criticism is the consciousness of art' (A: 11). It is at this point in the essay that Murry reveals the nearly suppressed competition at the base of his assertions:

> The essential activity of true criticism is the harmonious control of art by art. This is at the root of a confusion in the thought of Mr Eliot, who, in his just anxiety to assert the full autonomy of art, pronounces that the true critic of poetry is the poet . . . No, what distinguishes the true critic of poetry is a truly aesthetic philosophy. (A: 11)

Another unconscious intrusion of the contemporary politics of competition into his critical theory is Murry's fondness for the word 'hierarchy', as when he insists that the 'function of true criticism is to establish a definite hierarchy among the great artists of the past, as well as to test the production of the present' (A: 14). This emphasis on ranking has for Murry a moral implication:

> The critic has not merely the right, but the duty, to judge between Homer and Shakespeare, between Dante and Milton, between Cézanne and Michelangelo, Beethoven and Mozart. If the foundations of his criticism are truly aesthetic, he is compelled to believe and to show that among would-be artists some are true artists and some are not, and that among true artists some are greater than others. (A: 14)

Mansfield appears to have shared Murry's penchant for judging and ranking. In her review of Dorothy Richardson's *The Tunnel* in the *Athenaeum* on 4 April 1919, she valorises 'Memory' and its important function in both life and art, in judging 'all that is in our minds – appointing each his separate place, high or low, rejecting this, selecting that – putting this one to shine in the light and throwing that one into the darkness' (Mansfield 1930: 6). Clare Hanson comments on Mansfield's trope as 'a powerful, institutionalised, male memory', which suggests her ambivalent stance towards feminism in its seeming approval of 'male authority' (Mansfield 1987: 19). Nonetheless, Mansfield might have felt uneasy with Murry's blatant reliance on the traditional male 'hierarchy' of greatness for his ranking system. She wrote many reviews of books by women for the *Athenaeum*, and as Hanson notes: 'On the whole KM is more lenient with these writers than with their male counterparts' (Mansfield 1987: 17).

This clearly was not the case when Mansfield approached Virginia Woolf's *Night and Day*. Murry only exacerbated the competition between the two women by assigning the book to her, for even before reading it she had complained to Ottoline Morrell on 21 August 1919 that 'it will be acclaimed a masterpiece & she will be drawn round Gordon Square in a chariot designed by Roger after a supper given by Clive' (KMCL 2: 352). When she finally read *Night and Day*, after she had once again returned to the Riviera for the winter, she found herself in a real quandary. She disliked Woolf's novel intensely and yet did not want to say it outright in the review for fear of offending her. She wrote to Murry on 14 November 1919 that Woolf's novel 'is a lie in the soul. The war never has been, that is what its message is', but that she must 'be very careful and do my best to be dignified and sober. Inwardly I despise them all for a set of cowards. We have to face our war – they wont' (KMCL 3: 82).[15]

Murry was pressed to explain Mansfield's review to Woolf at a dinner with her on 22 November. His letter to Mansfield the next day reveals a complicated nexus of theoretical differences, personal competition and group dynamics. To bolster his own position, he quickly let Woolf know that *his* friends (Tomlinson, Waterlow and Sullivan) 'all thought it explained itself perfectly', and then told her that what Mansfield meant was that Woolf 'made an abstraction from life'. He recognised that this did not comfort her, as she then responded by saying that Mansfield's 'novel reviews showed that [she was] not interested in novels' (LJMM: 221). Murry considered that 'a very illuminating remark, illuminating Virginia of course. What she really meant . . . was that you related novels to life. Virginia can't abide that' (LJMM: 221).

Yet Murry must have found himself in a conundrum. He did not want to have his friendship with Woolf destroyed over his defence of Mansfield's review. Despite his hesitations about her approach to writing, he hoped to maintain a relationship with her – and with her sister, Vanessa Bell. Thus in his letter to Mansfield the next day he softened his tone:

> I think that Virginia & Vanessa, however much we disagree with them – and, as I said, I think we are profoundly at cross purposes with Virginia, at least – are the two women with whom you & I have most in common (except, perhaps, Brett). At all events, when I'm with any of those three I don't feel that my nerves are all ragged and being jagged with a blunt saw. I suppose it's because they are all, in their way, sincere & devoted artists. They don't make that continual, ghastly enervating personal claim on your attention that other women do. If you disagree with them, they don't visibly hasten to agree with you. There's something hard & definite & self-contained about them. (LJMM: 223)

I find Murry's merging of himself in Mansfield here very suggestive in terms of gender politics: 'the two women with whom you & I have most in common'. In one way, his statement could be said to feminise himself, but almost as if unconsciously drawing back from that unacceptable assumption, he finds it necessary to assign to them the hardness and self-containment usually attributed to men. There is also a possibility that he uses that sense of likeness to counter Mansfield's enduring suspicion of his attraction to other women. His gratuitous contrast of these female artists with ordinary women works both to eliminate any elements of sexual attraction and to bolster Mansfield's exceptionality, her difference from the conventional femaleness she had always scorned. But Murry was not sensitive to the fact that Mansfield no longer cared to be identified in terms of her androgynous qualities. Her physical vulnerability, her loneliness, her jealousy were all in a seeming conspiracy to undermine her old defiant independence. In response to Murry's praise of the three women, Mansfield was more concerned with letting him know the cost of his sociability with them:

> How I envy you seeing people – & yet of course it means nothing to you. I mean you are not like me, dependent upon contact with people. I am, yes, I am. By people I mean – not being alone. I'd live all the rest of my life without seeing another human being if I had you. (KMCL 3: 125)

Notes

1. Dennis McEldowney astutely remarks, apropos some of Mansfield's biographers' criticism of Murry's behaviour: 'None seems to have explored more recent awareness of the strains placed by long-term illness on patients and those about them' (McEldowney 1985: 116).
2. The French writer Georges Duhamel (1884–1966), was an army surgeon during the war and wrote two collections of wartime observations: *Vie des martyrs* (1917) and this new one, *Civilisation 1914–1917*, published under the pseudonym of Denis Thevenin. Murry's review, 'The Great Hallucination', was published on 8 June 1918 in the *Nation*. He had also written a review of *Vie des martyrs*, 'The Discovery of Pain', which had appeared in *TLS* on 7 June 1917. Both reviews are reprinted in Murry's *The Evolution of an Intellectual* (1920).
3. Murry's review 'Mr. Sassoon's War Verses' appeared in the *Nation* on 13 July 1918. It is reprinted in *The Evolution of an Intellectual* (Murry 1920).
4. See Sassoon's *Memoirs of an Infantry Officer* for his account of the events which followed and which resulted in his hospitalisation for 'shell-shock'.
5. In comparison, it may be of interest to note that in 1919, Virginia Woolf earned about £153 from her writing; Leonard Woolf earned £578. His editorship of the *International Review* (which was also funded by Rowntree) paid him £250 of that total. See Leonard Woolf, *Downhill All the Way* (New York: Harcourt Brace Jovanovich, 1975), p. 17.
6. The *Athenaeum*, founded in 1828, became the most illustrious literary periodical of the Victorian period, but by the early twentieth century it was in decline. During the war it was changed, by its editor Arthur Greenwood, into a monthly 'Journal of Reconstruction'. For an incisive discussion of the history of the reconstruction movement and the *Athenaeum*'s role in it, see Goldie (1998: 12–22). For a useful description of Murry's editorship and his recruitment of contributors see Oscar Wellens (2001).
7. See Kinkead-Weekes (KW: 497–501) for a detailed discussion of Lawrence's reactions to the rejection of his work. He points out how Murry's memory failed him in *Reminiscences*, when he wrote that he had only rejected one piece: 'Lawrence had certainly sent three, very probably four, possibly five' (KW: 500).
8. Lawrence's 'Whistling of Birds' was published in the second issue of the *Athenaeum*, 11 April 1919, under the name of 'Grantorto'. The annotated

publisher's copies of the periodical at City University in London indicate that Lawrence was paid £4 for his contribution.

9. See Kaplan (1991: 161–8) for a fuller discussion of the critical dialogue between Mansfield and Woolf. Woolf's essay appeared in *TLS* on 10 April 1919. She later revised it as 'Modern Fiction', in *The Common Reader* (Woolf 1925).

10. See Goldie (1998) for the most fully developed analysis of that debate.

11. Mansfield's reviewing for the *Athenaeum* receives comprehensive attention in two recent articles. See Angela Smith (2009: 3–18); and Jenny McDonnell (2009: 727–42).

12. Murry's poem was written in 1913 (L: 37). Lilley's *Bibliography* (Lilley 1974) lists its date of publication as October 1919, but Woolf's diary comment of 12 May 1919 contradicts that attribution (see DVW 1: 271).

13. The term 'genius' seems nearly absent in the discourse of postmodernism, however. According to David Bromwich, 'the word dominated nineteenth-century discussions of interpretation and community, and it is only beginning to pass from view' (Bromwich 1985: 143).

14. Patricia Moran remarks that the men in each of the circles around Mansfield and Woolf 'championed one woman by undermining the other . . . And there is room for only one' (Moran 1996: 13–14).

15. Mansfield compares *Night and Day* to Jane Austen's novels: 'There are moments, indeed, when one is almost tempted to cry it Miss Austen up-to-date. It is extremely cultivated, distinguished and brilliant, but above all – deliberate. There is not a chapter where one is unconscious of the writer, of her personality, her point of view, and her control of the situation' (Mansfield 1930: 113).

Chapter 6

'The Coming Man and Woman'

I

'You are evidently a genius as an editor – nothing short of that – a perfect genius', Mansfield tells Murry on 13 October 1919, after reading through a particularly lively issue of the *Athenaeum* (KMCL 3: 21). Murry is equally complimentary in his response to her letter on 17 October, exclaiming that she is 'the only *genius* in the whole bunch of good ones among us' (LJMM: 187). He also magnanimously suggests she help Lawrence by writing something on *Sons and Lovers*, 'saying how it stands out etc. You know what the average is like nowadays & you can speak your mind' (LJMM: 188). In this optimistic mood, he lays out his plans for her to consider: 'I have two determinations – one to make the paper a success against all competition this winter – the other to write a novel with among other things some real you and me love in it'.[1] As editor, Murry is now able to control the direction of his own literary criticism without interference. He can select the books he wants to review and use them for his own purposes, especially as vehicles for his developing aesthetic principles. In fact, the *Athenaeum* provides the opportunity for both Murry and Mansfield to cultivate their critical talents and to articulate the theoretical bases for their critical practices. Mansfield's 'novel page', as Murry calls it, is 'one of the features most appreciated in the paper', and he believes that it is 'quite unlike – in a different class to – anything that's being done in the way of reviewing anywhere to-day' (LJMM: 210).

Murry's praise is justified. Mansfield's reviews can be read with enjoyment even today, long after most of the novels she wrote about have been forgotten.[2] Yet her production of 111 reviews of fiction between April 1919 and December 1920 represents an enormous expenditure of energy from a woman struggling to stay alive. She took on two or three novels at a time and spent hours crafting each review, working against the paper's deadlines; consequently, she was unable to write much fiction. Nonetheless, as Clare Hanson remarks, 'it seems reasonable to suggest that the clarification of certain precepts in her *Athenaeum* criticism contributed to the sureness of tone in the fiction from this period on' (Mansfield 1987: 34).

Mansfield's critical practice during this time parallels Murry's. I should emphasise here, however, that Murry's and Mansfield's views are so intertwined that it is difficult to be sure of the origin of any particular component of a concept. How much Murry was influenced by Mansfield can only be inferred, since his letters contain no discussion of the content of her reviews nor the aesthetic principles she puts forth in them. Instead, he praises the beauty of her prose, the delicacy of her touch. If she might be impatient with the infelicities of his style of expression, the same cannot be said of his reaction to hers. In fact, there is not a word of disagreement in his response to any of her reviews, and it is probably reasonable to assume that he was in complete accord with her judgments.

Mansfield shares Murry's disdain for writing that ignores the extent of the change in consciousness brought about by the war, as we have seen with her criticism of Woolf's *Night and Day*, to which he had responded: 'The War *is* Life; not a strange aberration of Life, but a revelation of it. It is a test we must apply; it must be allowed for in any truth that is to touch us' (LJMM: 211). Nevertheless, their mutual rage against post-war complacency and hypocrisy is not easily assuaged by the current manifestations of the 'new', the prevalence of experimentalism as the motor of modernist aesthetics. About that they both seem ambivalent. Their writing about experimental literature during the *Athenaeum* period is cautious rather than radical (as it had been in their embrace of avant-garde practices during the *Rhythm* period at the start of their relationship). This caution is in keeping with the general progression of their thought towards a consolidation of modernist principles instead of an automatic reaction *against* traditional conventions, as it had been much earlier. A review by Mansfield on 15 October 1919 indicates that she is fully aware that

> we live in an age of experiment, when the next novel may be unlike any novel that has been published before; when writers are seeking after new forms in which to express something more subtle, more complex, 'nearer' the truth; when a few of them feel that perhaps after all prose is an almost undiscovered medium and that there are extraordinary, thrilling possibilities. (Mansfield 1930: 96)

Her wholehearted enthusiasm for this 'almost undiscovered medium' relates to her own discoveries as a writer of fiction. She had been appreciative in her review on 13 June 1919 of Woolf's *Kew Gardens*, understanding almost from inside the text how Woolf 'begins where the others leave off' (Mansfield 1930: 39), and perhaps some of her later disappointment with *Night and Day* had to do with the absence of experimentation. On 28 November 1919, only a week after she reviewed Woolf's novel, Mansfield reacted similarly to several other current works of fiction:

> However deep the knowledge a writer has of his characters, however finely he may convey that knowledge to us, it is only when he passes beyond it, when he begins to break new ground, to discover for himself, to experiment, that we are enthralled.

Nonetheless, she hesitated before offering full approval to experimentation, preferring to see it as the culmination of a process rather than the start of one: 'The "false" writer begins as an experimentalist; the true artist ends as one' (Mansfield 1930: 119).[3]

Where Mansfield and Murry seem most troubled about experimentation is in its then current popularity in the form of various types of literary impressionism in fiction and poetry. Mansfield's uneasiness about impressionism is already apparent in her first review for the *Athenaeum* on 4 April 1919. She criticises Dorothy Richardson's 'passion for registering every single thing that happens in the clear, shadowless country of her mind', and expresses the need for an organising principle to 'judge' the significance of 'each' in 'its appointed place in the whole scheme' (Mansfield 1930: 5–6). In her review of May Sinclair's *Mary Olivier* on 20 June 1919, Mansfield asks: 'Is this to be the novel of the future?' and considers how 'the difference between the new way of writing and the old way is not a difference of degree but of kind. It's aim . . . is to represent things and persons as separate, as distinct, as apart as possible'. She argues that this kind of atomisation of experience into perceptual fragments removes 'what Blake beautifully calls the bounding outline' (Mansfield 1930: 44–5).[4]

It cannot be entirely coincidental that only two weeks earlier, Murry applied a similar critique to 'modern poetry', which 'like the modern consciousness of which it is the epitome', is in a state of 'indecision, which it manages to conceal from itself by insisting that it is lyrical, whereas it is merely impressionistic'. Murry insists that the

> value of impressions depends upon the quality of the mind which receives and renders them, and to be lyrical demands at least as firm a temper of the mind, as definite and unfaltering a general direction, as to be epic. (A: 52)

He would continue in a similar vein nine months later when he derides 'the queer spectacle of a whole race of very young poets who somehow expect to attain poetic intensity by the physical intensity with which they look at any disagreeable object that happens to come under their eye'. Here he acidly remarks: 'to register the mere facts of consciousness, undigested by the being, without assessment or reinforcement by the mind is, for all the connection it has with poetry, no better than to copy down the numbers of one's bus-tickets' (A: 182).

The philosophical underpinnings for Murry's complaints here are articulated in 'The Function of Criticism', where he objects to Hegel's 'thesis that all the events of human history, all man's spiritual activities, are equally authentic manifestations of Spirit', and insists that the true critic must 'distinguish between intuitions and to decide that one is more significant than another' (A: 7). Murry's statement is reminiscent of Mansfield's remark about Dorothy Richardson, written five months earlier, 'that everything being of equal importance to her, it is impossible that everything should not be of equal unimportance' (Mansfield 1930: 146).

Murry's insistence upon 'the quality of the mind which receives and renders' the impressions as the primary locus for his critical attention is characteristic of that same tendency to rank writers according to the comprehensiveness of their vision that I discussed in Chapter 5. While Mansfield shares this insistence, as well as its implied hierarchy of values, her critical practice –at least as far as she was able to develop it through her work for the *Athenaeum* – does not display the same penchant for praise of 'great' writers as does Murry's. This is largely the result of her having to review so many trivial books, especially those she called 'pastime novels'. Murry reserved for himself, or for other reviewers, the books by or about canonical authors. For instance, he had Sydney Waterlow write an article for the centenary of George Eliot's birth, even though Mansfield had told him she wanted to do it.[5] In an even more blatant example of appropriation, in August 1919 Murry had taken on the review of a book of Chekhov's short stories, recently translated by Constance Garnett, despite the fact that Mansfield had been a devotee of Chekhov for years and at present was working with Koteliansky on translations of Chekhov's letters for publication in the *Athenaeum*.[6]

Nonetheless, Murry's decision to write about Chekhov makes sense within his own developing critical framework; it allowed him to articulate, more precisely than he had been able to do before, his understanding of the philosophical and aesthetic bases of the current expressions of literary impressionism. Mansfield's objections to it must have been in the forefront of his mind while he prepared his article, less than two months after her review of May Sinclair's *Mary Olivier*. In it he singles out

Sinclair as his only contemporary example to contrast with Chekhov, although his reference to her is more generous than was Mansfield's. There is an implication in Mansfield's critique that Sinclair had suddenly taken up experimentation almost as if she were doing so to be part of the fashionable avant-garde. Mansfield suggests that 'it is too late in the day for this new form' (Mansfield 1930: 45), but Murry interprets Sinclair's 'latest experiment' as an indication of how the modern need 'to reconcile the greatest possible diversity of content with the greatest possible unity of aesthetic impression . . . is beginning to trouble a writer with a settled manner and a fixed reputation' (A: 79).[7] Murry decides that Chekhov 'faced and solved' that problem, and in so doing 'is, in fact, a good many phases in advance of all that is habitually described as modern in the art of literature' (A: 79). Chekhov is 'not what he is so often assumed to be, an impressionist' (A: 76). Murry recognises that Chekhov's 'comprehension radiates from a steady centre, and is not capriciously kindled by a thousand accidental contacts' (A: 76). Unlike the Impressionists, Chekhov 'had slowly shifted his angle of vision until he could discern a unity in multiplicity' (A: 76–7).

Murry complains that, among his contemporaries, 'how rarely do we see even a glimmering recognition of the necessity of a unified aesthetic impression! The modern method is to assume that all that is, or has been, present to consciousness is *ipso facto* unified aesthetically' (A: 79). He understands that Chekhov 'decided on the quality of aesthetic impression he wished to produce, not by an arbitrary decision, but by one which followed naturally from the contemplative unity of life which he had achieved' (A: 80).

Murry's distinction between the 'arbitrary' and the 'natural' here reveals the degree to which his aesthetics are grounded in Romantic notions of organicism. (This grounding is also apparent in his frequent use throughout the essay of terms such as 'organic connection', 'flowering of a plant' and 'emanation from life'.) He establishes a similar dichotomy in his contrast between the 'classical' and 'modern' methods:

> The classical method consisted, essentially in achieving aesthetic unity by a process of rigorous exclusion of all that was not germane to an arbitrary (because non-aesthetic) argument . . . The modern problem – it has not yet been sufficiently solved for us to speak of a modern method – arises from a sense that the classical method produces over-simplification. It does not permit of a sufficient sense of multiplicity. (A: 79–80)

Murry's desire for 'a unified aesthetic impression' bears some similarity to Virginia Woolf's earlier call for 'some unity, significance or design', when she reviewed Dorothy Richardson's *The Tunnel*.[8] Woolf's reaction to Richardson's impressionistic method was more favourable than Mansfield's, however. She recognised that it was a method that 'if triumphant, should make us feel ourselves seated at the centre of another mind' (Woolf 1965: 121). The success of such a method depends for Woolf on 'the artistic gift of the writer', which is expressed through the creation of the appropriate pattern or 'design'. It is important to differentiate this from Murry's emphasis on how the writer's 'comprehension' should 'radiate from a steady centre'. Murry assumes a stable subject underneath the manifestations of multiplicity. His insistence upon 'a unified aesthetic impression' is still related to his long-standing theory of harmony and the humanist conception of an essential self that is its grounding principle.

Woolf's famous description of 'a myriad impressions', 'an incessant shower of innumerable atoms' which 'shape themselves into the life of Monday or Tuesday', tends to put the burden of the creative process on the activity of shaping rather than upon the essence of the shaper (Woolf 1925: 154). This is a crucial difference from Murry's belief in a 'radia[tion]' from a steady centre'. Murry's concept is one in which the artist *resists* the passivity of *being shaped*. Thus he is interested in the 'sense of the rhythm of an achievement' and looks for 'the organic progression' in a poet's work (A: 52). Furthermore, Woolf's emphasis falls more upon 'design' as an aspect of technique. Murry's interest in technique is less emphatic, as is evident in his letter to Mansfield on 23 November 1919, where he states that he feels himself to be 'always notoriously weakest in the examination of the technical side of a work' (LJMM: 223).

In retrospect, we can discern how Woolf's objections to current modes of impressionism might lead her to a more abstract formal structure for her novels, corresponding with her strong affinities with post-Impressionism. We can also discern how Murry's objections might lead him to a critical practice centred upon the integrity of the individual author, one that valorised the 'steady centre' he found in Chekhov and would be further elaborated in his later studies of Keats and other canonical writers.

Murry's problem with 'technique', however, is another matter. It is directly related to his failure as a novelist. For unlike Woolf and Mansfield, who were able to use their respective critiques of current literary impressionism productively to their own advantage as writers of fiction, Murry lacked 'the artistic gift' that might enable him to imagine a new structure for his fiction. He seemed to realise his deficiency when he told Mansfield on 17 October 1919 that he wanted to write another novel (unlike 'rotten old *Still Life*'), and admitted:

> I don't know how I shall tackle it; I can't get a scheme, and don't see what good it would do if I had one. I'm sure I wasn't built to work with schemes. One door suddenly opening out of a dark chamber, then another, and another – that's the only way my mind ever works. (LJMM: 188)

Despite Murry's complaint that the 'modern method is to assume that all that is, or has been, present to consciousness is *ipso facto* unified aesthetically' (A: 79), there is considerably irony in this description of his own artistic method, which seems to follow the same principles he had criticised only two months earlier.

II

Woolf's questioning of Richardson is related to her own struggles to discover a method that would allow her both to explore the stream of consciousness and to avoid 'the danger' of 'the damned egotistical self; which ruins Joyce and Richardson' for her (DVW 2: 14). In this respect, Woolf resembles Mansfield, who had complained of Richardson that 'her concern is primarily, and perhaps ultimately with herself. "What cannot I do with this mind of mine!" one can fancy her saying' (Mansfield 1930: 5). Mansfield's distaste for self-display is also apparent in a letter to Murry on 5 December 1919: 'I think as a critic that me or *us* is superfluous' (KMCL 3: 141); and it is related to another point of intersection between her critical practice and Murry's, namely their interest in the concept of impersonality.

Only ten days before her outburst to Murry about his self-focus, Mansfield had become intrigued with the idea that artists 'should surrender something of their personality'. Yet she also wanted to discover what an artist 'is subduing, to mark that side of him being gradually absorbed (even as it were without his knowing it) into the side of him he has chosen to explore, strengthening it, reinforcing it even while *he thinks* it is subdued away' (KMCL 3: 119). It is notable, however, that she considers that the disturbing elements – those which must be 'subdued' – do not disappear. They persist within a self now larger, and *strengthened* because of them. What she may be struggling to clarify resembles the Freudian distinction between repression and sublimation. The artist's 'subduing' does not result in unproductive symptoms of illness, but in a greater creative power. She, like Murry, here seems to value the impersonal as an achievement that is the culmination of experience 'absorbed' and understood rather than wilfully suppressed.[9]

Yet Mansfield's notion of 'subduing' became more severe and restrictive as the crisis in her relationship with Murry continued into the new year. By 25 January 1920, she would remark in a letter to Murry's younger brother: 'People today are simply cursed by what I call the *personal* . . . What is happening to ME. Look at ME. This is what has been done to ME' (KMCL 3: 196). And in her diary two days later she would comment on her 'philosophy – the defeat of the personal' (KMN 2: 190).[10] Nonetheless, there is a great difference between those two remarks. The diary entry includes her comment that she is 'wretched' and is struggling 'to *work*'. The day before she had written: 'Felt ill with fatigue and cold & my lungs hurt. It is because I am not working . . . My temper is so bad! I feel I am horrid and can't stop it. It's a bad feeling' (KMN 2: 190). In contrast, the letter to Murry's brother presents her public face, where she takes on the role of a teacher advising a young person, and urges this aspiring artist to accept life and give himself up to it.

Here again, Mansfield and Woolf seem to parallel Murry and Eliot in a shared (if not directly stated to one another) concern about the complexities of artistic impersonality. In an essay on Thomas Hardy in the *Athenaeum* on 7 November 1919, Murry refers to the 'unity which comes of the instinctive refusal in the great poet to deny experience, and subdues the self into the whole as part of that which is not denied', and which 'gives . . . to personal emotion what is called the impersonality of great poetry' (A: 127). Six months later, in 'The Function of Criticism', he defines the 'great artist' as someone 'whose work manifests an incessant growth from a merely personal immediacy to a coherent and all-comprehending attitude to life' (A: 13–14). Similarly, in 'The Condition of English Literature', published in *TLS* on 7 May 1920, Murry suggests that 'true artistic individuality comes only after an arduous effort to discipline a merely personal otherness' (DR: 71). The latter essay reflects what David Goldie has described as an evolution in Murry's work 'coincidental with Eliot's attempts to articulate a traditional structure that curbs a merely personal utterance' towards a greater emphasis on 'both the necessity and the difficulty of incorporating the tradition' (Goldie 1998: 47, 48).[11]

Nonetheless, whatever emphasis Murry places on impersonality, his more enduring impetus as a critic during this time remains his interest in the individual artist, in the 'rhythm of personality' expressed through an 'organic progression' in the work of 'poetic genius' (A: 52). This possibly is a manifestation of Murry's continued fascination with the mystery of creative talent, which he feared he lacked, but admired (and envied?) in Mansfield, Lawrence and Eliot.

Despite Murry's shared interest with Eliot in the concept of impersonality, Eliot was becoming annoyed with Murry's tactics as a critic.

In a letter to Sydney Schiff on 30 November 1920 he complained that Murry's 'criticism is dictated by emotion, which is not the same thing as saying that he feels strongly about the things he criticises'. He also charges Murry with 'a sort of irreverence for reason', and decides that he is 'an egoist . . . hopelessly isolated from both persons and causes' (Eliot 1988: 422).[12] Eliot's denigration of Murry here probably relates to some immediate disagreement, but it does come to rest on a central characteristic of Murry's criticism: its emotionality. Eliot's charge 'of irreverence for reason', however, does not hold up against the evidence of Murry's carefully argued critical responses. Nonetheless, Murry actually took pride in the fact that his reasoning had its foundation in feelings. When Virginia Woolf once told him that he 'was the most intellectual of all modern critics', he disagreed vehemently: 'I am an absolutely emotional critic. What may seem intellectual is only my method of explaining the nature of the emotion' (LJMM: 223).

Murry's reaction to Woolf's comment is a component of his and Mansfield's long-standing opposition to Bloomsbury. It seems a resurgence of that old Lawrentian brand of 'vitalism' in battle against bloodless abstraction, a penchant for evaluating both writing and 'living' within an increasingly severe ethical framework. Coincidentally, only two days before Woolf's remark about Murry's intellect, Mansfield wrote to him that he had a 'fine intelligence capable of detachment'; but unlike Woolf, she did not mean it as a compliment. She continued with barbed words of comparison: 'but God! God! Im *rooted* in Life' (KMCL 3: 107), knowing that Murry would be wounded by her assumption that he was not.

As if in defence at such an assumption, Murry tried to explain to her how the intellectual and emotional are combined in his writing:

> It is true I try to give my views an intellectual statement, because that is the only method I have. If I were a born writer, I should express myself in your way. But my attitude is almost exactly like yours. I can't treat art as a clever game, and I am (to myself anyhow) always notoriously weakest in the examination of the technical side of a work. My test is extremely simple. If a work awakens a profound response in me, then I sit up and try to find what it is that is working on me. (LJMM: 223)

Ironically, it was Murry's insistence on emotion as the foundation of his critical practice that brought about Mansfield's strongest condemnation of his writing style. In her letter of 5 December 1919 she warns him not to bring himself into his literary criticism, that he antagonises his readers by his insistence on openly proclaiming his sincerity. When he does so, it makes her feel 'a queer kind of shame' over his self-exposure:

If you speak for your generation *speak* but don't say I speak for my generation – for the force is then gone from your cry. When you know you are a voice crying in the wilderness *cry* but dont say 'I am a voice crying in the wilderness'. (KMCL 3: 141)

III

Murry's greater sense of achievement as a critic, as well as his increasing power in the literary establishment as the editor of the *Athenaeum*, are evident in his letter to Mansfield of 6 April 1920: 'You know we're very much more famous than we were a year ago. Lots of people are beginning to look upon us as the coming man and woman'. He then adds a revealing parenthesis: '(that shd. be the other way about, but it comes natural)' (LJMM: 306). His belief in Mansfield's potential fame had been intensifying. On 9 February he had told her: 'You are a *big* writer. You are as classic as Tchehov in your way' (LJMM: 276); and three days later remarked: 'There's nothing like your work; and I am convinced its the only real achievement of our generation in prose – outside Sons & Lovers. Lawrence has gone mad. You are the only person who is the real thing' (LJMM: 280). He would shortly refer to her fiction explicitly in one of his reviews, calling 'Prelude' (along with Eliot's 'Portrait of a Lady' and a couple of other contemporary poems) an example of contemporary writing in 'which the vital act of intuitive comprehension is made manifest' (A: 179).[13]

In his letter, Murry makes certain to differentiate his professional achievement from Mansfield's.[14] He calls the *Athenaeum* his 'experimental farm', his 'testing station' where he will 'learn [his] job':

> For you the case is different. Compared to you I am intolerably immature. You will be doing your best work long before I shall. Your work now – stories & criticism – seems to me hardly possible of improvement. And I *know* that within three years you will be famous as a story-writer throughout the English speaking world. (LJMM: 306)

Murry's letters to Mansfield while she spent the winter of 1919–20 on the Italian Riviera contrast greatly in tone from those he sent her in 1918. Then, he seemed in a morass of depression, overwhelmed by the combined force of the war and Mansfield's illness, smarting from his sense of exclusion, and only ameliorating his despair by indulging in the shared fantasy of The Heron. Now he seems enlivened; he is suddenly important: an emerging critic, a powerful editor of a paper who is in a position to affect the reputations of his contemporaries. He is suddenly popular too, invited to parties, dinners, week-ends in country houses. Now, instead of imagining The Heron, Murry is actively working to achieve it. He traverses the countryside on weekends in search of the perfect house for them, 'the real thing – an old farmhouse' (LJMM: 258) perhaps, and impulsively buys expensive objects – a clock and 'one exquisite writing table' (LJMM: 230) at Ottoline Morrell's sale of furnishings from her house on Bedford Square. At moments (whenever he hears of a slight improvement in Mansfield's physical condition), he becomes elated: 'I have the conviction that we have turned the corner of our futures; that good things are waiting for us in the hedges & ditches, good things for us, for *Athenaeum*' (LJMM: 217).

In contrast, Mansfield has no such illusions about the future, and her recognition of the disparity between Murry's situation and her own only exacerbates her growing fury over her isolation and sense of abandonment. In this regard, 'The Man Without a Temperament', written between 10 and 12 January 1920, during what she called 'the worst days of my whole life' (KMN 2: 188), parallels her earlier 'Je ne parle pas français' as a response to her belief in Murry's rejection. The story enacts the very dilemma she had described to Murry on 4 December 1919: 'It would spell failure for you to live abroad with me . . . I can imagine what hours we should spend when I realized and you realized the sacrifice' (KMCL 3: 134). The tedium and emptiness of those imagined hours shape the story of Robert and Jinny Salesby, who are living in a hotel on the Riviera, listlessly passing the hours between meals and bedtime in a state of either polite boredom or suppressed emotions of regret and anger.

There appears to be no critical disagreement about the model for Robert Salesby. For example, Antony Alpers, in his first biography of Mansfield (1953), suggests that 'Mr. Salesby seems to be sketched from the Murry of the bitterest journal-entries – self-imprisoned, self-absorbed, resignedly a martyr, and heartily disliked by the other guests'; and Pamela Dunbar remarks that the 'biographical parallel helps to explain the apparent unfairness in the portrait of the dutiful Robert, who is everywhere crucified for his suppressed resentment; nowhere given credit for the apparent generosity of his conduct' (Dunbar 1997: 128). Yet there is nothing in Mansfield's imaginative reshaping of Murry's personality into Salesby that approaches the level of criticism Murry tended to heap on himself, what Lawrence had called his 'self-wriggling'. Maurice's behaviour in *Still Life* is far more damning than Robert Salesby's in 'The Man Without a Temperament'. In fact, Murry might not have even recognised the portrait as a criticism of himself. When he first read the story he told Mansfield that it was 'extraordinarily beautiful' (LJMM: 275), and that it was 'absolutely sure, not a wavering line from beginning to end, & so sweet'. He felt that she had 'hit the middle of an extremely delicate note & the tone goes reverberating on in the memory' (LJMM: 284). When Murry read Alpers' biography of Mansfield in 1953, he rejected its negative interpretation of Robert Salesby, telling Alpers: '"If ever a character was drawn with loving admiration, Salesby was. I should be very well content to go down to posterity as his original"' (JJMM: 305).

Perhaps Murry was able to overlook Salesby's forbidding demeanour which made the children run away, screaming in terror '"The Englishman!"', and the adults' grimaces and remarks about him behind his back. As his own biographer explains: 'All his life long, Murry retained [a] singular gift for stirring up violent emotions in nearly everybody who came into touch with him' and he finds it 'mysterious' that Murry was unable to understand 'the noisy petulance he provoked' (L: 134, 136). Perhaps Murry preferred to believe that Mansfield was sympathetic to the contradiction in himself, the disparity between his apparent unresponsiveness and the feeling man hidden behind the unapproachable exterior. Consequently, the 'loving admiration' he discerned must have been revealed to him through details that might be read as a secret code, such as Robert's memories of their previous happiness, 'Heron'-like moments, such as a dinner with Jinny and close friends (one, suggestively named 'Dennis', evoking the character in *Still Life*), where 'everybody's laughing', and Dennis says '"Oh, we all know Robert"' (KMCS: 138). There is also Jinny's reference to the smell of 'freshly ground nutmegs', to which Robert responds with a smile (KMCS: 131), a hint perhaps of Murry's verse play, *Cinnamon and Angelica*, in which all the characters are named after spices.

Only two months earlier Murry had completed the play and told Mansfield that although it had ended in 'pure pain', he had hoped to 'get this indistinguishable mixture of gloom – the black pit you see in me – and exquisite happiness & unshakeable faith, expressed. They exist together, & they do not merely co-exist; but are utterly fused' (LJMM: 208). On 5 December 1919, Mansfield had sent Murry a few suggestions for revision of the play, but then wrote the following:

> At that moment I tried to *think* out what I wanted to see and instead – bending my mind to your play I saw you instead – in all your innocence and beauty. I saw that you which is the *real rare secret* you. Oh if only I could lift this dark disease from me. It did lift for the instant but then I realised how dark it is – and how it has poisoned me . . . And I also feel I must make very very plain that I never want you here. Dont think that for one instant. I DONT. You must stay where you are. I must get through this

and find my way out or not alone . . . The time is past when we might have been together in such a case. Now it would only spell tragedy for us both. (KMCL 3: 140)

Mansfield encapsulates this conflict in a passage close to the end of the story. She describes Robert lying in bed, remembering that the doctor had said that he should go abroad with her, as he does not have

> a regular job like us wage earners. You can do what you do wherever you are – 'Two years'. 'Yes, I should give it two years. You'll have no trouble about letting this house you know. As a matter of fact . . .'
>   . . . He is with her. 'Robert, the awful thing is – I suppose it's my illness – I simply feel I could not go alone. You see – you're everything. You're bread and wine, Robert, bread and wine. Oh, my darling – what am I saying? Of course I could, of course I won't take you away.' (KMCS: 142–3)

Murry seemed to have missed the effect of Mansfield's decision to embed the sentence 'He is with her' inside the remembered conversation. The effect of this placement increases the ambiguity of Robert's feelings, relying on the reader to decide whether it is an expression of exasperation, resignation or ironic despair. Murry also may have missed the even more pronounced ambiguity in the last lines of the story, when Jinny asks Robert:

> 'do you mind awfully being out here with me?'
>   He bends down. He kisses her. He tucks her in, he smoothes the pillow.
>   'Rot!' he whispers. (KMCS: 143)

In a superficial reading, Robert's slang expression would seem merely an attempt to reassure Jinny by dismissing her worries, that of course he does not 'mind'. This usage is similar to that in a later story by Mansfield, 'Honeymoon', where the newly wed George dismisses his bride's worry about him swimming in the Mediterranean with '"People talk an awful lot of rot about the danger"' (KMCS: 403). But the word 'rot' in 'The Man Without a Temperament' flows outside the context of a syntactical unit so it can function as either a noun or a verb. Moreover, as the last expression in the story, the word 'rot' carries with it all the accumulated meanings of disease, disintegration, dissimulation and despair.[15]

If Murry appeared to others as a 'man without a temperament', he did not believe it of himself. The epistolary Murry frequently displayed a self that was a cauldron of conflicting emotions. When Mansfield sent him a telegram on 9 February 1920, saying 'your coldness is killing me' (KMCL 3: 213), he wrote back frantically:

> Why, why! Why do you think I have withdrawn? . . . Do you think the anguish of your letters doesn't tear my heart in bits? Do you really think I

don't feel? . . . Here am I – this is my voice – these are my lips, my eyes. Am I that stone? (LJMM: 277, 279)

Only the day before he had displayed his 'temperament' extravagantly in his response to a denunciatory letter from Lawrence, which he sent on to Mansfield with the following expressions of outrage:

> Don't let it make you angry. But may God do so unto me & more also if I ever enter into any communication whatever with him. If ever I see him, no matter when or where, the first thing I shall do is to hit him as hard as I can across the mouth. He seems to have become so degraded that I feel he is something of a reptile, and that he has slavered over me in his letter. *Please keep it*: because I am just writing to him to tell him that I intend to hit him whenever & wherever I see him again. And if anything happens I want people to know why I did it. (LJMM: 268)[16]

Lawrence's letter of 30 January 1920 had been a furious reaction to Murry's rejection of some articles he had sent – with Murry's encouragement – to the *Athenaeum*. In it he calls Murry 'a dirty little worm' three times, and tells him to 'deposit your dirty bit of venom where you like' (LDHL 3: 467–8). Lawrence also seems to have sent a contemptible letter to Mansfield, possibly at the same time as the one to Murry. That letter has not survived, except in the excerpts she includes in her own letter of 7 February – in the midst of a barrage of anger and disappointment with Murry – telling him that Lawrence 'spat in my face & threw filth at me and said "I loathe you. You revolt me stewing in your consumption"'. She then urges Murry not to forgive Lawrence: 'I do beseech you if you are my man to stop defending him after that & never to crack him up in the paper. *Be proud*' (KMCL 3: 209).[17]

Mansfield was delighted to see Murry's violent reaction to Lawrence's letter (written before he realised she had received an even more despicable one), and remarked on the 'coincidence' that they had each used the same epithet, 'reptile', in their separate responses to Lawrence. In a curiously retrogressive move towards the archetypal female, she manoeuvred a reversal of an earlier attack on Murry for not being enough of a 'man':

> Oh, when I read your reply do you know I *kissed* it . . . *As* I read it *as* I kissed it I had the queer, the *queer* feeling as though somehow one was caught in some wave of tradition that passes round & round the earth – as though hundreds & hundreds of years ago – a woman . . . like I was . . . had been handed a letter from her lover who swore to smite his enemy and she kissed it & laid it against her cheek. Thats NOT nonsense. But you must hit him when you see him – there's nothing else to do. (KMCL 3: 214)

Consequently, Lawrence's attack on the two of them re-established – at least temporarily – the bonds of embattled moral superiority that had sustained them in the past. If the issues that had brought on the crisis resulting in 'The Man Without a Temperament' had not been resolved, this momentary surge of energy fuelled by rage altered the mood of their epistolary conversation.

It is no surprise to find traces of Murry's anger with Lawrence later that year in his review of *The Lost Girl*, which appeared in the *Athenaeum* on 17 December 1920. The date of publication suggests that Murry was working on it while he was becoming involved in an emotional relationship with Princess Elizabeth Bibesco.[18] This was not the first time that Murry had strayed, however. A year earlier, Mansfield had been suspicious of his friendship with their mutual friend, Brett. It is not really possible to know the 'truth' about the extent of Murry's involvements, but he did seem compelled to return to these situations again and again in his journals later in his life, as an attempt to state for posterity the 'fact' that those flirtations were never consummated. He admits, for example, on 23 May 1954, that they never went further than touching the women's breasts. He says he was suffering from 'progressive sexual starvation' and 'craved the warmth of a woman's body':

> I suppose it was impossible for Katherine to have the same attitude to me as I had to her over the Carco affair: at the same moment to allow absolute freedom, and to feel absolute trust. Phthisis had begun, and with it a new kind of demand upon me, which I really accepted. But it seems, in retrospect, a little hard. While she was well, I had to be the companion of her 'innocent' self; and when she was ill, I had to be 'the man without a temperament'. I was content, nay positively happy, to be that, provided we could be together; but then she must always go away. (MSX 4159: 52)

Accordingly, it is not difficult to see a connection between Murry's 'progressive sexual starvation' and the elements of envy, competition and barely concealed rage submerged beneath the surface of his review of *The Lost Girl*; even its title, 'The Decay of Mr. D. H. Lawrence', seems more appropriate to Murry's condition at that moment than to Lawrence's.

Murry focuses his review on 'the obvious loss of creative vigour' (RDHL: 213) in this novel. He insists that Lawrence has 'lost some power of immediate contact with human beings that he once possessed; his intuitive knowledge has weakened under the pressure of theory', so that the novel's central character, Alvina Houghton, is 'more the idea of a woman than a woman'. That *theory* is 'sex theory', and Murry believes that it had 'falsified and dominated' Lawrence's earlier novel, *The Rainbow*, but at least there it had been redeemed by 'passages of darkly beautiful writing, so remarkable that at times they aroused a sense that the latest flowering on the tree of English literature might be one of the most mysterious' (RDHL: 212, 211).

Complicating Murry's approach to *The Lost Girl*, is, of course, his still-smarting anger over Lawrence's letters to Mansfield and himself earlier that year. That anger is apparent in the rising animosity of his language as the review continues:

> [Lawrence] writes of characters as though they were animals circling round each other; and on this sub-human plane no human destinies can be decided. Alvina and Cicio become for us like grotesque beasts in an aquarium, shut off from our apprehension by the misted glass of an esoteric language, a quack terminology. Life, as Mr. Lawrence shows it to us, is not worth living; it is mysteriously degraded by a corrupt mysticism. Mr. Lawrence would have us back to the slime from which we rose. His crises are all retrogressions. (RDHL: 213)

Nonetheless, Murry's distaste for a 'phrase like "his dark receptivity overwhelmed her"' (RDHL: 212), and his use of such terms as 'grotesque beasts', 'this sub-human plane' and 'slime from which we rose', combine to suggest a deep resentment over his own necessary suppression of sexual drives.

Murry's review partakes as well in an interchange between himself and Mansfield evident in a letter she wrote to him somewhere around 6 December, soon after she had read the 2 December review of *The Lost Girl* in *TLS*, which had annoyed her: 'The Times gave no inkling of what it was – never even hinted at its dark secret' (KMCL 4: 138). (Although Mansfield was not aware of it, the unsigned review had been written by Virginia Woolf.) Mansfield's imagery in her remarks about Lawrence's novel surely must have influenced Murry's:

> Lawrence denies his humanity. He denies the powers of the Imagination. He denies Life – I mean *human* life. His hero and heroine are non-human. They are animals on the prowl. They do not feel: they scarcely speak. There is not one memorable *word*. They submit to the physical response and for the rest go veiled – blind – *faceless* – *mindless*. This is the doctrine of mindlessness. (KMCL 4: 138)

Mansfield is particularly outraged by Lawrence's treatment of his central female character's physicality. She complains about Alvina 'thriving on the horse-play with the doctors. They might be beasts butting each other', and 'the scene where the hero throws her in the kitchen, possesses her, and she returns singing to the washing-up. It's a *disgrace*.' But nothing riles her more than Lawrence's description of Alvina's intimation of her pregnancy: 'Oh, don't forget where Alvina feels "*a trill in her bowels"* and discovers herself with child. A TRILL – what does that mean – And why is it so peculiarly offensive from a man? Because it is *not on this plane* that the emotions of others are conveyed to our imagination. It's a kind of sinning against art' (KMCL 4: 138).

In contrast, Woolf seems less offended than Mansfield about Lawrence's treatment of sexuality, and more open to exploring its deeper significance than Murry. Woolf writes that she came to the book with a 'belief in Mr Lawrence's originality', and a sense of him as:

> a writer . . . with an extraordinary sense of the physical world . . . for whom the body was alive and the problems of the body insistent and important. It was plain that sex had for him a meaning which it was disquieting to think that we, too, might have to explore.

Yet she finds that 'sex, indeed, was the first red-herring that crossed our path in the new volume'. On the contrary, her disappointment with the novel lies more with its relentless realism: 'Details accumulated . . . and sex disappeared'. She remarks that she does not want to read Lawrence 'as one reads Mr Bennett – for the facts, and for the story'. Rather than considering the novel as representing 'the Decay of Mr Lawrence', she titles her review 'Postscript or Prelude?', leaving open the possibility that this novel, which 'is probably better than any that will appear for the next six months', might be 'a stepping stone in a writer's progress' (Woolf 1965: 158–60).

It had not been accidental that Murry's seemingly final break with Lawrence occurred in connection with his editorship of the *Athenaeum*. Murry's newfound power to make decisions that would have an effect on others' professional lives would bring about other contentious situations before his editorship ended in February 1921 and the paper was merged with the *Nation*. Afterwards, Lawrence wrote to Koteliansky on 2 March 1921 with spiteful glee: 'I hear the Athenaeum lost £5000 a year under our friend the mud-worm' (LDHL 3: 675).

Notes

1. Murry was finishing his verse play, *Cinnamon and Angelica*, and still preferred to think of himself as a creative writer first and foremost, even if most of his energies were devoted to running the paper and writing articles for it.
2. Mansfield's reviews in the *Athenaeum* are collected in *Novels and Novelists*, edited by Murry and published in 1930.
3. When Mansfield's *Bliss and Other Stories* was reviewed by Malcolm Cowley in *The Dial* 71 (September 1921), he remarked: 'She has borrowed

just enough from the new experiments in prose without trying to swallow them whole' (p. 265).

4. See Kaplan (1991: 163–8) for a fuller discussion of Mansfield's reactions to Dorothy Richardson and May Sinclair, especially in terms of the notion of 'feminine style'. See also in this context, Hanson (Mansfield 1987: 17–20).

5. George Eliot had been one of Mansfield's favorite authors since her adolescence. See Kaplan (1991: 85–7).

6. Vincent O'Sullivan pointedly remarks:

> One of the lesser mysteries of her relationship with her editor-husband is why, in the light of his extravagant praise of her as a critic, he persisted in sending her such dull fiction, while he saved Chekhov for himself, and commissioned long and serious literary essays from a range of friends. Mansfield liked to joke that she was quite uneducated alongside highbrow Jack. Murry may have agreed with this more than he declared. (KMCL 3: viii)

7. It appears that May Sinclair was deeply hurt by Mansfield's review. At a dinner party some months later, she told Murry that 'she admired [Mansfield's] work more than any'. His hostess then took him aside to tell him that Sinclair '"had been terribly upset by K. M.'s review of her novel, because she thought that K M. is the only person who really knows how to do it"' (LJMM: 280).

8. Woolf's review of *The Tunnel* had first appeared in *TLS* in February 1919. It is reprinted in *Contemporary Writers* (Woolf 1965: 120–2).

9. Mansfield's attitudes about impersonality have a longer and more complex genealogy than I have room to discuss here. See Kaplan (1991: 169–87) for a more comprehensive examination of this issue.

10. Such comments have made it easy for critics to discuss Mansfield in relation to Eliot's theory of impersonality. An early example of this is in a 1953 review by Sam Hynes, who discerned in Mansfield 'a turn from romantic egocentricity, in which the external exists as stimulus for internal disturbances, toward the cold classicism that Eliot postulates when he says, "The progress of the artist is a continual self-sacrifice, a continual extinction of the personality"' (Eliot 1975: 560).

11. Goldie's (1998) discussion of how Murry's interest in the tradition is interrelated with Eliot's addresses a major development in Murry's critical practice, but one that is outside the framework of this chapter.

12. Woodfield considers Eliot's complaint 'hypocritical', resulting from an intensifying competition with Murry. See his discerning analysis of Eliot's letter to Schiff (DR: 19).

13. Originally published as 'Poetry and Criticism' in the *Athenaeum* on 26 March 1920.

14. Murry's delight in his own success is evident in a letter two days later where he mentions that 300 copies of his new book, *The Evolution of an Intellectual*, had been taken by an American publisher: 'so the first edition will certainly be sold out' (LJMM: 310).

15. W. H. New discusses Robert Salesby's use of the word 'rot' in relation to 'a corruption within himself that has contributed to the decay of their relationship' (New 1999: 78–9).

16. Murry's reply, dated 8 February, was added to the typed manuscript copy

of Lawrence's letter to Murry: 'This is to tell you that it is my fixed intention, when ever or wherever I meet you again, to hit you in the face. There
is no other way of treating you' (LDHL 3: 468). For a more complete
discussion of the conflict over Lawrence's letters to Murry and Mansfield
see Kinkead-Weekes, 'Rage Against the Murrys' (Kinkead-Weekes 1999:
116–34).

17. In 'Rage Against the Murrys', Kinkead-Weekes (1999) surmises that
Lawrence turned his anger against Mansfield because he mistakenly
believed that Murry had rejected his essays because of her influence.

18. For details of the 'Bibesco affair', see Alpers (1980: 322–4, 332–3). See also
Woolf's allusion to the 'Bibesco Scandal' in her diary entry of 16 February
1921. Woolf's description of her conversation with Murry at his farewell
dinner is of particular interest (DVW 2: 91).

Chapter 7

The Things We Are

I

Unlike Robert Salesby in 'The Man Without a Temperament', Murry appeared to settle into his new life abroad with Mansfield in 1921 without apparent signs of repressed resentment. Robert Salesby had been cast adrift with nothing to occupy himself but the daily rituals of taking tea with his wife and bringing her a shawl. The one essential quality that Mansfield had neglected to give him was a dedication to the act of *writing*. In contrast, Murry would find himself suddenly freed from the exhaustive entanglements – professional and social – of the *Athenaeum*, and now ready to pursue his creative endeavours. It should be noted here also – as Alpers has suggested – that Murry's removal from the editorship meant 'the parting of the ways between the Murrys and Bloomsbury as a whole' (Alpers 1980: 331). For, without Murry's influence as an editor to consider, Woolf and her friends had no need to pretend to interest in him and their barely submerged hostility need no longer be held in check.

During his stay in Menton in the first months of the year, Murry started work on his second novel, *The Things We Are*, and completed a series of lectures which he delivered at Oxford in May, and published the next year under the title *The Problem of Style*. By the end of June, he had joined Mansfield in the mountains of Switzerland, at the Chalet des Sapins in Montana-sur-Sierre, where they lived in productive intimacy and tranquillity. Alpers describes the months of 1921 that Mansfield spent with Murry in Switzerland as 'the summit of her creative life' (Alpers 1980: 334). She wrote some of her greatest stories there, including 'At the Bay', 'The Garden Party' and 'The Doll's House'. And Murry, freed from the relentless labour of editing the paper, could finally allow himself the luxury of writing full-time and immersed himself in *The Things We Are*.[1]

It was only a few months after writing 'The Decay of Mr D. H. Lawrence', his review of *The Lost Girl* published in the *Athenaeum* on 17 December 1920, that Murry began writing *The Things We Are*. Moreover, in July 1921, when it was well underway, he read and reviewed *Women in Love*. Although the general plot structure of his novel must have been firmly in place by this time, Murry's reactions to *Women in Love* might well have affected its development, and even more so, his process of revision.[2] Mansfield read it also, and exclaimed to Ottoline Morrell on 24 July, that Lawrence's novel 'is so *absurd* that one cant say anything; it after all is almost purely pathological, as they say'. Her derisive tone belies the pain she must have felt when she contrasted her present reality with Lawrence's depiction of a world of emotional adventure and sexual discovery; for, as her off-handed remark to Ottoline Morrell suggests, she well knew the novel's connection with her own life: 'You know I am Gudrun?' Her ordered and self-disciplined life with Murry at this moment was exactly the obverse of Gudrun's in the novel: 'M. and I live like two small timetables. We work all the morning & from tea to supper. After supper we read aloud and smoke; in the afternoon he goes walking & I crawling' (KMCL 4: 252).

It is noteworthy that in mood and temperature, *The Things We Are* and *Women in Love* are completely antithetical. The 'five hundred pages of passionate vehemence' (RDHL: 216) of Lawrence's contrast greatly with Murry's own three hundred pages of chill lassitude. But in his review of *Women in Love* published in the *Nation and Athenaeum* on 13 August 1921, Murry's tone matches Lawrence's. It heats up, becomes fierce and agitated, swelling with righteous emotion about Lawrence's

> wave after wave of turgid exasperated writing impelled towards some distant and invisible end; the persistent underground beating of some dark and inaccessible sea in an underworld whose inhabitants are known by this alone, that they writhe continually, like the damned, in a frenzy of sexual awareness of one another. (RDHL: 216)

Murry's rhetoric becomes even more heated as the passage continues. He says Lawrence's characters 'grope in their own slime to some final consummation, in which they are utterly "negated" or utterly "fulfilled"' (RDHL: 216). He insists that Lawrence believes that

> these convulsive raptures, these oozy beatitudes [are] the only end in human life. He would, if he could, put us all on the rack to make us confess his protozoic god; he is deliberately, incessantly, and passionately obscene in the exact sense of the word. He will uncover our nakedness. It is of no avail for us to protest that the things he finds are not there; a fanatical shriek arises from his pages that they are there, but we deny them. (RDHL: 217)

The degree of Murry's animosity is indicated by his use of the word 'obscene'. For it could be considered a red flag to the censors. Surely he must have remembered how it was a reviewer's similar charge in 1915 that set into motion the government's assault on *The Rainbow*.

Murry might have had a glimmer of doubt at this point in the review, however. His next paragraph hesitates for a moment – but only a moment – in its first sentence: 'If they are there, then it is all important that we should not deny them'. Yet he immediately counters that with: 'Whether we ought to expose them is another matter'. His oppositional pairing of the words 'expose' and deny' is connected also with his defence of 'civilisation' earlier in his review.

> We stand by the consciousness and the civilisation of which the literature we know is the finest flower; Mr. Lawrence is in rebellion against both . . . The things we prize are the things he would destroy; what is triumph to him is catastrophe to us. He is the outlaw of modern English literature; and he is the most interesting figure in it. But he must be shown no mercy. (RDHL: 215)

His use of the adversarial binary is more than a rhetorical strategy, however. It exemplifies Murry's own unresolved ambivalence about the meaning of that very word, 'civilisation'. For, after all, like Lawrence he had spent the war years in conflict over the uses to which its overwhelming inventiveness and will to power had been applied.

Murry insists that Lawrence 'has sacrificed everything' (RDHL: 222) in his attack on the modern consciousness, and has thereby 'murdered his gifts', which 'were valuable to the civilisation which he believes he has transcended' (RDHL: 222), in order to reveal a 'consummation' that 'is a degradation', a 'knowledge' that is 'subhuman and bestial, a thing that our forefathers had rejected when they began to rise from the slime' (RDHL: 223). That last phrase of the review seems itself a 'rise' from analysis to near hysteria. It is overheated to the degree that one cannot help but suspect *denial*.

Earlier in the review Murry had taken up a pose of humorous befuddlement to trivialise – and thus undermine – the seriousness of Lawrence's exploration of sexuality. In referring to the 'essential crisis of the book' in the 'Excurse' chapter, where 'Rupert and Ursula, who are said to reach salvation at the end of the history, have a critical and indescribable experience', Murry insists that 'it is not a matter of sexual experience, though that is, of course, incidentally thrown in; but there is a very great deal to do with "loins"', which he mockingly repeats as 'loins of a curious kind' (RDHL: 219):

> Mr. Lawrence calls them 'his suave loins of darkness'. These Ursula 'comes to know'. It is, fortunately or unfortunately, impossible to quote these crucial

pages. We cannot attempt to paraphrase them; for to us they are completely and utterly unintelligible if we assume (as we must assume if we have regard to the vehemence of Mr. Lawrence's passion) that they are not the crudest sexuality. Rupert and Ursula achieve their esoteric beatitude in a tearoom; they discover by means of 'the suave loins of darkness' the mysteries of 'the deepest physical mind'. They die and live again. (RDHL: 219–20)

We might suspect that much of that so-called 'unintelligibility' is a pretence on Murry's part. Years earlier, in 1914, he had written in his diary that Frieda 'accuses [Lawrence] of taking her "as a dog does a bitch"' (MSX 4147: 40), which suggests that he might have known what Lawrence was insinuating. Moreover, as I mentioned in Chapter 2, I do not believe for a moment Murry's later claim in *Reminiscences of D. H. Lawrence* (1933) that he

> did not, even in 1921, regard that crucial novel as having any special refer-
> ence to *me*, and I had no suspicion that it had been written in 1916, or that
> the real core of it was precisely that abortive struggle between a conscious
> Lawrence and an unconscious Murry at Higher Tregerthen. (RDHL: 10)

Murry's overheated reaction to the novel betrays his personal involvement, even if his awareness of 'the real core' remains suppressed. His
surface disgust at the 'frenzy of sexual awareness of one another' in
which Lawrence immerses his characters deflects him from defining that
'real core'. Perhaps that deflection is itself a symptom of Murry's denial
of the power of homosocial desire and the evidence of its traces in the
very novel he himself was engaged in writing. Was he not disturbed
by the homoerotic suggestiveness of the relationship between Birkin
and Gerald, the loss of rigid definitions of what constitutes 'masculine'
sexual energy? Murry's repeated references to 'loins' reveal more than
an attempt at ridicule. They might suggest an unresolved reaction to the
threat of homosexuality which underlies Lawrence's text.

A noticeable feature of Murry's style in this review is his reliance on
the vague and protean word 'things' to carry a multiplicity of conflicting
and sometimes euphemistic connotations: 'the things he finds are not
there'; 'it may indicate many things'; 'the things we prize are the things
he would destroy'; 'a thing that our forefathers had rejected'. These
'things' are then referred to in following sentences as if 'they' had been
already defined: 'If they are there, then it is all-important that we should
not deny them'; 'they should not be exposed', and so on. This momentary inability – or refusal – to name seems awkward in a writer who had
so recently defined 'prose' in *The Problem of Style* as 'the language not
merely of exact thinking, but of exact description' (Murry 1925: 58). In
his brief moment of praise for the earlier Lawrence at the beginning of

the review, Murry referred to his once 'exquisite discrimination in the use of language' (RDHL: 214). Murry's own verbal inexactness could be a symptom of resistance, an avoidance of coming to terms with himself.

Most obviously, that avoidance is at play in his choice of title for his novel: *The Things We Are*. The plural form makes the title particularly ambiguous. Does it mean that each one of us is many things? Or, are all of us one thing? Murry includes an epigraph on the title page from Shakespeare's Parolles in *All's Well that Ends Well* : 'Simply the thing I am/Shall make me live'. In its singular form, the allusion could suggest a unitary, coherent, essential self (although that would not be the case with Parolles, a seemingly duplicitous character).[3] But Murry's shift to the plural in both subject and object tends to open further complexities, suggesting multiplicity, the self as divided, changing, evolving. The ambiguity of the title signals the emotional ambiguity underlying the text.

Although Murry's relationship with Lawrence is not the subject of his novel, that relationship seems to leaves its trace, nonetheless, in an emotional undertow, a contrary libidinal energy that once had been so damaging to their friendship (and Murry's with Gordon Campbell as well). Greatly diminished, no doubt, but at some level of awareness – perhaps not fully acknowledged – Murry lets it intrude. Superimposed over the older, tormented and contested relationship with Lawrence now appears Murry's more recent one with J. W. N. Sullivan, almost a parodical reversal of the other.[4] Murry simply could not leave alone his penchant for triangular relationships, and despite his wide reading of literature, his imagination seemed to be unable to reach beyond that paradigm for an appropriate 'plot' for his new novel.

Sullivan was the man who had supplanted Lawrence as Murry's closest friend during the dreary years at the War Office (when he had been Murry's partner in those late-night speculative, overly-intellectualised conversations that so used to irritate Mansfield), and who later became his assistant editor at the *Athenaeum*. With Sullivan, moreover, the power dynamics were the reverse of those with Lawrence: Murry was clearly the one in command. Although Sullivan might have been the model for Bettington, aspects of Murry himself seem blended into his character. Thus both Bettington and Murry's persona, Mr Boston, become manifestations of his continued sense of self-division. (Murry uses the formal title 'Mr' for Boston for a good part of the novel, but not for Bettington, which accentuates the imbalance in status between them.) Since writing *Still Life*, Murry had learned that the creative process could involve a re-apportioning of the multiplicity of the self into separate characters. In this respect, *The Things We Are* cannot be said to escape from the dilemma Murry had put forth in *A Problem of Style*, where he questions whether

> it were really a literary merit for an author to be recognizable at all times and all places in his work: on the whole it is far more likely to be an impertinence. In how many novels of recent years is the all-important dialogue carried on between so many obvious hypostatisations of the novelist's self! (Murry 1925: 9)

Such questioning of authorial intrusion exemplifies one of Murry's central concerns in *The Problem of Style*, which David Goldie considers 'Murry's most sustained attempt to define the relations between authorial personality and style' (Goldie 1998: 80). It is an element of Murry's continuing preoccupation with the concept of artistic impersonality – which had been interconnected with Eliot's during the period of the *Athenaeum* – that he highlights in the conclusion to his lectures:

> Nothing will teach a man to feel distinctly: but probably the best way for him to discover whether he does is to leave himself out of the reckoning. To be impersonal is the best way of achieving personality, and it gives him far less chance of deceiving himself. (Murry 1925: 143)

In fact, Murry had been thinking about Eliot's ideas during the time in Menton when he composed the lectures on style. His journal records on 11 March 1921: 'Began T. S. Eliot'; on 14 March: 'Article on T. S. Eliot'; and on 15 March: 'article on Eliot sent' (MSX 4145). That article was a review of *The Sacred Wood*, in which Murry interprets Eliot as suggesting that 'an artist's seriousness . . . is measured by the degree to which he sacrifices all desire for immediate and unrestrained expression, all personal idiosyncrasy, to the impersonal task of building the solid object which is the work of literary art' (DR: 95).[5] Eliot later told Murry that it was 'on the whole the best review I have had' (Eliot 1988: 447), and it appears to have prodded him to seek a rapprochement with Murry after some kind of falling-out during the final weeks of the *Athenaeum*.[6]

Murry's diary records 'Tea with Eliot' on 5 June 1921, three days before he left London to join Mansfield in Switzerland. Neither man seems to have left a record of their conversation on that occasion, but its impact might have elicited a few of the details in the novel suggestive of Eliot. After all, Eliot was the one man of Murry's acquaintance whom he later described, in his journal of 29 May 1954, as having 'lived in the same kind of isolation' as himself (MSX 4159: 59). Did Murry's choice of the name 'Boston' for his persona in the novel suggest some level of identification with Eliot?

Despite Murry's pronouncements about impersonality and artistic creation, it happened that he still could not 'leave himself out of the reckoning' when he constructed his novel, which is suffused with elements of his life, opinions and emotional conflicts. Incidentally, Virginia Woolf had no doubts about the novel's personal connections, writing to Ottoline Morrell on 1 August 1922: 'He has a mania for confession. I suppose his instinct is to absolve himself in these bleatings and so get permission for more sins' (LVW 2: 540), and remarking in a follow-up letter on 6 August that 'all his characters were embodiments of his own faults and his own entirely sentimental and unreal aspirations' (LVW 2: 542).

II

As its title suggests, *The Things We Are* is centred on the process of self-discovery, but a number of obstacles hinder that effort, primarily that it must take place in a modern society that has 'seen the complete decay of the whole Victorian system. It simply dissolved in the night during the war' (Murry 1922b: 31). That breakdown of the 'system' is the necessary background for the atmosphere of uncertainty and alienation permeating the novel as a whole. And Murry makes it clear that this breakdown is related to an even larger change in consciousness, a change that in itself is the hallmark of modernity. At the beginning of the novel, Boston approaches life in a passive acceptance of the domination of impersonal forces of control. His place in the universe is infinitesimal; he is helpless under the rule of science, economics and psychology. He sees no purpose to his existence, and has 'read much history, and enough astronomy to know that in all probability there are a hundred thousand universes like our own swimming in the infinite of space; enough anthropology to be aware that morality is the product of an unsteady evolution' (ibid.: 26). Boston's reaction to these markers of human insignificance and moral relativism is resignation, rather than shock or denial. These are the conditions in which modern life adjusts itself. In temperament, however, he contrasts greatly with his friend Bettington, who tries 'to explain to Mr. Boston that life, in spite of astronomy and anthropology, was exciting' (ibid.: 30).

It is not surprising to find parallels between the kind of modernist alienation Murry depicts in *The Things We Are* and that of Eliot's *The Waste Land*, published later the same year.[7] The two works seem to share the same diagnosis of the underlying malaise of modernity and a similar emotional tenor, even if they differ greatly in genre and style. Mr

Boston's daily life at the beginning of the novel resembles that of one of Eliot's walking dead 'flowing' into the city:

> Mr. Boston worked at Cadogan Square from 10 a.m. to 6 p.m. . . . and he saw no reason why it should not go on for forty years. In the evenings he read, or wandered interminably in the London streets. He was accosted by women, he watched street-fights, he sat in the remote seats of cinemas, drank at coffee-stalls, saw women sleeping in mid-winter on the Embankment, women fighting each other amid a crowd of cheering men in Seven Dials, stared over bridges at the filthy yet regal Thames, listened to men preaching exasperated atheism in the Park, wondered at piercing solitary cries in the night. It was a sharp and jagged world, irremediably alien to him. (Murry 1922b: 24–5)

The fascination of the early Eliot with 'the thousand sordid images' ('Preludes') garnered through the accumulation of such kinds of urban details had already become a characteristic of modernist treatments of the city. Not that Murry would have needed Eliot's 'Prufrock' or 'Preludes' as his models. We should not forget that he was one of the first British critics to recognise the significance of Baudelaire.[8] It was only that past October that he had written:

> Truly Baudelaire was the *poète maudit* of the city, the vast and loathsome growth which then first and most terribly had begun to poison human life. With fascination and hatred he contemplated this triumph of civilization, this instrument of torture for the poor and the poet. Perhaps he may become more palatable if we describe him as the first poet of modern industrialism, and the only great one. (DR: 87)[9]

Nonetheless, there is a countermovement to Murry's description of Mr Boston's evenings, quoted above. In the same paragraph, following the words 'alien to him', Murry's prose begins to flow. That 'sharp and jagged world' begins to soften and there is a shift from the impersonal omniscient narration of Boston's activities to a form of free indirect discourse, illuminating Boston's internal responses to what he perceives:

> He liked London best when a heavy rain was falling. The sudden sprouting of innumerable umbrellas, the sharp scream of the cab-whistles, the police-men standing unperturbed in their gleaming waterproofs, the soft sound of hurrying footsteps, the eager rush of water in the gurgling gutters, the bright shining of the wet roadways, the touch of the drops on his own face, comforted and thrilled him; he felt in these moments that he had become a member of the great city. (Murry 1922b: 25)

The movement from 'exasperated' to 'unperturbed', from 'piercing solitary cries' to 'the soft sound of hurrying footsteps', climaxes with 'the eager rush of water' and 'the touch of drops on his own face'. Murry had used the verbs 'watched', 'saw', 'stared' and 'listened' in the first section of the passage. The senses of sight and hearing only serve to intensify the separation of Boston from his environment, but the shift to the sense of *touch* in the second section intimates the possibility of release. Boston is 'comforted' and 'thrilled' by even this kind of physical contact. Accordingly, it is through the sense of touch that his alienation momentarily dissolves, allowing him a glimpse of human solidarity in becoming 'a member of the great city'.

Murry's choice of the word 'member' here is suggestive – especially if it is linked with the other images of 'sprouting' umbrellas and 'the eager rush of water' – given that Boston's sexual repression is the central problem of the novel. It is obvious that his street wandering is voyeuristic. He watches 'women sleeping', 'women fighting'. He sits 'in the remote seats of cinemas'. That Murry was familiar with the Freudian symbolism of umbrellas is certain. (He surely remembered Mansfield's quip about *Howards End*: 'And I can never be perfectly certain whether Helen was got with child by Leonard Bast or by his fatal forgotten umbrella. All things considered, I think it must have been the umbrella' [KMN 2: 93]). In fact, he sets his story into action through an incident involving an umbrella, which cannot help but remind us of Forster. Boston first meets Bettington and Felicia when he loans them his umbrella during a downpour 'when the theatres were emptying'. Boston's friendly gesture impresses Bettington, who later remarks: 'I've been working in London ten years now, and I've never had an umbrella lent me by a total stranger before' (Murry 1922b: 30).

If Murry shares Eliot's diagnosis of the malaise of modernity, and like him focuses it on the misplacement of sexual desire amidst the anonymity of the city, his prescription for treating that malaise seems to be – perhaps unwittingly – an acknowledgment of Lawrence's influence. For it is the transfer of a phallic object from one man to the other that initiates Boston's awakening from a half-life of passive acceptance of his dutiful role in the mechanistic functioning of the system. The umbrella thus becomes both a sign of the emerging bond between the two men and a harbinger of their later rivalry, a presentiment of a final conveyance of a far more emotionally significant 'object'.

Murry treats Boston's memories in a way that emphasises the domination of self-enclosure. Near the beginning of the novel – in an echo from *Still Life*, which itself harks back to Murry's own formative experiences in Paris in 1910–11 – Boston remembers his time in Paris when he was around eighteen, where he 'listened to Bergson and Durkheim and Seignobos without any enthusiasm; he put most of that into the long letters which he wrote his mother every day' (Murry 1922b: 18). Although Boston heard about Picasso and 'saw a painting by Monet', he was always distanced from his experiences in Paris, unlike Murry himself, who had a profoundly erotic, as well as intellectual awakening there. To Boston, in contrast, these 'two years in Paris had been no more than a spectacle' (ibid.: 20).

Significantly, there is no Margueritte figure in this reversion to the Parisian scene. Instead there are echoes of Mansfield's Dick Harmon of 'Je ne parle pas français' (also a version of Murry), whose Parisian adventure was aborted by his need to return to his mother. Boston is similarly the victim of maternal fixation. His only love interest in his youth had been his mother, and he knows that her 'death had shaped his life' (Murry 1922b: 14). He remembered that

> when they walked arm in arm, he had felt that every one who passed must be admiring her and envying him. Often they were. For the love he gave her was of such a kind that it made her eyes brilliant; it was a delicate and tempered air in which she could breathe and flower. When he was only ten he knew this, knew more than this, that they lived mysteriously by one another. Away from her . . . he was uprooted and like to wither. (Murry 1922b: 14–15)

Murry draws on his feelings for his own mother in this description. He writes in his autobiography: 'I had been since I was a little boy, her cavalier' (BTW: 94), and explains that she was 'only nineteen years of age' when he was born, 'a beautiful woman, or rather a beautiful girl; and to me, she is still'. Moreover, Murry describes himself as having been 'a beautiful baby" and 'very much my mother's son' (BTW: 9). Like his author, Boston apparently shares in a mother's good looks: 'from her one could have told that he was her son. Their eyes, brown and clouded, were the same; so were their long lashes' (Murry 1922b: 12). Despite the similarities in appearance between Murry's mother and Boston's, their childhoods were completely antithetical. The enclosed world in which Boston had lived with his mother, 'alone . . . in the little white house in Brittany' (ibid.: 14), would have been, for Murry himself, a dream fantasy. It would be the fulfilled desire of the boy who might happily have disposed of his intrusive, tyrannical father, a man to whom it 'never occurred . . . that it was a little hard for a girl so naturally gay and loving as my mother, to be alone in the house from eight in the morning till after midnight'. (Murry's father worked at two jobs to support the family.) If Murry understood the necessity behind his father's drive, he detested the way it was carried forth: 'All that my father did – as he not infrequently said – was done for us' (BTW: 19).

The wish-fulfilment behind Murry's depiction of Boston's childhood is also apparent in his providing to Boston an inherited income, 'four pounds a week of his own' (Murry 1922b: 86), which makes possible his eventual escape from the alienated urban environment and the daily routine of the business world. In fact, Murry gives to Boston exactly the kind of privileged background that he had pretended to as a student at Oxford, when he told people that he 'had a mother who lived abroad on a pension' (L: 17). Boston becomes a version, then, of a Murry who had never experienced the burden of an impoverished childhood. Yet Murry really could not eliminate that burden in himself, and that is where the bifurcation of self into two characters becomes most evident in the novel. Murry takes the harsher, more realistic details from his memories of his childhood and gives them over to Bettington:

> Why had it always been so dark? Now he came to think of it, there was no sunlight in his memory at all. There was only gloom and grit and sordidness, amid which he had run like a drop of water in grey dust, complete and separate and hidden . . . Oh, yes, he had been loved by his mother and he had loved her. But somehow it had made no difference; it had never lighted the darkness or driven the terror away. Why did he always see her, as he saw her now, in an ugly grey cloth cap of his father's stuck through with an evil-looking hat-pin, her hair looped untidily under it, her arms pink with soap and water, pegging out washing in a dank and mildewed garden? Why was the clasp of her fingers always soft and slimy with soapsuds, and the balls of her fingers so puckered and rough that he shrank under the touch? (Murry 1922b: 227–8)[10]

In his autobiography, Murry says he resented 'the squalor in which my mother was involved', and had never been able to forget an incident on 'washing day', when – as a child of only two or three – he accidentally set his room afire by upsetting a 'mean and sordid' little penny lamp:

> my mother came running in with a fibre doormat in her hand, and beat out the flames with it. I thought it very brave of her, as it was. But printed on my memory ever since is the figure of my mother with bare arms, with an old cloth cap pinned on her hair, beating the flames with a dirty doormat. The bare boards, the stink of oil, the evil little lamp lying empty on the floor – and my mother. It may be that I afterwards invested this memory with a total sordidness which I, at the moment, did not wholly feel. But of one thing I am certain. The cloth cap pinned to my mother's hair was ugly to me then; and I resented it that my mother was involved in this ugliness. (BTW: 10)

Bettington's memories of the 'grim process' of his early education also greatly resemble Murry's: 'He had worked and worked ever since he was a tiny boy. He saw himself wandering years ago into the dark arches of a board school' (Murry 1922b: 226). Murry uses nearly the exact image in *Between Two Worlds* when he describes himself at the age of two and half, entering 'the infants class of the Rolles Road Board School' for the first time: 'There were many gloomy arches, and I was frightened' (BTW: 11).[11]

Significantly, their differing reactions to childhood experience makes for the greatest contrast between Boston and Bettington. Bettington says: 'It often seems to me that my life is only a desperate fight away from my childhood'. Boston's response is the reverse: 'It was the other way with me . . . As far as I've fought at all, it's been to live back in my childhood. That's far more deadly' (Murry 1922b: 266). Bettington has trouble imagining what that kind of childhood could mean:

> I've always thought . . . that if you've had a childhood worth living back in, you have something that can never be replaced, a kind of stored-up richness that you can never get in any other way. Without it, you become prematurely hardened; you can never receive things into yourself again. (Murry 1922b: 266–7)

Bettington's reaction again comes closest to Murry's own. Mansfield had often complained to others of 'this jealous passionate love of himself . . . which comes from his wretched childhood and poor stifled youth' (KMCL 4: 9). She once told him: 'Your childhood horrifies me. You came upon things so late & then they were so few' (KMCL 3: 224). The absence of that 'stored-up richness' Bettington spoke about was Murry's major problem as a novelist and poet. In *The Problem of Style* he describes a type of writer who

> may have the power to attain to an emotional comprehension of life, and to frame or recognise a plot that is an adequate and natural symbol of it, but he may be poor in the faculty of vivid sensuous perception which alone will enable him to cover the skeleton with the living flesh and blood of a style that is vital in all its parts. (Murry 1925: 108)

That 'faculty of vivid sensuous perception' he knew he lacked, and he also knew that Mansfield and Lawrence had it in abundance.

Yet, despite Boston's seemingly blissful childhood, he remains emotionally blocked, unable to make creative use of his advantages. He tells Bettington:

> 'I've often felt that my capacity for happiness, even more my capacity for love, was used up when I was small; that I reached a kind of pinnacle then, and all the rest of the time has been slowly slipping down from it. There's something paralysing in a perfectly happy childhood.' (Murry 1922b: 267)

III

While Murry worked on *The Things We Are*, Mansfield was composing 'At the Bay', that magnificent story based on her own memories of childhood. Did she and Murry talk about their childhoods again in those long evenings at the Chalet, unwinding from their mutually intense hours at their separate writing tables? He might have felt about hers somewhat like Bettington did about Boston's, even though he knew well that Mansfield's perception of her childhood was complex and ambivalent, full of the dualities that were a constant feature of her personality. If Murry bifurcates the real and the fantasy mother into the separate memories of his doubled characters, Mansfield's representation of the mother distances her from the emotions and desires of her children. Mansfield depicts Linda Burnell in 'At the Bay' as a woman with her own complicated, contradictory interior life, unlike Boston's static memory of a mother embalmed in her 'exquisite' perfection.

Yet Linda does share one characteristic with Murry's *real* mother (at least the mother as she is described in his autobiography): the desire for escape. Linda's girlhood fantasy of sailing 'up a river in China' with her father, 'two boys together' (KMCS: 221), oddly resembles Murry's memory that his 'mother had her dreams. Once, in a desperate burst of confidence, she told me that she wanted to be a gipsy and live in a caravan' (BTW: 19). (Murry also uses this same recollection in his novel, applying it to another maternal figure, Mrs Williams. Boston imagines that she might 'dream when she goes to bed at night of some wonderful man – a gipsy in a caravan'.) The major difference between Mansfield and Murry here, obviously, is that Murry never imagined that his mother's desire for escape might have been from *himself*, as well as from his father. Rather it must have fed into the oedipal fantasy of being alone with her that is demonstrated in his construction of Boston's 'perfectly happy childhood'.

In contrast, it seems clear that Mansfield intends the mother's desire for escape to be from her *children*, as well as her husband. Mansfield describes her as a woman whose

> whole time was spent in rescuing [her husband], and restoring him, and calming him down, and listening to his story. And what was left of her time was spent in the dread of having children . . . She was broken, made weak, her courage was gone, through childbearing. And what made it doubly hard to bear was, she did not love her children. (KMCS: 222)

The difference between Murry and Mansfield in this respect is striking: too much mothering opposed to too little.

Neither Mansfield nor Murry had studied Freud, and their resistance to his ideas goes back to the Rose Cottage days, when Murry reacted with antagonism to Lawrence's Freudian-style pronouncements, and later to Cornwall, when Mansfield ridiculed Lawrence's phallicising discourse. Perhaps there lurks an unconscious admission of Murry's continued emotional connection with Lawrence in his use of Freudian concepts in *The Things We Are*. Nonetheless, Freud's ideas – even in their diluted, popularised form – had become so absorbed into the matrix of contemporary thought by 1921 that it would have been impossible to escape them. Murry suggests as much in an essay he wrote on Proust in July 1921. In considering the 'epoch-making changes in the intelligence and the sensibility' which 'mark the historical advance of one period upon the other' in 'the evolution of literature', he makes the following observation, which neatly ties together the two major intellectual influences of the novel he was writing at the same time:

> A man who has absorbed into his consciousness the aimless principle of Natural Selection develops a new nerve of sensibility which perceives, isolates, and emphasises a quality of aimlessness in all experience. Similarly, a man who has assimilated the Freudian psychology will respond with a new awareness to every manifestation of the sex impulse in the life before his eyes. Every atom of new knowledge that is really apprehended and digested by the mind serves, if not positively to enlarge, at least to rearrange the mechanism of the sensibility. (D: 105)

Murry not only suggests the Freudian oedipal paradigm as the explanatory motive for Boston's sexual repression, but he includes the very subject of psychoanalysis itself as a topic of conversation in the novel. In a scene late in the story, Murry lets Bettington try to describe it:

> 'The theory is, I think, that most of one's vital being goes on out of reach of our consciousness. We have all kinds of desires that are extremely important; and we keep them under in the unconsciousness. There they ferment and fester, and produce all kinds of mental illnesses. If they can be made conscious, they disappear, either by being dragged into the light, and dissolved, as it were, or by becoming so imperative that they have to be satisfied. The psycho-analysts say that one's dreams are symptomatic of these unconscious repressions. They follow the clues of your dreams, and so drag the repressions into daylight.' (Murry 1922b: 236–7)

Although Murry depicts Bettington making this explanation in all seriousness, he undermines its significance by placing it in the midst of a superficial social scene, ripe for satire, with one of the other characters declaiming: '"There *are* no healthy people, from the psycho-analytical point of view"', and another deciding to have her '"complexes" . . . "looked at"' and being told: '"It's not in the least like sounding your heart with a stethoscope, you know"' (ibid.: 237–8). This is exactly the same device Murry used in *Still Life*, when he let Maurice Temple defend his theory of harmony to another similarly satirised group of fashionable pretenders to the intelligentsia.

This brief moment of meta-critical discourse both calls attention to the Freudian paradigm underlying the text and questions its adequacy. Murry is still as divided about the validity of Freudianism as he is about the nature of the self. It is then rather amusing to read his diary entry of 6 February 1922, where he seems surprised when some press cuttings in advance of the 27 March publication date of *The Things We Are* 'continually refer to it as "a psycho-analytical" novel. I wonder what the game is. They must have had the tip from somebody' (MSX 4145).

Despite Murry's ambivalence about psychoanalysis, his figurative language throughout *The Things We Are* easily lends itself to Freudian interpretation, as it had in *Still Life*. The most egregiously Freudian moments in *The Things We Are* occur in Murry's treatment of Boston's dreams, which seem to reflect his disturbance over the visit of Bettington and Felicia to his rural retreat, and his realisation that he 'resented the happiness of the other two', and that his feelings for them 'swung from pole to pole like a quivering needle' (Murry 1922b: 147, 149). In his first dream, Boston

> seemed to grow bigger and bigger, heavier and heavier, to become monstrous; and Felicia became smaller and smaller, daisy size. Yet she remained grown-up, while he sank back into a gross and idiot child. She tugged and tugged at his huge hand. Suddenly one of his great fingers came off, and she fell backward into the sunlight, crying with pain and terror. And he only laughed an imbecile laugh. (Murry 1922b: 193)

With its obvious allusions to tumescence and detumescence, this has all the hallmarks of an ejaculatory dream, and Murry suggests as much by adding that when Boston 'woke gasping, trying to drive the horror of the dream from his mind . . . it *stained* him somehow' (my emphasis). The dream reveals the extent of Boston's fear of his own sexuality, which has been for so long repressed that its release might return him to the omnipotent irresponsibility of infantile sexuality. The *monstrous* big baby cannot be controlled by the 'grown-up' mother-substitute, but she still has the power to castrate him, as the loss of the finger suggests.

It is not possible to know if Murry had one of Mansfield's fictional dream sequences in mind while he was writing, but it seems more than a coincidence that in 'Prelude', the earlier, companion story to 'At the Bay', Linda Burnell has a dream about walking with her father and coming upon a 'tiny bird', 'strok[ing] its head with her finger' and finding it suddenly growing 'bigger and bigger' until it 'had become a baby with a big naked head and a gaping bird-mouth' (KMCS: 24). Accordingly, the dreams juxtaposed reveal neatly gendered oppositions. For the woman, sexual arousal leads inevitably to pregnancy: the fear is about having a baby. For the man, sexual arousal makes him *become* a baby.

The unacceptability of his dream haunts Boston: 'The memory of it would lie in wait for him', and he seems almost to will another, ameliorating dream to take its place when he dozes off again. In the second dream, Boston finds himself 'in a great dancing room' in which 'there were many people, but none . . . as young as he . . . It was like an Embassy ball, and though he felt well dressed, he wanted to remain in obscurity'. When a 'woman in black with a long train' enters the room, a woman 'very sure of herself', who was 'yet looking undecidedly round the room', Boston suddenly

> felt in his hand a bunch of unreal white flowers – daisies with blanched centres – which had not been there before, and he knew she was looking for these. He went forward and pinned the posy under her right breast. He saw her breast heave with his eyes, felt it heave with his fingers. He did not know who she was; he knew only that he had played his allotted part; he did not know whether it was right or wrong. Nobody seemed to be surprised or glad, not even the woman herself. He sank back into the obscurity again. (Murry 1922b: 194)

While the first dream evokes the potency of the id, the second dream seems under the domination of the super ego. The room is filled with representatives of paternal authority and societal power, men with 'white, clipped beards'. Boston must somehow redeem himself in their eyes by making the right gesture: 'play[ing] his allotted part'. Notice how he does not participate in the 'dancing' (with its analogous relationship to sexual intercourse). His gesture rather is chivalrous, conforming to the accepted codes of *civilised* behaviour. It alters the symbolic valences of the terms 'daisy' and 'fingers', and seems to control the forbidden incestuous impulses related to this mysterious woman in black, whom 'he did not know'. Yet despite his obeisance to the social codes, he still does 'not know whether it was right or wrong'. Beneath the gestures of civility still lurks the anarchy of desire.

In terms of the novel's plot, however, the second dream might be considered one possibility for Boston's resolution of his untenable dilemma. He is falling in love with a woman whom he believes belongs to his best friend. Should he follow the code of honour, play his allotted role, seek fulfilment through the sacrifice of his feelings for a greater good? Much of the novel that follows is taken up with various incidents and discussions between Boston and Bettington revolving around such a renunciation. But revealingly, it is Felicia herself who draws attention to the homosocial dynamics in both men's behaviour towards her. She finally exclaims in sarcastic exasperation:

'So you two stand there admiring each other's nobility, while I wait for the first who will degrade himself sufficiently to marry me . . . Wouldn't it be simpler . . . if you both had me as a mistress, turn and turn about. You'd have so much opportunity for renunciation. You could go on admiring each other quite indefinitely.' (Murry 1922b: 248)

Felicia easily recognises how in these masculine competitions, the woman herself is 'left out of the reckoning'. As Murry portrays her, Felicia is an independent woman, intelligent, witty and astute. Bettington had described her to Boston soon after their acquaintance as a woman who had 'been mixed up with the suffrage' and was 'dead against marriage' (Murry 1922b: 32). Nonetheless, Felicia's personal qualities and her own internal struggles to determine her life's trajectory are not Murry's concern in the novel. Her perceptive comments may expose both men's egocentricity and self-delusion, but they punctuate the text, not control it.

Appropriately, given the psychodynamics of the novel's plot, when Boston eventually realises that he is in love with Felicia, she 'seemed to remind him of some one he had known long ago, in a life far simpler than this of ours' (Murry 1922b: 316). Ironically, this final allusion at the end of the novel to what Freud called 'the most perfect, the most free from ambivalence of all human relationships' (Freud 1989: 133) invokes the novel's only reference to an actually *passionate kiss*. (Murry never allows for one between Boston and Felicia.) At the beginning of the novel, the enervated, isolated Boston had opened a cardboard box filled with mementoes and drawn out a small, mother-of-pearl mirror:

He held it close to his eyes and gazed into their reflection. They were brown, and clouded as though they had been frozen; long dark lashes fringed the lids. When he had looked into them till he was almost dizzy, he snatched the mirror to his lips and kissed it passionately. (Murry 1922b: 9)

At first, a reader might be startled by this moment's revelation of such intense self-absorption, what Mansfield had described of Murry as 'his jealous passionate love of himself'. But Murry actually has deeply complicated this moment of Boston's self-reflection. For he then reveals that the mirror belonged to Boston's mother, and he had bought it for her when he was a student in Paris. He remembers how he had put 'that mirror in her hands' as she lay dying, and she 'raised the mirror slowly to her face, and smiled into it', telling Boston as he 'kneeled beside the bed. "I want to look pretty when I die. Do I?"' (ibid.: 13).

The kiss then also suggests the fusion of mother and son, that longed-for return to the undifferentiated pre-oedipal condition of inseparability. Yet its passion contains immeasurable degrees of regret and longing. And here, the most painful (and suppressed) dimension of the novel's subtext comes into view. If Felicia is intended to be a representation of Katherine Mansfield at the manifest level of the text, Boston's mother is her representative in its latent subtext. The genuine 'passion' in the novel, then, is revealed in the intensity of Murry's prose when he describes the dying mother. The details have nothing whatever to do with his own mother (who was still very much alive and vigorous), but with 'the fragile and doll-like beauty' he associated with Mansfield. There is mention of 'the books they had loved. Dark-blue *David Copperfield* simply stared at him'[12] (a book so loved by both Mansfield and Murry that its very name seems a secret code between them) and of 'a tray with a purple rose in a little brown pot set in the corner of it' (Murry 1922b: 11):

> But the unchanging centre of this picture was a bed, heaped high with pillows, the white sheet so neatly folded that it seemed impossible that the girlish head and hands resting upon them should belong to a living woman. The placing of the red on the cheeks, high on the cheekbones, and the smudge of the red itself suggested the brush of a clumsy workman marring an exquisite doll, marring the work of the artist who made her eyebrows with two single strokes of a sable pen, and her lips, which she held parted a little save when she smiled at him. (Murry 1922b: 11)

We should not forget that the scene of Murry's writing of *The Things We Are* was alongside a woman he knew (even if he resisted that knowledge) would not survive. He began his novel in the frustration of his impotence in the face of her illness. Boston's reaction to his mother's statement when she tells him she wants to look pretty when she dies, must surely reflect Murry's own agonising incapacity:

> He wanted to call out, in an astonished, incredulous voice, 'Why you're not going to die, darling! But a weight lay on his tongue. 'You're lovely, lovely,' he said.
>   She closed her eyes and lips, as though she would lock the truth into her body. He went outside and crept up and down the passage, muttering 'Devil . . . devil . . . devil. . .'.
>   Mrs. Boston died while he was in the passage. Though she looked just the same when he opened the door – her eyes and lips sealed and the mirror held loosely in her fingers – he knew she was dead. A wasp circled stupidly round her sticky medicine-glass. (Murry 1922b: 13–14)

There is an eerie sense of foreknowledge in Murry's description of Mrs Boston's death. Nearly a year and a half later, on 9 January 1923, Mansfield suffered an enormous haemorrhage while climbing the stairs. Murry ran for the doctors, who 'pushed Murry out of the room before Katherine's eyes' (Alpers 1980: 383). She died while Murry was in the passage.

Notes

1. Lea mentions that Murry also wrote most of the essays in *Countries of the Mind* and the first half of his third novel, *The Voyage*, during his stay at the Chalet between July and December 1921 (L: 85). He also remarks that the Bibesco 'episode, so innocent in itself, and yet because he had kept it secret, so deleterious to their relationship was the germ of *The Voyage*' (L: 81).
2. Murry's diary records that he began typing *The Things We Are* on 8 August 1921, and finished typing and revising on 5 September (MSX 4145).
3. In an essay, 'Shakespeare and Love', written in September and published unsigned in *TLS* on 13 October 1921, Murry stated: 'In *All's Well that Ends Well* – supremely cynical title – Shakespeare seems deliberately to take revenge on his own idealism of love. He deliberately makes Bertram detestable and shows that the bragging coward, Parolles, is the better man' (Murry 1922a: 24). In her notes on Shakespeare, undated, but placed by Murry after entries of late November 1921, Mansfield wrote: 'Parolles is a loveable creature, a brave little cock sparrow of a ruffian' (KMN 2: 265).
4. As Michael Whitworth points out, Murry 'modelled' the character of Bettington in *The Things We Are* on Sullivan, and notes that 'Bettington is a journalist, an enthusiastic talker, a devoted reader of Dostoevsky, and a former part-time student at London University' (Whitworth 2001: 153–4). Whitworth suggests that Bettington's name might be a derivation from 'Eddington', the famous physicist, who like Sullivan, reached a wide audience by writing on recent developments in science.
5. The review was originally published in *The New Republic*, 13 April 1921.
6. See Eliot's letter to his mother on 22 January 1921 for his explanation of his animosity towards Murry at this time (Eliot 1988: 432–3).
7. *The Waste Land* was published initially in the *Criterion* on 20 October 1922.
8. Murry's earliest piece on Baudelaire was 'The Influence of Baudelaire' in the *Rhythm Literary Supplement* (March 1913).
9. This essay originally appeared in the *Athenaeum* on 22 October 1920. Murry also wrote another important essay on Baudelaire for *TLS* (7 April 1921), which is reprinted in *Countries of the Mind* (Murry 1922a: 153–79).
10. In a letter to Ottoline Morrell on 18 July 1922, Woolf used Murry's reference to 'mildew' for her own purpose of ridicule: 'If Murry lives next door to you, I assure you the mildew will sprout in every room'. She had just mentioned that she had 'dropped The Things We Are, half paralysed with disgust and boredom' (LVW 2: 538).
11. It may be impossible to disentangle the threads of memories belonging to Murry and details he might have culled from conversations with Sullivan. Sullivan uses a similar incident in *But For the Grace of God*:

> My earliest recollection is of standing near a high wall in a little dark alley-way, with my mother trying to disengage her hand from mine . . . For this was my first visit to a dame-school, and I was to go alone, as

a 'good boy,' through a terribly forbidding entrance in that high wall. (Sullivan 1932: 9)

12. In *Still Life*, Anne's special book is also *David Copperfield*. Shortly before beginning his novel, Murry had written on 'The Dickens Revival' for the 29 May 1922 edition of *The Times*. Another essay, 'On Seriousness: Dickens and George Eliot' appeared in *The Times* on 11 July 1922.

Chapter 8

Circulating Mansfield

I

Katherine Mansfield's death did not follow a period of heightened intensity in her relationship with Murry, rather the contrary. Her last year displayed yet another cycle, similar to those in the past, of closeness, misunderstanding, disappointment and separation. Even during the relatively peaceful and productive months alone together at the Chalet, there had been signs of difficulty, which Murry did not completely perceive. On 7 September 1921, two days after he had sent *The Things We Are* to his publishers, Mansfield wrote to Ida Baker requesting that she take on the job of managing the household again, realising that she could not handle both 'housekeeping' and her writing. She asked her to 'accept this situation as the outcome of our friendship', which she considered 'every bit as sacred and eternal as marriage' (KMCL 4: 277).[1] By late October, she would describe Ida Baker as 'the official wife of both of us' (KMCL 4: 303).

Mansfield's reference to the 'sacred and eternal' nature of friendship bears so much Lawrentian weight that it again reveals how much *Women in Love* had invaded her consciousness that past summer, and the loss of Murry's closeness to Lawrence underlies her concern over his isolation with her at the Chalet, as is evident in her letter to Sydney Schiff on 25 December 1921, where she mentions that he 'craves friends', but men he knows are too 'frightened . . . to ever show him more than a kind of head sympathy'. She understands that it is the kind of longing that she cannot satisfy, and she tells Schiff that she is 'sure men need men in a way few women understand' (KMCL 4: 351). She returns to the topic of friendship in her letter to Schiff on New Year's Eve, this time turning it back to herself, confessing that although she would like to have real friends, she probably never will. Nonetheless, she has had 'moments' when she has understood what genuine friendship might be. She recalls a conversation she once had with Lawrence when he exclaimed: "'We must swear a solemn pact of friendship. Friendship is as binding, as solemn as marriage. We take each other for life, through everything – for ever'" (KMCL 4: 359). Mansfield admits that when he said it, she thought it was 'extravagant – fanatic', but now, considering the state of the world, she can understand what he meant.

Thinking about Lawrence during the Christmas season inevitably would bring back Mansfield's memories of that far-off Christmas in Chesham in 1914. She reminisced about it with Koteliansky: how Lawrence had been so nice that evening, and how Frieda had worn her Bavarian dress. She now feels love for Lawrence, and even for Frieda, when she considers them through the misty lenses of time. In her melancholy mood, she remarks 'how strange it is, how in spite of everything, there are certain people, like Lawrence, who remain in one's life for ever, and others who are forever shadowy' (KMCL 4: 343).[2]

At this moment, however, Murry was still happy with their isolation at the Chalet, especially since it allowed him so much time for work. On 28 January 1922 Mansfield praised the improvement in his writing: 'All sounds so easy, so to flow off his pen, and that hard dogmatic style has quite gone. He is a real *critic*' (KMN 2: 321). It may also be the case that Murry's perennial sexual frustration was – at least partially – allayed by his intense physical activity: skating and skiing. He liked to ski in front of their chalet so that Mansfield could watch him, and she seemed to appreciate such displays of his physical prowess, calling him 'a glorious object' and 'excessively handsome' in her diary on 6 January (KMN 2: 314). In reading Murry's and Mansfield's diaries in tandem, I am struck by the ease and warmth of their responses to each other in these last weeks before Mansfield's journey to Paris to seek help from Dr Manoukhin.[3] On 29 January, for example, Mansfield says 'I feel there is such love between us. Tender love. *Let it not change*! (KMN 2: 321). The next day, after she left for Paris, Murry describes how it moved him to watch her slip just before she had climbed into the sleigh to take them to the station because she was so 'unused to walking in snow . . . "Bless her!"' (MSX 4146). In Mansfield's account of that same trip to the station through the heavy snow, she claims that their 'happiness . . . reached its zenith that day' (KMN 2: 322).

Murry expected Mansfield to return following her consultation with Dr Manoukhin, but she decided she wanted to stay and begin treatment immediately. Murry was hesitant about joining her in Paris. He worried about what it would mean to live in a hotel: 'I shan't really be able to work. I can't have my books and I shan't be able to settle down to the regular grind of my novel', he wrote to her on 2 February (LJMM: 352).

He had started his third novel, *The Voyage* (which would not be finished and published until after Mansfield's death). Yet he quickly realised his loneliness without her and wrote again on 5 February:

> For the life of me I don't really know what's best. I do want to break the back of this novel; I do want to get some articles done. But at the same time just as sincerely I want to be with you if I'm any help – even if it's only as a cribbage partner. (LJMM: 355)

Mansfield was already aware of Murry's hesitancy towards joining her. In her diary on 4 February she had written:

> Heard from M. saying he prefers to remain in Montana. All his letters now are the same. There breathes in them the relief from strain. It is remarkable. He does not believe a word about Manoukhine & talks of coming to 'fetch' me in May. Well, if I am any better there will never be any more *fetching*. (KMN 2: 323)

Four days later, she wrote to Murry with a barbed tongue: 'Please do not come here to me', apparently in response to his telegram telling her he was going to join her after all:

> I want you to have your freedom as an artist . . . You were willing to join me *if I wanted you* – you were prepared, like a shot, *to be of help to me*. (But that is exactly like saying to a person: If you want to borrow money, borrow from me . . . It is not the gesture of people who deeply understand each other.) On the other hand your own personal feeling was not that at this most critical of all the moments in her life I could not leave Wig. Golly – no! It was my work – May would be too late – my novel – and so on. Reverse the positions, darling. *Hear* me saying that to you! (KMCL 5: 52)

The crisis was resolved by Murry's decision to come to Paris after all. His diary of 11 February records: 'Arrived Paris 5:45 . . . Lovely to be with Tig again. She looked so wonderfully well' (MSX 4146), and his arrival appears to have reversed the tone of increasing hostility in Mansfield's diary: 'In half an hour it seemed he had been here a long time. I still regret his leaving there for *his* sake. I know it is right for our sake' (KMN 2: 325). Her daily diary entries peter out by the end of February, and the brief notations give little indication of the quality of her relations with Murry at the present moment. It seems that they play many games of chess, that Murry reads Chekhov aloud to her, that one day he goes out and buys them a teapot. Instead, the diary entries are overwhelmed by the evidence of her physical suffering. She feels 'rather like being a beetle shut in a book, so shackled that one can do nothing but lie down – and even to lie down becomes a kind of agony' (KMN 2: 326). The story she managed to complete during her stay at the Victoria

Palace Hotel is 'The Fly', that unnerving portrait of victimisation, grief and suffering.

Murry's diary dutifully records each of Mansfield's 'seances' [treatments] and each tiny weight gain, for example: 'Feb. 17 Tig's third seance – gained 400 gr.'. He notes when the doctor seems pleased with her progress, and tells him that 'Tig's cough would begin to get better'. On 31 March he remarks that 'Tig regained her confidence. Tig walked out for the first time down the rue de Rennes as far as the Vivarium.' It is painful to read these entries; their alternating hope and disappointment reverberates far beyond their minimalist prose. Only occasionally does Murry mention his own emotional reactions to the daily struggle, such as on 20 April:

> A bloody depressing day, even though the weather was beautiful & we drove in the Bois de Boulogne . . . Tig has been really ill this week – pains in her lungs continually – intense pains in the abdomen. She says she feels weaker than she has felt for months – and her cough to my ear seems to have taken on the deep lung-tearing sound.
> And we were madly happy on Friday – absolutely confident. O for an end to the doubts-! (MSX 4146)

II

What bitter irony must it have been for Murry and Mansfield to be in Paris – the heart of international modernism – in that banner year of 1922! In the midst of the flowering of 'High Modernism', along with *Ulysses*, *The Waste Land* and *Jacob's Room*, their own books were published. Yet, given the context of physical and emotional suffering, neither of them makes much of what should have been significant moments in their careers: the appearances of Mansfield's *The Garden Party and Other Stories* on 22 February, and Murry's *The Things We Are* on 27 March. Murry simply notes the publication date of his novel in his diary without comment, and casually mentions on 24 May that he had been told that it was selling better than expected (MSX 4146). Mansfield, in turn, modestly expresses satisfaction when she receives, very soon after its publication, letters from readers about *The Garden Party*.[4]

In the interludes between Mansfield's treatments with Dr Manoukhin, she and Murry had a number of encounters with notable writers living in Paris, which brought them again – as it had early in their careers – into proximity with proponents of international modernism. Sydney Schiff arranged for James Joyce to visit them for tea at their hotel; Manoukhin introduced them to expatriate Russians, such as Ivan Bunin and Dimitri Merzhovsky; and Murry finally met those French writers 'to whom he was already well known as the "presenter" of Proust and Gide to the English public – Valery and Charles Du Bos, for example, who became his friends and lifelong admirers' (L: 89).[5]

Murry had published his first review of Proust in the *Nation and Athenaeum* on 12 November 1921, while he and Mansfield were still living at the Chalet des Sapins. Mansfield had praised the review to Sydney Schiff on 3 December as 'by far the best thing he has done', and exclaimed that both of them had 'lived Proust, breathed him, talked and thought of little else for two weeks – two solid uninterrupted Swiss weeks' (KMCL 4: 329). (I doubt that Mansfield was aware of a circuitous connection between Murry's seemingly obsessive interest in Proust and his recent relationship with Elizabeth Bibesco. I suspect that during some of Murry's intense conversations with Elizabeth Bibesco the previous autumn, she had told him of her friendship with Proust, and described for him Proust's cork-lined bedroom, and how he had taken her to eat at the Ritz and sat there 'in his fur coat in the suffocating restaurant drinking black coffee and eating nothing' [Bibesco 1989: 187].)

Murry's biographer comments that 1922 was 'as barren a period in his life as 1921 had been fruitful' (L: 91), and in quantitative terms Lea's statement is accurate. Murry, nonetheless, continued to produce his weekly reviews for the *Nation and Athenaeum* as well as occasional pieces for other periodicals, and amongst these are articles that still hold interest for twenty-first-century readers of modernist literature, such as his review 'Mr Joyce's "Ulysses"' and his essay 'The Break-Up of the Novel'. These demonstrate his most far-reaching engagement with the theoretical implications of literary modernism. Murry's reaction to *Ulysses* in both of these pieces reveals how his concerns over the validity of literary impressionism (which I discussed in Chapter 6) are now taken to a higher level, incorporating a more comprehensive analysis of the problem of subjectivity in relation to the larger question of the condition of modern consciousness itself.

In the 22 April review of *Ulysses*, Murry sets up Joyce as 'the egocentric rebel', the 'anarchist' who would

> blow what remains of Europe into the sky. But he is so individual that very few people will know when the bomb has exploded . . . By the excess of his anarchy, Mr. Joyce makes himself socially harmless . . . The head that is strong enough to read 'Ulysses' will not be turned by it. (DR: 118)

Accordingly, Murry considers that 'the driving force of this remarkable book is an immense, an unprecedented, liberation of suppressions'. Not surprisingly, considering Murry's earlier response to Lawrence's treatment of sexuality in *Women in Love*, he is ambivalent about the ultimate value of overthrowing all limitations and inhibitions of European civilisation:

> The best European is the one who bears his restrictions with the best grace, as recognizing their necessity. Mr. Joyce's book will possibly serve others as an indication of the limits they must not pass. It may help them to free themselves of inhibitions which are really destructive of vitality, and, at the same time, make it easier for them to accept those which are the conditions of civilization, and perhaps of art itself. For just as Mr. Joyce is in rebellion against the social morality of civilization, he is in rebellion against the lucidity and comprehensibility of civilized art. (DR: 118–19)

Nonetheless, Murry appreciates that *Ulysses* is 'a reflection of life through a singularly complex consciousness' and that Joyce achieves an extraordinary effect in the Nighttown section of the novel, which he calls 'a kind of "*Walpurgisnacht*"' where Bloom and Stephen Dedalus 'become human quintessentialities, realised potencies of the subconscious, metaphysical egos'. There Murry sees 'a genius of the very highest order, strictly comparable to Goethe's or Dostoevsky's' (DR: 119).

The review reveals that Murry is still concerned with 'the quality of the mind which receives and renders [impressions]', as he had expressed it in 1919 (A: 52). Accordingly, he pays attention to Joyce's 'superhuman effort to empty the whole of his consciousness' into his novel (DR: 119). Yet he hesitates when he realises that

> there is a vast difference between emptying a man's mind of all its possible thoughts during an hour on to paper, and producing the impression of an hour of a man's thinking. The thoughts of an imaginary half-minute may give us that far better than the thoughts of an actual hour. Again and again in 'Ulysses' we lose the circumstance in the circumstantiality. (DR: 120)

Partially, Murry's response is the impatience of a critic who recognises that his 'negative judgments are only provisional, and that fuller illuminations would make the dark places clear. Possibly. But we cannot spend our life with "Ulysses"' (DR: 120).

Murry's ambivalence about Joyce is also apparent in 'The Break Up of the Novel', and it is epitomised by his statement there that '*Ulysses* is a work of genius; but in spite of its objective moments, it is also a *reductio ad obsurdum* of subjectivism' (D: 146).[6] Again Murry's impatience comes to the fore: 'We long to escape from this incessant web of consciousness in which we are everywhere entangled, and to be allowed to trust to the revelation of the object' (D: 146). He insists about Joyce that 'rather than sacrifice one atom of his truth of detail, he is arcane and incomprehensible; and it is impossible not to feel he enjoys his own mysteriousness' (D: 147).

Mansfield said that during Joyce's visit on 29 March, he and Murry 'simply sailed away out of my depth' in their conversation about the relation between *Ulysses* and *The Odyssey*, and that she was 'almost stupefied'. She sensed that it is 'absolutely impossible that other people should understand *Ulysses* as Joyce understands it. It's almost revolting to hear him discuss its difficulties' (KMCL 5: 138). Nevertheless, according to Alpers, Joyce told the Schiffs 'that Mrs. Murry seemed to understand his book better than her husband which would have surprised her' (Alpers 1980: 358).[7] Mansfield's letter to Brett on 29 April suggests the quality of her response to the novel:

> Marion Bloom and Bloom are superbly seen at times. Marion is the complete complete female. There's no denying it. But one has to remember she's also Penelope, she is also the night and the day, she is also an image of the teeming earth, full of seed, rolling round and round. (KMCL 5: 156)

Mansfield's surer grasp of the metaphorical complexity of Joyce's novel distinguishes her approach to it from Murry's. Murry seems overwhelmed by the barrage of detail, although he recognises that 'Ulysses is a magnificent attempt by an extreme subjectivist to overcome the formlessness into which the method must so easily degenerate' (D: 145).

In 'The Break-up of the Novel', Murry undertakes a sustained analysis of the evolution of 'the process which has ended in the abolition of the story', which 'may be traced back far into the nineteenth century', and reached a turning point in 1913–14 when 'three significant books, calling themselves novels made an unobtrusive and independent appearance' (D: 133, 136). Describing the innovations of Proust's *Du côté de chez Swann*, Joyce's *The Portrait of the Artist as a Young Man* and Richardson's *Pointed Roofs*, Murry writes:

> These books had points of outward resemblance. Each was itself incomplete, a foretaste of sequels to come. Each was autobiographical and, within the necessary limits of individuality, autobiographical in the same new and peculiar fashion. They were attempts to record immediately the growth of a consciousness. Immediately; without any effort at mediation by means of an interposed plot or story. All three authors were trying to present the content of their consciousness as it was before it had been reshaped in obedience to the demands of practical life; they were exploring the strange limbo where experiences once conscious fade into unconsciousness. (D: 137)

Typically for Murry, he arranges a mini-hierarchy amongst these three explorers of consciousness. Of Proust's *À la recherche du temps perdu*, Murry already predicts that 'even though the work is still unfinished', it will come to 'an end strictly and necessarily identical with the beginning'.[8] Murry considers Proust's a novel that 'is at once a philosophical justification of its own existence and the history of its own creation' (D: 138). Thus Proust's

> internal completion . . . gives him the position of conscious philosopher of a literary impulse which arose, quite independently, in two other minds at the same moment. Simply because it is the most conscious, Marcel Proust's effort subsumes those of James Joyce and Dorothy Richardson, though it is not for that reason more important than they. But common to them all is an insistence upon the immediate consciousness as reality. (D: 138–9)

Murry also betrays some gender bias when he goes on to observe that Dorothy Richardson's 'insistence upon the immediate consciousness as reality . . . is probably instinctive and irrational; it has a distinctively feminine tinge'.

The article nicely outlines the historical development of 'the extreme and deliberate subjectivism of the latest developments of the novel', which Murry situates 'as the culmination of Rousseauism'. The nineteenth century intensified the divide between 'the instinctive individualism of the artistic sensibility' and the 'new demoplutocratic' society which 'had neither room nor respect for such an unprofitable activity of the human spirit as art'. Murry then recapitulates some elements of Boston's world view in *The Things We Are* into his argument by using the 'rational reinforcement from the advance of science' to explain how the 'anthropocentric conception of the universe was finally abandoned, and an indifferent universe lent its weight to a hostile society in thrusting back the individual upon himself' (D: 139).

Murry's analysis of the cultural background of the emergence of the new fiction of consciousness pulls together many of the same issues that later critics of modernism are still continuing to pursue. He includes in his discussion such examples as the influence of Baudelaire's prose poems, the impact of Dostoevsky and Tolstoy who 'exploded the novel' and the 'conception of the artist as a superman' (D: 136, 140). As he develops his thesis, however, the same kind of impatience with superfluity that he expresses in his review of *Ulysses* becomes more apparent. In a phrase comparable to Virginia Woolf's call for 'some pattern or design' in her essay on 'Modern Fiction', Murry says 'a consciousness is a flux, it needs to be crystallized about some foreign object to have an intelligible shape' (D: 145):

> Marcel Proust's historical and philosophical preoccupations supply such a thread; but even he can be excessively tedious when his grasp on the external world is slackened. Miss Richardson can be as tiring as a twenty-four hour

cinematograph without interval or plot. And in Ulysses, James Joyce at times carries his effort of analysis to such lengths as to become as difficult as a message in code of which half the key has been lost. (D: 145)

Murry's rhetorical strategy in this essay is at first surprising and then transparently obvious. He builds a carefully considered argument for the inevitability of the rise of 'extreme subjectivism' in the novel and then finds it wanting in order to elevate another *kind* of 'modern fiction':

> The two significant methods in the most modern fiction are, on the one hand, the presentation of a consciousness, on the other, the presentation of the vivid moments of a consciousness. Both are equally subjective. They differ, however, in this important particular that, whereas the subjectivist novelists seem to be chiefly moved by a desire to express the truth alone, the story-writers aim at an *art* which is compatible with the truth. The most obvious consequence is that the second are much more easily comprehensible than the first, because they speak a universal language. A writer who presents an object perceived, interests us immediately, because there is common ground between his perceptions and our own. It is also easier for us to feel the individual quality of such a writer's consciousness than it is to disentangle it from the work of a writer who is busy in insisting upon the nature of his consciousness. (D: 144)

In a characteristic move, Murry next takes the opportunity to praise the emerging hero in his pantheon of literary 'Greats': Anton Chekhov, who epitomises the writer attempting 'to reconcile subjectivism with objectivity' (D: 141):

> Like the subjectivists, Tchehov was obsessed by a passion for truth; like them, he believed that the only reality was the individual consciousness; like them, he had conceived a deep mistrust of the machine of story. But in a higher degree than they, he possessed the purely creative genius of the writer, which is an instinct for objectivity and concreteness. He reconciled the two conflicting impulses in an individual creation. The short story of Tchehov was an innovation in literature. The immediate consciousness remains the criterion, and the method is based on a selection of those glimpses of the reality which in themselves possess a peculiar vividness, and by virtue of this vividness appear to have a peculiar significance. (D: 142)

Murry's appreciation for Chekhov slyly allows him to reveal the submerged subtext of his discussion in 'The Break-up of the Novel'. Attempting to show the persistence of what he calls 'the Tchehov tendency' (D: 141), he concludes that the 'most finished modern example is to be found in the short stories of Katherine Mansfield' (D: 143). He does not want Mansfield to look like a mere follower of Chekhov, however:

It is quite impossible to imitate, almost impossible to be influenced by a method so completely intuitive as Tchehov's. It is simply that Katherine Mansfield is a similar phenomenon: her work is of the same kind as Tchehov's, and precisely because it is of the same kind it is utterly different from his. (D: 143–4)

Murry frames their likeness metaphorically: 'In a short story by Tchehov or Katherine Mansfield it is as though an intense beam of peculiar light were cast upon a fragment of reality' (D: 144). Here is Murry's fullest attempt so far to *circulate* Mansfield. This is a process which will be greatly intensified after her death, but in the last years of her life is already in operation. For example, in his lectures on style the previous year, Murry had made a point of quoting a long paragraph from Mansfield's 'Prelude' to illustrate 'the vital difference between true and false descriptive writing' (Murry 1925: 103). Murry's promotion of Mansfield was an enduring feature of his relationship with her. When he was editor of the *Athenaeum*, he had been able to give her an outlet for publication and also ensure that she receive major reviews by assigning them to friends, such as Sullivan and de la Mare. When he had left the *Athenaeum*, his approach had to be less direct, but he found he could bolster her reputation by embedding discussion of her work within his general criticism, as he did in 'The Break-up of the Novel', where she assumes importance by being linked to Chekhov, or as in *The Problem of Style*, where he uses her as a counterweight in her 'vigour' as 'a contemporary author' in her 'prime' against 'Mr. Arnold Bennett's decrepitude' (Murry 1925: 103).

Murry's rather tentative appreciation for modernist experimentation quickly dissolved after Mansfield's death. Less than a year afterwards he would write in the 1 November 1923 issue of the *Adelphi* (in the now transformed, confessional style that he had taken up for his new venture in journalism) about his *personal* reactions to the emergence of Proust and Joyce:

I examined them, for I am a top-heavy person who has to examine things. Essentially, from my point of view essentially, they are nothing. Landmarks, perhaps, to tell me twice again that the intellectual consciousness is utterly *kaput* . . . What Tchehov had done sincerely and simply and perfectly, they were trying to do fashionably, elaborately and unnecessarily. It was a waste of time. Possibly it may be art. I know it is not the kind of art that deeply interests me. I am a detective by profession, and I can interest myself deliberately, in a professional kind of way, in anything. But neither Marcel Proust nor James Joyce interest *me*. There is more really profound thought-adventure in one of Tchehov's stories like *The Black Monk* than in all their work put together. They have talent, buckets of it, but talent – what's the use of talent except to help you to say something of importance for life? (Murry 1924b: 299–300)

What accounts for this belligerence towards the intellectually 'fashionable' and this insistence on the importance of individual taste? Murry's turn against Proust and Joyce signals a dramatic break with modernist literature and – as a subtext – its exponents, the Bloomsbury intellectuals, from whom by then, he was nearly completely alienated.

III

The Victoria Palace Hotel in Paris turned out to be the last 'home' Murry and Mansfield lived in together for any length of time. After their four months there they returned to Switzerland in June, but apparently their miserable journey set off both a rapid decline in Mansfield's health and a rupture between them.[9] On 29 July, Mansfield moved down to Sierre with Ida Baker, leaving Murry in Randogne. Considering Mansfield's evident annoyance over Murry's apparent lack of empathy with her suffering, and knowing how many-layered were the complexities of both partners' emotional lives, we cannot accept as completely reliable Murry's explanation that it was Mansfield's involvement with 'occult doctrines' that caused their separation. Undoubtedly, that shielded other elements of discord. Alpers mentions that even Ida Baker, 'the only other person who might have described the event in detail, never did so to [him] leaving the impression that she did not really know what had taken place'. Alpers surmises that 'it may well be that Murry himself hardly knew and had to reconstruct it afterwards' (Alpers 1980: 362).

Murry did not realise that this apparently temporary separation would turn out to be permanent. Never again would he live with Katherine Mansfield. When she decided suddenly to travel back to London in mid-August, Murry came also, but Mansfield stayed at Brett's house and Murry at Boris Anrep's next door. During her six weeks in London, Mansfield involved herself more fully with the ideas of Ouspensky and attended his lectures, which was a precipitating factor in her sudden decision to travel to France on 2 October 1922. Having recognised that Manoukhin's treatment was a failure, and that medical science had nothing left to offer her, she had decided to investigate the possibility of joining Gurdjieff's community at Fontainebleau.[10] Murry was shocked and dismayed when he heard that Mansfield was planning to meet with Gurdjieff: 'You've passed clean out of my range & understanding . . . I feel our ships are sailing away from each other & that we're just waving' (LJMM: 365), he wrote in bewilderment on 14 October, Mansfield's thirty-fourth birthday.

For the rest of his life, Murry would circle back to those last months of 1922, analysing them and reinterpreting them according to his current preoccupations. He described them in the public format of his books and articles, and in the private format of his personal journals. Although he tended to portray himself as a rationalist standing firm against the onslaught of occultist doctrines, he was actually beginning to look beyond the framework of rationalism for emotional support in the midst of this present crisis, such as reading about Yoga and trying to breath 'rhythmically' to make 'his mind a blank' (MSX 4162: 251).

Murry does not seem aware of the ironic implications of either his attraction to 'rhythmic' breathing or of the name of Gurdjieff's 'Institute for the Harmonious Development of Man'. 'Rhythm' and 'Harmony', as we have seen, had been the dual centrepieces of his philosophy ever since his first venture in publishing, *Rhythm*, and the concept of 'harmony' was his answer to Lawrence's theory of polar oppositionality.

As it had in 1921, the topic of Lawrence would begin to intrude again in Mansfield's correspondence as the year drew to its close. The Christmas season seems to have been indelibly linked with memories of Rose Tree Cottage. Late in November, Mansfield had asked Murry if he would ever like to meet up with him again, and mentioned that Lawrence (and Forster) would have been able to understand what she was experiencing at the Institute, although she recognised that Lawrence's 'pride would keep him back. No one person here is more important than another' (KMCL 5: 326).[11] Perhaps her seeming willingness to allow Lawrence back into her life might have begun to soften Murry's opinion as well. He mentions 'the times when you & I used to sit with the Lawrences in their kitchen', in his letter to her on 17 December.

Murry's unfinished manuscript of 1947, which he states is a 'sequel' to his published autobiography, *Between Two Worlds* (1935), contains his most fully articulated analysis of this last stage in his relationship with Katherine Mansfield. Nearly a quarter century separates this analysis from the experiences described within it and its interpretation is coloured by the events in Murry's life during those intervening years: his tragic second marriage to Violet Le Maistre (who also died of tuberculosis), his tortured third marriage to the abusive Betty Cockbayne, and his final happy pairing with Mary Gamble. Thus, what he discerns as the 'pattern' of his relationship with Mansfield can be placed within the larger 'pattern' of his subsequent relationships. He sets up here a basic dichotomy in his younger self, between the passive Murry who 'numbly acquiesced' to Mansfield's demands, and the active, assertive Murry who held fast to his own sense of 'intellectual' integrity. The 1947 analysis is full of carefully structured oppositions: mind and body, discipline and doctrine, life and death. Yet it also softens the intensity of the differences as it clarifies their structural relationship. Its description of the end of Mansfield's life is abrupt and in its pretence of artlessness, oddly moving.

He begins by describing the course of Mansfield's illness, and his regrets about how it was handled, both by her doctors and by himself. Should he have insisted she go to a sanatorium? Should he have gone along with Dr Sorapure in reassuring her despite the 'death sentence of the specialist'? Should he have 'allowed her to go in pursuit of health from Dr. Manoukhin in Paris'? He explains how he could not accept her decision to enter the Gurdjieff Institute, but blames himself for not being able to give 'her a faith – a real faith, not an animal one – a faith that could face death undismayed'. He recognises that she was braver than he and 'took a plunge' that he 'could never have taken':

> We said Goodbye. We loved one another very deeply. But the old anguished love was buried – the love which had been our life. When I went, at her pressing & unexpected summons, to visit her some twelve weeks later, I saw a creature radiant with love & tenderness, renewed, prepared for the *vita nuova*. On the evening of the day I arrived she died, of a sudden & violent haemorrhage. She was not expecting death. There was anguish & terror in her eyes when the blood poured from her mouth. The two doctors shut me out of the room. (MSX 4162: 248–9)

The convergence of Mansfield's sudden death and Murry's growing openness to spiritual renewal seems to have led him a month later to the profound mystical experience that he described as 'the one entirely revolutionary happening' in his life (quoted in L: 102). Distraught and disoriented, he had returned to England feeling himself to be 'an automaton, completely unable to make contact with [his] fellow human beings' (Murry 1929: 32). One night, isolated in a cottage in Sussex, sitting 'motionless for hours' trying to 'face the truth that [he] was alone', Murry says he realised himself 'as a little island against whose slender shores a cold, dark, boundless ocean lapped devouring' (Murry 1924b: 43). He had reached 'the pinnacle of personal being' when he realised completely how his physical consciousness could only extend as far as the ends of his 'hands and feet' and beyond them was 'that frontier [which] stretched out vast immensities, of space, of the universe, of the illimitable something that was other than I' (Murry 1924b: 42–3). And then suddenly he underwent one of those overwhelming experiences that fill the pages of writings by mystics:

> a moment came when the darkness of that ocean changed to light, the cold to warmth; when it swept in one wave over the shores and frontiers of myself; when it bathed me and I was renewed; when the room was filled with a

presence, and I knew I was not alone – that I never could be alone any more, that the universe beyond held no menace, for I was part of it, that in some way for which I had sought in vain so many years, I *belonged,* and because I belonged, I was no longer I, but something different, which could never be afraid in the old ways, or cowardly with the old cowardice. And the love I had lost was still mine, but now more durable, being knit into the very substance of the universe I had feared. (Murry 1924b: 44)[12]

Murry would quote from this account of his mystical experience six years later and add to it the information that he had 'passed over deliberately' in 1923. He now mentions that the 'presence' he had felt 'was definitely connected with the person of Katherine Mansfield'. He clarifies this by stating that he does 'not mean that the room was filled with her "presence"; but that her "presence" was given to [his] consciousness simultaneously with the "presence" that filled the room', and that assured him that 'all was well with her' (Murry 1929: 37–8).

In Murry's construction of his life as a spiritual journey, this incident takes central stage in his personal drama. He quickly discovered that it could serve the purpose of explaining his new direction as a writer – and most significantly, as an editor. He used it as a public justification for his new publishing venture, the *Adelphi*, which first appeared in June 1923, less than six months after he returned from Fontainebleau. Its purpose was threefold: to propound the discovery he had made that 'we are not isolated . . . We believe in life' (Murry 1924b: 18); to further the ideas of D. H. Lawrence (a subject I will take up in the next chapter); and most essentially, to circulate the writings and image of Katherine Mansfield.

Murry must have been surprised by the magazine's enormous success. Its first issue sold more than 15,000 copies and by the end of its first year, more than 100,000 were in circulation, according to John Carswell, who nicely describes its initial reception:

> The main effect of the *Adelphi* . . . was outside London, and especially in the north of England where its vaguely religious and cultural message, mixed with modernity, struck home for those with a chapel childhood and an adolescence of doubt mingled with regret . . . Murry had enough of the evangelical to reach many who could never have tolerated Virginia Woolf or E. M. Forster. (J. Carswell 1978: 199–200)

Lea remarks that despite Murry's ostensibly 'mystical' motivation, the prospectus that he drew up for the *Adelphi* before its publication suggests that 'it is at least as eloquent of Murry's revulsion from Bloomsbury as of any more positive belief' (L: 106). The prospectus emphasises Murry's assault on the preoccupations of avant-garde culture:

We are bored to death by modern dilettantism. We are sick of 'Art'. Inspired by no living purpose, it has brought us nowhere. If modern literature is to be anything better than a pastime for railway journeys or a parlour game for effete intellectuals, it must be built upon some active conviction. Those who have something to say will know how to say it. Therefore, we hope that although the contents of THE ADELPHI may not be 'literary', they will be literature. (quoted in L: 107)

That such a turnabout on Murry's part would not be well received by Bloomsbury is not surprising, as evidenced by Virginia Woolf's remarks on 30 July 1923:

Poor Middleton Murry has had a conversion, which has had an odious Bantam – the Adelphi – . . . As literature, it seems to me worthless – (only strong words are out of place): it seems to me mediocre then. The spirit that inspires it, with its unction and hypocrisy, and God is love, which still leaves room for flea bites, pin pricks, and advertising astuteness, would enrage, were it not that there's something so mild and wobbly about that too that I can't waste good wrath. Most of my friends find it deplorable. (LVW 3: 59)

By the end of the year, Woolf would be even more annoyed with Murry's 'new' direction. He clearly had become a figure of ridicule, as is clear from her comment that 'Eliot says he has unbuttoned his waist-coat and found his level. One might as well listen to a half starved clerk spouting religious revival on a tub at Hyde Park Corner' (LVW 3: 80).

But it was Murry's willingness to write about his personal 'revelations' about Mansfield's death in the *Adelphi* that bothered Woolf more than anything. On 8 July 1923 she complained: 'I dont object to opening the heart, but I do object to finding it empty. Murry has nothing whatever to reveal. Yet he has sold his reticence' (DVW 2: 253).

Murry probably dismayed his friends when he began to work on Mansfield's papers nearly immediately after her death, which would have been evident to them when they read his letters to the editors of *TLS* and the *Nation and Athenaeum* on 15 and 17 February (just over a month after his return from Fontainebleau), seeking copies of her letters for future publication (Lilley 1974: 94). In each subsequent issue of the *Adelphi* , Murry would publish work by Mansfield: poems, drawings, sketches, fragments of stories and, most controversially, extracts from her notebooks, often prefaced with his own self-conscious 'introductions'.[13] Many years later, on Mansfield's birthday, 14 October 1931, Murry recorded in his journal that 'she would have been 43 to-day', and indicates how the impact of her death continued to reverberate:

Katherine is complete, immortal, – not personally mine. She gave me myself by leaving me. The shock of that bereavement was the one crucial happening of my life. Everything afterwards grows out of that. And if I go down to posterity simply as the husband of Katherine Mansfield, – well, it won't be far from the truth. (MSX 4149: 19–29)

Notes

1. See Burgan (1994: 142–68) for an astute, sensitive analysis of Mansfield's gradual acceptance of her dependence on Ida Baker as a caretaker.
2. Despite Mansfield's softening towards Lawrence at this time, she still could be critical in her old way. She had complained to Schiff on 3 December: 'when he gets on to the subject of maleness I lose all patience' (KMCL 4: 330).
3. Like so much in Mansfield's and Murry's lives, even this medical situation has a literary connection. According to Catherine Carswell, Dr Ivan Manoukhin had been Gorky's doctor, and it had been Gorky who announced to the press in November 1921 that Manoukhin had discovered a cure for tuberculosis (C. Carswell 1932: 179).
4. *The Garden Party* was an immediate success. The first edition sold out and it was reprinted in March, April and May of 1922. The American edition came out on 26 May 1922, and it also went through many re-printings, six in 1923 alone. See Kirkpatrick (1989: 22–5).
5. René Wellek (1986: 111) comments that 'Murry had the singular merit to have written first in English' about Proust's novel.
6. The article was originally published in the *Yale Review* in January 1923, but Murry dated it as March 1922 when he reprinted it in *Discoveries*, suggesting that it was probably written during his time in Paris.
7. Alpers quotes remarks in letters from Mansfield to Violet Schiff and from Violet Schiff to Wyndham Lewis to support this supposition.
8. In his 'M. Marcel Proust: a New Sensibility', first published in the *Quarterly Review* in July 1922, Murry similarly writes: 'If . . . M. Proust's book ends, as we believe it will end, in its own beginning, it will have a unity – in spite of the apparent discrepancy of certain of the parts – of a kind which has never been achieved in a work of literature before: it will be the first book in the world that has been the psychological history of its own creation, and a philosophical justification of its own necessity' (D: 121).
9. See Ida Baker's description of this 'dreadful journey' (Baker 1972: 197–9).
10. Mansfield's experiences at the Institute for the Harmonious Development of Man lie outside the framework of this book. For information and analysis of her Gurdjieffian involvement see the differing views of her biographers: Alpers (1980: 424–5); Meyers (1978: 238–52); and Tomalin (1988: 228–37). For an account by a follower of Gurdjieff, see James Moore's *Gurdjieff and Mansfield* (Moore 1980).
11. Lawrence had sent her a postcard from Wellington, with the word 'Ricordi' [Remembrances] written on it, and she had also mentioned Lawrence in the will she signed in August (Tomalin 1988: 190–1).
12. This description first appeared in the *Adelphi* in its second issue in July 1923; it was reprinted the next year in *The Unknown God* (Murry 1924b).

13. These numerous publications were only the beginning of Murry's efforts to circulate Mansfield. He would gather many of them together with additional stories that he had already published in various periodicals to form the two posthumous collections of her stories: *The Dove's Nest* (1923) and *Something Childish* (1924). He followed these in 1927 with Mansfield's *Poems* and with his construction of the *Journal of Katherine Mansfield*. Next came a collection of *The Letters of Katherine Mansfield* in 1928, and a compilation of her *Athenaeum* reviews, *Novels and Novelists*, in 1930. This editorial productivity continued throughout the greater part of Murry's life. For example, he published more material from Mansfield's notebooks in *The Scrapbook of Katherine Mansfield* in 1939, *Katherine Mansfield's Letters to John Middleton Murry, 1913–1922* in 1951, and a fuller, supposedly 'definitive' edition of Mansfield's *Journal* in 1954. These books kept Mansfield's reputation alive and their success allowed Murry to realise a considerable income from their sales.

Chapter 9

Circulating Lawrence

I

Mansfield's softening of heart towards Lawrence during the last months of her life allowed for a gradual reconciliation to begin for Murry as well. Apparently, some time in December 1922, Murry wrote to Lawrence in New Mexico, 'suggesting' that their 'relation should be renewed' (RDHL: 98). He responded, cautiously, on 30 December: 'Heaven knows what we all are, and how we should feel if we met, now that we are changed. We'll have to meet and see' (LDHL 4: 364). Lawrence's softening might have been hastened by Murry's positive review of *Aaron's Rod* in August. Nevertheless, Murry's need for Lawrence had only become acute after Mansfield's death. As it was in 1915, when Lawrence had offered a distraught Murry emotional intimacy to assuage the pain of Mansfield's (temporary) abandonment, so now, in 1923, Lawrence would offer a similar – if more guarded – sympathy to a Murry devastated by his awareness of an abandonment that was final. The letter he received from Lawrence on 2 February 1923 made certain the possibility of genuine reconciliation:

> Yes, I always knew a bond in my heart. Feel a fear where the bond is broken now. Feel as if old moorings were breaking all. What is going to happen to us all? Perhaps it is good for Katherine not to have to see the next phase. We will unite up again when I come to England. It has been a savage enough pilgrimage these last four years. Perhaps K. has taken the only way for her. We keep faith – I always feel death only strengthens that, the faith between those who have it. (LDHL 4: 375)

The language of this letter must have echoed in Murry's mind for the rest of his life. In his unpublished manuscript of 1947, from which I quoted in the preceding chapter, he referred to his 'parting of the ways' with Mansfield over the issue of Gurdjieff, and exclaimed: 'It was a sad business after so long a pilgrimage together' (MSX 4162: 249).[1]

Lawrence also mentions in the letter that he was having his publisher send Murry a copy of *Fantasia of the Unconscious*: 'I wanted Katherine to read it. She'll know though. The dead don't die. They look on and help' (LDHL 4: 375). Such consoling fiction could only have bolstered Murry's growing mysticism and his tendency to place enormous significance upon coincidental phenomena. He nearly leapt at the chance for another revelation through Lawrence to equal his mystical experience in relation to Mansfield. Thus Murry made his reading of *Fantasia* into a turning point in his own spiritual 'pilgrimage'. Clearly, the conjunction of Lawrence's sympathetic response to Mansfield's death and Murry's reading of *Fantasia* would structure the next phase of the relationship between the two men.

In *Reminiscences of D. H. Lawrence* (1933) Murry describes how he eagerly read Lawrence's book

> late into the spring night in a solitary cottage in Ashdown Forest. . . . I had just emerged from an experience which changed me radically. Lawrence's declaration of faith in the *Fantasia* was completely convincing to me in my new half-convalescent, half-confident condition. Here was something in which I did veritably believe with all my heart, and all my mind, and all my soul . . . If this was what Lawrence believed and stood for, then I was his man: he should lead and I would follow. (RDHL: 99–100)[2]

Murry's rhetoric resembles here a conversion narrative, and to some extent, that is what it is. Murry's tendency to conflate Lawrence and Jesus is easily detectable in this passage, as it is also when he attributes his founding of the *Adelphi* to this new relation to Lawrence: 'I would prepare the place for him. I would make a new magazine, and begin by publishing the essential chapters of the *Fantasia*' (RDHL: 100).[3]

Murry's use of the words 'solitary cottage' emphasises his isolation and evokes his earlier reference to the same setting for the mystical experience I discussed in the last chapter. In reality, Murry's life was not nearly so lonely as he later made it seem. He actually had taken the cottage as an escape from the growing complexities of his relations with women. His 1947 manuscript describes how shortly after he returned from Mansfield's funeral he became embroiled in another manifestation of his predilection for triangular relationships, this time with the wife of his mystic friend Dunning, who had tried to make him become her lover, with her husband's acquiescence. That was followed by a complicated relationship with Dorothy Brett, which although it did not end in marriage, as Mansfield three years earlier had prophesied,[4] did involve a sexual union, consummated – according to Brett's diary – on 20 April 1923, only three months after Mansfield's death (Hignett 1984:

135). Murry's relationship with Brett lies outside the concerns of this book, however, interesting though it may be.[5] I mention it largely to suggest the emotional confusion of Murry's life during the months after Mansfield's death and to suggest that it is one element in his complicated friendship with Lawrence, becoming part of the subtext of his later, most provocative, circulating of Lawrence: *Son of Woman*. Another part of that subtext – and a far more significant part – is Murry's sudden blossoming of interest in Frieda Lawrence, later that same year.

Frieda had arrived in London at the end of August 1923, during a particularly difficult period in her marriage. Murry had expected that Lawrence would accompany her, and begin to work with him on the *Adelphi*, but he delayed his trip and asked Murry to 'look after F. a bit. You know what a vague creature she is' (LDHL 4: 483). Without Mansfield's critical eye and without Lawrence's domination, Murry relaxed into a friendly appreciation for Frieda's warmth and emotional openness. He spent much time in her rooms and even accompanied her to Freiburg that September. According to Ellis, Murry stopped sleeping with Brett during this time, only resuming it once he realised that Lawrence was soon to arrive (Ellis 1998: 149). Hignett believes that 'Brett seems not to have realised that an affair had developed between Frieda and Murry' (Hignett 1984: 142). Not surprisingly, all of this evoked a great deal of gossip amongst their mutual friends. Whether or not an actual affair ensued remains a continuing matter of speculation. Lea accepts Murry's explanation, quoting from Murry's journal about his love for Frieda and how he held back from sleeping with her because of his loyalty to Lawrence (L: 118). In their late-life correspondence, both Murry and Frieda refer to their trip together and discuss whether it was a mistake not to have consummated their union at that time.[6]

Whatever the 'truth' of the matter, Lawrence clearly was suspicious when he returned, as is apparent in the animosity against the 'Murry' figure in three stories he wrote soon afterwards, which I will discuss in the next chapter. The whole situation seems an ironic reprisal of the one in 1920, when Mansfield suspected that Murry was sleeping with Brett. In both cases, Murry maintained his innocence by insisting that he had not gone 'all the way'! In both cases, the 'affairs' would be fully consummated after the deaths of their respective spouses.

Lawrence's stay in England occasioned another incident that has become legendary in the varying accounts of the Murry/Lawrence relationship. Again, a familiar pattern repeats itself. Again it takes place around Christmas time, at a party, sometime between 21 and 24 December 1923 (Ellis 1998: 148). Most of its attendees – Lawrence, Frieda, Murry, Koteliansky, Gertler and Mary Cannan (Gilbert had long since dropped out of the picture after the break-up of his marriage to Mary) – had been participants at that other famous party at the Cannan's windmill in 1914. Lawrence had rented a room for a dinner at the Café Royal and invited in addition to the above, Catherine and Donald Carswell and Dorothy Brett. As with the earlier party, there was far too much drinking by people who were not used to doing so. Koteliansky 'smashed a number of the Café Royal's glasses' following his speech in praise of Lawrence, and Lawrence himself ended the festivities by vomiting at the table and then falling into unconsciousness, having to be carried down to a taxi to be taken home. Ellis's description of this evening seems to me the most reliable and balanced, taking into account the differing interpretations of the evening by Brett, Catherine Carswell and Murry. During the evening Lawrence asked all those present to come with him to New Mexico and make the beginnings of a new kind of life there. It was the 'Rananim' ideal all over again. There were different reactions from the guests. Ellis explains:

> Drink, and the perception some of those appealed to felt they had of Lawrence's desperate loneliness, must explain why all but one of those present responded in the affirmative [Mary Cannan] . . . Of those who indicated that they were willing to follow Lawrence to the New World, only Brett and Murry made it clear after the dinner (as they almost certainly had before) that they were to be taken seriously. (Ellis 1998: 149–50)

The symbolic moment of the evening for Murry came as the climax of an ascending crest of emotionality. Catherine Carswell describes it with considerable distaste:

> what I next remember is Murry going up to Lawrence and kissing him with a kind of effusiveness which afflicted me. He must have been sensible to my feeling, because he turned to me.
> 'Women can't understand this,' he said. 'This is an affair between men. Women can have no part or place in it.'
> 'Maybe,' said I. 'But anyhow it wasn't a woman who betrayed Jesus with a kiss.'
> At this Murry again embraced Lawrence, who sat perfectly still and unresponsive, with a dead-white face in which the eyes alone were alive.
> 'I *have* betrayed you, old chap, I confess it,' continued Murry. 'In the past I *have* betrayed you. But never again. I call you all to witness, never again'. (C. Carswell 1932: 212)

Murry vehemently disagreed with Catherine Carswell's description, to no one's surprise. In his agitated self-defence over her depiction of himself in *The Savage Pilgrimage* he writes:

> It is perfectly true that on that night I did kiss Lawrence, for the first and last time in my life; it is quite untrue that I said the words 'I will not betray you.'

> What I said was: 'I love you, Lorenzo, but I won't promise not to betray you.' (RDHL: 169)[7]

Murry's description of the incident in *Reminiscences* is important enough in relation to the question of the homosocial dynamics of the Murry/Lawrence relationship to quote in full. Murry insists that it was impossible that Carswell 'should have understood the words as they were understood by me, who spoke them, or by Lawrence, to whom they were spoken':

> They had nothing whatever to do with the matter of my going or not going with Lawrence to New Mexico. They had no relation to any act of mine that was in contemplation at that moment. They had relation only to some final position of my 'principle' towards Lawrence's 'principle': of my impersonal self towards Lawrence's impersonal self. At the moment that I said the words, which were compelled from me, I knew exactly what they meant. They meant that Lawrence's secret was in my keeping. Not only that moment, and at that moment, did I understand that Lawrence had a secret, and that I knew it: somewhere I knew it. Not with my conscious mind. But I knew it was in my keeping; and that, if I looked, I should find it.
> To the end of Lawrence's life I forbore to look. I did not want to look. I was not strong enough to look. I had an almost superstitious fear of looking. I had never understood until that night, never come within a universe of understanding, how great had been his suffering. Suddenly, in a moment of vision, I saw it – an utterly impersonal thing: suffering, of a kind and magnitude and beauty, completely beyond my experience and until that moment beyond my extremest imagination. (RDHL: 170–1)

Ellis is unconvinced by Murry's further explanation that 'the secret he alone had discovered and could not promise that he would not betray, was that Lawrence had reached a stage when he was no longer committed to '"life" but to death and despair'. He wryly notes that for the others at the dinner

> who overheard the exchange between him and Lawrence, however, the significance would almost certainly have been local and particular. They would have taken the appeal which Murry claims preceded his own words ('Do not betray me') and those words themselves – whatever they were – as allusions to Frieda. (Ellis 1998: 151)

Ellis is right to describe Murry's long, convoluted explanation as written with 'characteristic if unconvincing ingenuity' (Ellis 1998: 151). Murry's rhetorical strategy in the passage I quoted above (as in the paragraphs following it) suggests subterfuge and a desire to tantalise the reader with some unstated 'secret'. Part of it might only be gloating: by the time of *writing* these remarks, Murry could boast to himself that he *had*, literally, betrayed Lawrence by finally sleeping with Frieda after all.

Yet it should be noted that an emphasis on secrecy and the attempt to establish a special understanding with the reader had long been a characteristic of Murry's critical method. As evidence, consider the following remarks in an essay of his from 1916, the year of his disastrous first break from Lawrence's attempted domination. Murry here is reflecting upon the relationship between 'creation' and 'criticism', a subject with deeply resonant meaning throughout his dealings with Lawrence (and Mansfield too, of course):

> In essence they are the same: creation is a man's lonely attempt to fix an intimacy with his own strange and secret soul, criticism is the satisfaction of the impulse of loneliness to find friends and secret sharers among the souls that are or have been. As creation drives a man to the knowledge of his own intolerable secrets so it drives him to find others with whom he may whisper of the things which he has found. (E: 24)

Murry's use of a similar kind of language of secrecy in his discussion of the Café Royal incident is then not unusual. But his circuitous sentences, his repetitions, his references to the matter as being that of his 'impersonal self towards Lawrence's impersonal self', his suggestion that the words were 'compelled' from him, that they emerged not from his 'conscious' mind, all seem to imply dynamics more complicated than whether or not he had – or would ever – take Frieda away from Lawrence. Further along in his explanation, Murry says:

> I had become aware that Lawrence was a living dead man, leading a posthumous life. To all but one person in a hundred thousand the very statement is nonsensical, meaningless. I am writing for the one person alone: for the person who knows, by experience or true imagination, something of the waste places which the lonely human soul can travel. Those who have no knowledge of these things can know only the outward and corporeal shell of such a man as Lawrence. (RDHL: 171–2)

By 1933, when he published these words, Murry would have had a much clearer idea about Lawrence's sexual problems than he might have had in 1923 (although even then, he likely knew some details from his many intimate conversations with Frieda). His repetition of the word 'secret' insinuates something that cannot be openly expressed. Something that only those who can read between the lines: 'the one person alone', who may identify with Lawrence's situation, could decipher. It might be too simplistic to accept totally the words of Murry's daughter, Katherine Murry, in her interpretation of these words, but she does provide a no-nonsense, late twentieth-century reaction to the whole situation:

> Other people there have given their versions of this strange scene, but in fact there were only two people who knew the meaning of those words: Murry

and Lawrence. The former was to explain that moment only after Lawrence's death. He said that he had had a sudden preternatural illumination and in a flash knew Lawrence's secret. In an unpremeditated gesture of profound pity and love he had leaned over and kissed his friend, and at that moment knew beyond all doubt that Lawrence had understood him and knew that he knew.

The secret was, I am absolutely convinced, Lawrence's homosexuality. Taboo in those days, it was Lawrence's tragedy in which Murry was powerless to help. He could only look on while his beloved friend, capable of such depths of love beneath all the venom and hatred, was cut off in a no-man's land, to live out an agony, lonely beyond all remedy.

Beyond veiled words, 'for those that have ears to hear',[8] Murry never betrayed Lawrence's secret. (K. M. Murry 1986: 23)

Katherine Murry's assurance that Murry 'never betrayed Lawrence's secret' might hold true if it was based solely on the evidence of his journals, of which she would have had access, but she oddly ignored some rather explicit attributions of homosexuality to Lawrence in *Son of Woman*, which I will discuss shortly. As to the journals, although Murry wrote there voluminously about Lawrence, returning over and over again to the illuminating incidents, the disagreements and quarrels, he did not – unless he later excised such references – 'betray . . . Lawrence's secret' in them.[9] Katherine Murry's 'absolute' certainty, while it seems to confirm the attribution of homosexuality to Lawrence, avoids consideration of Murry's own ambiguous feelings for Lawrence, which might better be interpreted through the theory of homosocial desire. Murry's libidinal energy seems to have re-directed itself into the intense rivalry over Frieda. Yet perhaps a surge of it – under the influence of alcohol – re-attached itself to Lawrence when Murry kissed him, 'with a kind of effusiveness' that 'afflicted' Catherine Carswell. Her memory of Murry insisting that 'Women can't understand this' and that 'This is an affair between men', might well reveal a momentary release of Murry's own repressed desire.

The fullest revelation of the *homosocial* dynamics in the triangle of Murry, Lawrence and Frieda appears in Murry's journal on 21 July 1932, when he was preparing *Reminiscences* for publication. There he questions himself about why he didn't follow Lawrence to New Mexico as he had promised, and attributes his refusal to the fact that Lawrence had invited Brett to come as well. He speculates that if he had gone, he and Frieda would have become lovers, and although he could not predict Lawrence's reaction, possibly 'there might have come out of it a strange *ménage à trois*. As woman, Frieda could have carried us both'. Murry remarks then: 'And – I feel – Lawrence knew it. And this is why he wanted Brett to go: to be my woman' (MSX 4149: 102–3).

Murry's imaginative projection here validates the essential core of homosocial desire between Murry and Lawrence. The ultimate fantasy of *sharing* the same woman allows for the closest possible transference of libidinal energy between the two men short of actual sexual relations. It is almost as if Murry intuited the danger of this conjunction, when he immediately followed his reference to the *ménage à trois* with the remark that Frieda would have become *his* woman. In this way he transformed the momentarily egalitarian relationship of the threesome back into the conventional – and acceptable – arena of sexual rivalry. He satisfied himself by assuming that he would have emerged the victor.

II

Murry's words were not always as 'veiled' with regard to Lawrence's possible homosexuality as Katherine Murry suggests in her memoir. *Son of Woman* contains several inferences of homosexuality drawn from Lawrence's fiction and applied to Lawrence himself. To a twenty-first-century reader, Murry's opening pages can easily suggest a subtext of homosexuality. He begins his book by analysing passages from *Fantasia of the Unconscious* about how men's sexuality is undermined when unhappy mothers use their sons as outlets for their own frustrations. Then he exclaims: 'That is Lawrence's history of his own life' (SW: 21). Murry insists that 'everything derives from it. He was, and he will say so plainly, at the last, a sex-crucified man'. Immediately following this statement, the language of secrecy begins to intrude:

> Even there he does not tell us everything. There is a secret which even he cannot reveal, and which he will strive to deny, to blot out of his consciousness, until the last. But it will emerge. It was Lawrence's destiny to be able to hide nothing of himself.
> In this book I shall reveal nothing which Lawrence himself did not reveal. There is nothing else to be revealed. There is, and can be, but one true life of Lawrence; and it is contained in his works. (SW: 21)

Consequently, Murry's critical approach to Lawrence's fiction is to assume that it is, 'indeed, almost wholly autobiographical' even if there is 'a certain amount of artistic transformation' (SW: 172). He tends to consider any character's statements or behaviour as equivalents of Lawrence's own. In fact, he often switches without warning from using a character's name, such as 'Paul Morel', to 'Lawrence'. When Murry states that 'what genuine and unhesitating passion there was in Lawrence's life before his mother's death went to a man, not a woman' (SW: 37), he bases this conclusion on 'Cyril's love for George' in *The*

White Peacock, with its 'description of the two young men bathing in the lake' (SW: 38), and quotes Lawrence's comment that '"our love was . . . more perfect than any love I have known since, either for man or woman"' (SW: 39). Later in the book, Murry merges Birkin with Lawrence in his discussion of *Women in Love*. He explains that when the 'hunger for a woman has proved disastrous, in spite of the assertions of actual, and the reports of imaginary fulfilment; it was inevitable that Lawrence should turn towards the possibility of a relation with a man' (SW: 119). Murry suggests that Birkin is trying

> to escape to a man from the misery of his own failure with a woman. This had always appeared to Lawrence a way out. In *The White Peacock* his love for a man is more perfect than his love for a woman; and, truly, in actual fact I believe it was a happier and less tortured relation for him. But always it was brief and fugitive. Lawrence was always, and inevitably, disappointed. (SW: 119)

Murry's use of the word 'fugitive' here, with its connotation of illegality, allows for his swerve towards the implicit attribution of homosexuality. More deeply embedded in the book, however, is an explicit charge in Murry's discussion of *Aaron's Rod*. He begins it with a provocative sentence: 'But what Lawrence was asking for was not even a disciple, but simply a lover' (SW: 208), and then continues with:

> He disguised it from himself, as he needed to do. But those who are responsive to the unconscious emotion no less than to the explicit thought of a book, cannot mistake the meaning of the beautiful chapter describing Aaron's illness in Lilly's little flat. The women are far away, the underlying tension of hostility which is always felt when Lawrence is describing a woman and a man together peacefully dissolves. Lilly is blissfully happy looking after Aaron, with a more than wifely tenderness. (SW: 208)

Murry directly states that 'Lilly wants a homo-sexual relation with Aaron to complete his incomplete hetero-sexual relation with Tanny. This he calls "extending" marriage. Other people might find another name for it' (SW: 211).

After finally using the word 'homo-sexual', Murry makes an interesting rhetorical move. By taking a space-break, he lets the reader pause for a moment – perhaps at the shock of him finally avoiding euphemism – and then begins the next section with two sentences that should have followed immediately without the break: 'It would be manifestly unjust, and manifestly ridiculous to condemn Lawrence for this. Lawrence was what he was, and we accept him whole' (SW: 212). Nevertheless, the reader should notice Murry's equivocation in the sentences that follow, regarding the differences between Lawrence's pronouncements on the social importance of the bonding between men in *Fantasia of the Unconscious* and his treatment of it in *Aaron's Rod*:[10]

> But it is absolutely necessary to distinguish what Lawrence, as a living person, is demanding, from what Lawrence, as a man of profound impersonal vision, declares to be necessary . . . To be united impersonally in creative and purposive activity on the basis of a true marriage fulfilment is one thing; to be homo-sexually united to a man of genius because he finds it impossible to achieve sexual fulfilment in marriage is quite another. The former is, we believe, a true and universal idea; the latter an individual indulgence, or an individual necessity. It is criminal to confuse them; but Lawrence wanted to confuse them. [Murry's use of the word 'criminal' here makes an insinuation similar to his earlier use of the word 'fugitive'.] He simply could not help it. Ultimately, he could not admit his own astonishing idiosyncrasy; he had to conceal it from himself, by representing it to himself as the universal constitution of a man. And this, in a sense, it is: for man does need man, as deeply as he needs woman. But these universal needs in Lawrence assumed an extreme form: the intensity with which he felt them made him, on the impersonal and spiritual plane, a symbolic and prophetic man; on the personal and actual plane, they simply tore him asunder. (SW: 212)

Murry's reference to 'being united to a man of genius' reveals a slippage between his ostensible reference to the relations between Aaron and Lilly in Lawrence's novel and an implicit reference to what he must have by now surmised was once Lawrence's aim in his relations with himself. This connection, although it remains unstated, seems to lie hidden behind Murry's belief that the 'nightmare' chapter in *Kangaroo* covers the years 1916–18, and is 'retrospective and autobiographical': 'In that record, which is of a veritable nightmare, and sometimes seems definitely to cross the border-line of sanity, there are clear traces of an endeavour by Lawrence to satisfy his hunger for a man' (SW: 123). Murry takes this opportunity to describe that 'painful failure' of their 'three months in close contact' during the Cornwall episode. He explains how Lawrence 'made a desperate call to Katherine Mansfield and me to join him and his wife and live together in unity. And we responded, because we loved him and his wife' (SW: 124).

Either Murry has forgotten his and Mansfield's intense dislike of Frieda at that time, or his recent affair with her has overpowered his desire for absolute accuracy in his recounting of the events. (He knew that Frieda would certainly read the book.) Murry also bends the truth slightly when he writes that

> All the knowledge of [Lawrence] contained in this book was completely hidden from me then; it was, in the main, concealed from me all through his life. When he died, something broke in my heart: but all I knew was that I had loved him, and that, at times at least, he had loved me . . . Only since his

death have I been driven by some inward compulsion to try to understand him. The attempt would have been impossible while he yet lived. (SW: 124)

Actually, Murry *did* have some knowledge of many things in *Son of Woman* even during that stay in Cornwall. He would have known, surely, the enormous effect of Lawrence's unhealthy relationship with his mother, and not only through reading *Sons and Lovers*. Certainly he must have recalled all those intense conversations about their parents in 1914. He had already written in the *Adelphi* about the 'long queer discussions in the Campbells' little drawing room, over Oedipus complexes and incest-motives, for it had been discovered that in *Sons and Lovers* Lawrence had independently arrived at the main conclusions of the psycho-analysts' (RDHL: 33). In fact, the entire book derives its thematic centre from Murry's perception that Lawrence's sexual problems are prefigured in

> Paul Morel's desperate attempts to break away from the tie that was strangling him. All unconsciously, his mother had roused in him the stirrings of sexual desire, she had, by the sheer intensity of her diverted affection made him a man before his time. (SW: 29)

As the title of his own book suggests, for Murry the oedipal struggle in *Sons and Lovers* is the key to Lawrence's life and work.

Although Murry's analysis of Lawrence as a 'sex-crucified man' conflates aspersions of the homosexual with manifestations of the homosocial, the latter brings forth from him the greater emotional charge. Throughout the book Murry insinuates the element of sexual rivalry by emphasising Lawrence's inadequacies (implicitly in contrast to his own sexual prowess). He declares in the first chapter that 'Lawrence was not a physically passionate man; he was not more passionate than the common run of men, but far less passionate – almost a sexual weakling' (SW: 52), and goes further in the same direction when he entitles the second chapter: 'The Sexual Failure'. Occasionally, Murry seems uncomfortable with his assertions, perhaps sensing that he was taking such an outrageous direction as a literary critic that he better take care to justify what he is doing:

> One shrinks from the necessity of thus laying bare the physical secrets of a dead man; but in the case of Lawrence we have no choice. To the last he conceived it as his mission to teach us the way to sexual regeneration, and he claimed to give the world the ultimate truth about sex. If we take him seriously, we must take his message seriously. Continually in his work we are confronted with sexual experience of a peculiar kind; it is quite impossible to ignore it. The work of a great man, as Lawrence was, is always an organic whole. If we shrink from following the vital thread of experience from which

it all derives, then we shrink from him altogether. It is all or nothing, with such a man as Lawrence; and, since it must not be nothing, it must be all. (SW: 88)

Murry's intricate and – at the same time – evasive analysis of how the depiction of 'sexual experience of a peculiar kind' is revealed in the novels allows allusions to Lawrence's possible impotence to surface (and not only through his apparently unconscious repetition of 'shrink' three times in the preceding paragraph!). This evasiveness can partially be explained by his worries about censorship. For example, following a long quotation from *The Rainbow* describing the 'terrible consummation' of Anton Skrebensky and Ursula Brangwen in the moonlight, after which Anton 'creeps away a broken man' (SW: 87, 88), Murry refrains from direct exposition and, in a rather fascinating rhetorical move, manages both to titillate the reader and escape responsibility for doing so:

> To discover all that underlies this fearful encounter, we should have to go to *Lady Chatterley's Lover*, to Mellors' account of his sexual experience with Bertha Coutts. That is, in the present state of affairs, unquotable. But in that page and a half the curious will find not only the naked physical foundation – 'the blind beakishness' – of this experience of Ursula and Anton, but also Lawrence's final account of the sexual experience from which both the sexual experience of Will and Anna, and of Anton and Ursula is derived. *The Rainbow* is, radically, the history of Lawrence's final sexual failure. (SW: 88)

Murry cannot define explicitly what he means by Lawrence's 'sexual failure', only by innuendo. Twenty-four years later, however, his journal reveals that he understood Lawrence's problem to be premature ejaculation, and that the 'peculiar' depictions of sexuality in his fiction are 'the result of a prodigious compensation for his simple sexual shortcomings' (MSX 4160: 32). In *Son of Woman* Murry could only allude to Lawrence's 'impotence' through guarded references to an inability to satisfy the woman and he could not reveal the *source* of his knowledge about Lawrence's sexual problems. He had to let inferences drawn from the novels and poems serve to support his argument about the man. (Ironically, in so doing, Murry was actually able to discuss sexuality itself with far greater complexity and subtlety than he had ever allowed himself to do in his own novels.) Most probably, his source of information about Lawrence's sexual problems was Frieda, perhaps during the conversations he had with her on their trip to Freiburg in 1923, but more likely when he slept with her shortly after Lawrence's death in 1930, and discovered that 'with her, and with her for the first time in my life, I knew what fulfilment in love really meant' (quoted in L: 165).

Murry's affair with Frieda makes itself felt in *Son of Woman*, I believe, in his great sympathy with the female characters in Lawrence's novels. His treatment of *The Rainbow* bears this out. In contrast to Katherine Mansfield's annoyed reaction to Anna Lensky dancing nude in the moonlight, when she read the novel in 1915, and his own complaint at the time that the novel had 'a warm, close, heavy promiscuity of flesh about it which repelled [him]' (BTW: 351), Murry's praise in *Son of Woman* for this very same scene reveals how much he had come over to Frieda's side. His own attraction to her is transparently present when he writes: 'I know nothing more beautiful or more powerful in all Lawrence's writing than the long chapter ominously entitled "Anna Victrix"', and refers to its description of the 'long world-forgetful ecstasy of passion with a carefree beautiful, passionate, unashamedly physical woman' (SW: 75).

Implicit in this moment of admiration is Murry's realisation that *he* would not have reacted to that 'ecstasy of passion' in the same way as Lawrence:

> We are, we have learned to be, afraid in Lawrence of that yielding of himself to the woman's leading. It is delightful, it is ecstasy; but it is also, to him, humiliation. It comes with sickening speed. 'Shame at his own dependence upon her desire drove him to anger'. (SW: 76)

Murry's statements about Lawrence's sexuality imply that he understands more than Lawrence what genuine sexual fulfilment should be,[11] as is apparent in his comment on the poems in *Look! We Have Come Through!*:

> She gives him fulfilment; he does not give it her, or this agonised fear of her leaving him would not exist.
> When the relation of sex is equal, there is on both sides simple security in the essential. Here is none. (SW: 66)

This emphasis on the importance of the woman's satisfaction is what most distinguishes Murry's ideas about sexuality from Lawrence's.[12] Throughout *Son of Woman* Murry takes note of instances of misogyny, which he clearly relates to Lawrence's fear of the power of women. For example, he decides that Ursula in *The Rainbow* 'is an unconvincing character' partly because she is 'made of the hated sexual woman' (SW: 89). In such ways, *Son of Woman* is a precursor to the feminist critiques of Lawrence which began with Kate Millett's *Sexual Politics* in 1970. Murry says of the poems in Lawrence's later collection, *Birds, Beasts and Flowers*, that he finds in them

> a profound resentment against the compulsion of sex upon the male. Only the point of view of the male – if it can be called the point of view of *the* male – is

considered. It is the male alone who bears the cross, who is humiliated, whose integrity is violated . . . we are reminded of Rupert Birkin's sudden outburst in *Women in Love*. 'On the whole he hated sex: it was such a limitation'. (SW: 231)

Murry points out the contrast between the popular conception of Lawrence, 'the habit of thinking that because Lawrence was so constantly concerned with sex, he loved it', and the more dire reality that Lawrence had the same 'intense hatred felt by the mediaeval monk against this humiliation and the cause of it – Woman. Love really *is* hatred for him' (SW: 231–2). Murry next connects this 'knowledge of humiliation' with 'the sheer detestation of woman which underlies *Aaron's Rod*':

The longing to escape from the love-mode is the longing to escape from the bondage to woman, from the bondage to woman so agonisingly felt by the unsatisfied and unsatisfying man. And whatever else the new life-mode which he is seeking will contain, we may be certain of one thing, that the basic union will be the union between men, and that the woman will be brought into complete subjection. (SW: 232)

Murry is certain that this 'complete subjection' involves the woman's 'surrender[ing] her claim to sexual fulfilment'. His interpretation of *The Plumed Serpent* brings out the centrality of this subjection to Lawrence's thematic structure. He quotes the description of Kate's sexual experience with Cipriano, which results in '"the death in her of the Aphrodite of the foam: the seething, frictional, ecstatic Aphrodite"', and points out how her 'surrender is completely one-sided', that it is the woman who gives up her claim to sexual pleasure. He is quick to notice that 'there is no indication, or faint hint, that the man forwent his physical "satisfaction"' (SW: 306–7). Murry uses this scene in the novel to elaborate – even more fully than he had earlier – his understanding of Lawrence's basic problem:

We need not dwell on this; but it would be criminal to slur it over. [Again, note Murry's use of the word 'criminal'] The sexual situation behind this imaginary consummation is fundamental in Lawrence; it is the physical cause of the extremity of his exasperation, and of his obsession with sexuality itself. Always, on the biological level, he felt himself inferior to the Woman: he was radically conscious that as a male he was a failure. And he could not accept the fact. He persisted that it was not he, but the Woman who was wrong. She claimed from him as male what she had no right to claim; her idea of sexual fulfilment was not the true idea of sexual fulfilment. Through Cipriano he makes her accept this perversion of the truth, just as years before, through Rupert Birkin, he had made Ursula Brangwen accept it. (SW: 307)

Murry instead argues 'that in life the Woman will never accept his perversion of the truth . . . You cannot by taking thought convince a woman that she is sexually fulfilled. She *knows*' (SW: 307).

Murry remains convinced that Lawrence's misogyny was present throughout his career as a writer; from his first novel to his last, he finds him 'brooding over the same experience . . . and all that is added essentially is a more bitter hatred of yet another woman – the woman with whom he has spent those eighteen years' (SW: 44). Murry's defence of Frieda – who remains unnamed throughout the text – animates his prose when he shortly declares that anyone who 'recognises the woman' behind Lawrence's depictions of women 'will be aghast at the intensity of loathing for woman in the sexual relation which Lawrence felt and uttered at the end of his life' (SW: 44).

The connection between this 'bitter hatred' of women and Lawrence's attraction to exoticism does not escape Murry's attention. He links the 'nostalgia that took hold of Lawrence so powerfully in Cornwall, for the "dark sensual magic" of a forgotten mode of life' to his later fascination with such peoples as Etruscans, Egyptians and Aztecs, those whom he called in his poem 'Cypresses', '"the silenced races and all their abominations"' (SW: 227). Murry recognises that in Lawrence's imaginative constructs, that 'mode of life' was 'the home of the mystery "beyond the phallic", of deliberate yet mindless sensuality between man and woman and, still more, between man and man'. He notes Lawrence's interest in 'the worship of the death mystery; of human blood sacrifice' and other elements of that life mode, but astutely comments that 'above all else it was a realm where Woman could not enter without putting off for ever her female nature: a realm where children are neither begotten nor born, and the great female demand upon the male is never made' (SW: 227).

Murry's remark about 'a realm where children are neither begotten nor born' relates to another component of his analysis of Lawrence's sexual difficulties: Lawrence's childlessness. He believes that Lawrence 'is denied that living thing on which in fact he could put forth the complete love that he can never give to a woman' (SW: 195). This lack, according to Murry's interpretation, contributed greatly to Lawrence's uncertainties over his masculinity:

> For a man who believed so passionately in marriage as Lawrence, to be married and childless was a disaster; and it must have filled him with misgivings, to find that the simple seal of fulfilment in marriage was denied him – and to know that it was he, not his wife, that was incapable. How far, how terribly far, he was from 'the hardy indomitable male' of his dreams! (SW: 194)

Accordingly, Murry takes note, rather acidly, that Lawrence creates a stallion in *St Mawr* who does not sire foals: 'The idiosyncrasy, by which the males are so male that they do not beget children, is now familiar' (SW: 337).

This remark seems almost gratuitous until one realises that it is a semi-transparent allusion to Murry's sexual competition with Lawrence. For by the time he wrote *Son of Woman*, he had fathered two children: Katherine, born in 1925; and John (Colin), in 1926. Yet if Murry had won this competition, it still could not be said that he had achieved 'fulfilment' in marriage by so doing. The most rewarding sexual experience he had had so far was that with Frieda Lawrence! Nonetheless, Murry's own sense of masculinity was bolstered by his paternity. It must have cleared up any doubts he might have had about his potency during his marriage to Katherine Mansfield.

III

Although Murry would be attacked for writing *Son of Woman* out of animosity towards Lawrence, or as an excuse to use his personal relationship with him for monetary gain, his motivations seem far more complicated than either of these suggests. It is important to emphasise here that Murry was writing that book in the midst of his own personal crisis. His second wife, Violet Le Maistre, was slowly dying of tuberculosis during the entire period of its composition.[13] Murry knew better than anyone the tragic irony of this repetition of Mansfield's fate. It intrudes at moments in *Son of Woman*, as when Murry remarks: 'The bliss of perfected love is but the prelude to the agony of inevitable separation, by disease or death' (SW: 379). His use of the two words so closely associated with Mansfield: 'bliss' and 'prelude', suggests the power of her continuing hold on his imagination.

By the time Lawrence died, Murry's relationship with him had actually ended. There were several stages to the ultimate deterioration of their friendship: the rivalry over Frieda; Murry's refusal to move to New Mexico; disagreements over the direction of the *Adelphi*, and Murry's cancellation of a trip to Italy to visit the Lawrences because of Violet's pregnancy. Murry describes this course of events in *Reminiscences* – minus those referring to Frieda – and dates the definite break as 'the beginning of 1926'. He declares that 'by that time I was prepared for it as inevitable' (RDHL: 107). Three years later, when he learned that Lawrence was very ill, he 'felt a great longing to see him before he died' (RDHL: 117), and wrote to ask if he could visit. Lawrence refused his offer and told him:

> I know well that we 'missed it' . . . We don't know one another – if you knew *how* little we know one another! . . . Believe me, we belong to different worlds, different ways of consciousness, you and I, and the best we can do is to let one another alone for ever and ever . . . It is no good our meeting – even when we are immortal spirits, we shall dwell in different Hades. Why not accept it. (LDHL 8: 295)

After such rejection, Murry's decision less than a year later to rush to the south of France to offer condolences to Frieda could be seen as the final resurgence of the homosocial triangularity that had marked his relationship with Lawrence throughout its history. If that triangularity had once involved Mansfield, whose power over Murry drew him away from Lawrence's domination, it had also once involved Frieda's desire to draw Lawrence away from Murry, when she had been jealous of the two men's preoccupation with each other during the days in Cornwall.[14]

Murry had no illusions that *Son of Woman* would be well received. When he heard about Catherine Carswell's book, which he surmised was 'largely an acidulous polemic against me', Murry felt the need to set down in his journal a justification for publishing *Son of Woman*, which he considered 'a discovery . . . of the essential Lawrence':

> My book was a necessary act of my own being . . . I submitted myself to Lawrence's work in a way in which – so far as I know – no other man has attempted to submit himself to it . . . There are things in it which I regret – the overwrought emotional tone of the end in particular – but even those I regret only egoistically – as a give-away of myself. The impersonal me is quite glad that they stand as a record that I was overwrought. (29 June 1932, MSX 4149: 92)

That readers would respond more to his 'overwrought emotional tone' than to his often brilliant close readings of Lawrence's writing should not surprise us. Murry's reputation amongst the intelligentsia had sunk so far since the days of the *Athenaeum* that Virginia Woolf could write on 15 April 1931: 'Murry – the one vile man I have ever known – has written a book about D. H. Lawrence, making out that he is Judas and Lawrence, Christ' (LVW 4: 312). There is no indication that she had yet read the book, yet she seemed to relish all the talk about it.[15] Nonetheless, its notoriety seems to have led her to read 'Sons and Lovers for the first time', and five days later she again assails Murry, whom she now calls 'that bald necked blood dripping vulture [who] kept me off Lawrence with his obscene objurgations. Now I realise with regret that a man of genius wrote in my time and I never read him' (LVW 4: 315).

Murry would continue to circulate Lawrence long after he published *Son of Woman* and *Reminiscences*. He would devote a large portion of *Between Two Worlds* to his friendship with Lawrence up to 1918 (where the book ends), and would write and lecture about him for the rest of his life. His responses to Lawrence would always be coloured by his own personal circumstances, but the intensity of emotion – that 'give-away' of himself – diminished with distance. Furthermore, Murry's approach to Lawrence becomes imbued with larger historical, political and religious issues.[16] This did not take long. After all, the publication of *Son of Woman* in 1931 coincided with the Great Depression. Lea mentions that Murry saw first-hand and was 'appalled by, the condition of the unemployed miners' when he lectured about Lawrence in Wales the next year (L: 189–90). It is noteworthy that the book Murry published in between *Son of Woman* (1931) and *Reminiscences of D. H. Lawrence* (1933) was *The Necessity of Communism* (1932). The title of one of his pieces in the *Adelphi*, in November 1932, was 'The Bourgeois, the Bolshevist and Lawrence'.[17] Murry's evolving politics might lie behind his remark in *Reminiscences* about his disagreement with Lawrence's desire to 'create the nucleus of a new society' in New Mexico, because if it 'depended upon people having money enough to go to New Mexico, and a profession which would comfortably maintain them there, then it was hardly worth thinking about' (RDHL: 106).

As the years passed, and Murry's political involvements increased, he attempted to situate Lawrence within a historical framework. In *Love, Freedom and Society* (1957), he describes Lawrence as 'the apocalyptic figure who marks the end of the age of Romanticism' and compares him to Rousseau, 'the apocalyptic figure who marks the beginning of it' (Murry 1957: 23). In this last published piece on Lawrence, Murry considers him within the context of 'a profound crisis' in Western civilisation: 'manifest at every level of human life: economic, political, moral, spiritual', which could lead to its total destruction: 'it is now quite conceivable that the human race will put an end to itself by atomic warfare or the preparations for it' (ibid.: 11). The traumatic events of the mid-twentieth century had only increased Murry's sense of Lawrence's significance as a thinker in whose 'quests' for new kinds of personal relationships and new kinds of relations between individuals and society 'one can trace a crucial moment of psychic upheaval, following a catastrophic inrush of unexpected experience' (ibid.: 29). Finally, Murry is able to see the strengths in 'Lawrence's objectifications of himself', so that in characters such as Birkin (whom Murry once derided) and Lilly, there is

a rare human reality. The vivid and impassioned dialectic of his search for a purpose, and of his relations with his wife, constitute a life and thought-exploration of the most absorbing interest. There is nothing remotely like it in English literature. The sensitive tip of an incomparable human consciousness, subtly and directly aware, through faculties which are lost or vestigial in the rest of us, of the whole environment in which it moves, is feeling its way through life on our behalf. (Murry 1957: 29)

Nonetheless, Murry is still disturbed by the instances 'of the victory of hate over love' (Murry 1957: 44) in Lawrence's later writings. And now, with the catastrophe of the Second World War behind him, Murry is doubly troubled by Lawrence's 'condemnation of democracy' (ibid.: 116). Therefore he is able to go further than he did in 1931 in recognising the dangers of the 'combination of tenderness and ruthlessness' in Lawrence's fascination with 'blood-consciousness' and 'pre-Christian human sacrifice' (ibid.: 46). Thus, when he now discusses *Kangaroo*, he notes that Jack Calcott's

> delight in his murderous fury is as much a fact of love and loving; so is the state of mind of those who ordered and those who executed the horrors of Belsen and Auschwitz, though I cannot imagine that Lawrence would have condoned these, had he lived to know of them. But where and how can he draw the line? This is where 'the belief in the blood' eventually brings Lawrence. (Murry 1957: 45)

The contradictions in Lawrence continue to trouble Murry to the end. Yet, to that end, he insists on 'the genius' of Lawrence, 'which communicates unique, comprehensive and profound experience so that we feel it on our pulses' (Murry 1957: 123). Murry allows the personal to surface once more in the last section of this last piece of his on Lawrence, but states it calmly and with a dignity he could not achieve in *Son of Woman*:

> It is easy, as it is tempting, to say that Lawrence's sensibility was excessive: particularly tempting for one who was his friend and tried, in vain, to endure the cataclysmic alternations of his moods. I cannot regret that I could not endure them: for my own integrity was at stake. Nor do I find myself abashed or smitten by pangs of conscience because a new generation has arisen which can, or believes it can, appreciate the genius while ignoring the contradictions of Lawrence. On the contrary, the longer I live, and the more I consort with Lawrence in imagination, the more certain I am that a criticism which will not honestly face his contradictions is unworthy of him and false to the ideal of integrity, for which on peril of its soul, criticism must strive. (Murry 1957: 121)

Notes

1. Murry's publication of much of this letter in the *Adelphi* in 1930 seems to have provoked the title of Catherine Carswell's controversial book *The*

Savage Pilgrimage: A Narrative of D. H. Lawrence (1932). There might also be an echo from the same letter in the title of Mary Middleton Murry's memoir of her life with Murry: *To Keep Faith* (M. M. Murry 1959).

2. In the 1947 manuscript, Murry remarks about himself: 'my half-superstitious way (of one who seeks meanings in all things)', but characteristically, Murry is only *half*-superstitious! (MSX 4162: 271).

3. Woodfield states that the *Adelphi* 'was intended to be the joint effort of a "Brotherhood" (J. W. N. Sullivan, H. M. Tomlinson, Koteliansky, Murry) and to be a voice for Lawrence. Instead it became virtually the sole effort of Murry' (DR: 42).

4. Mansfield wrote to Murry on 2 March 1920: 'I am so glad you love Brett so much. I used to feel in Italy that if I died you'd marry Brett very soon after . . . Shes wonderfully suited to you in a thousand ways' (KMCL 3: 236).

5. See Hignett (1984: 133–49) for the fullest account of Murry's affair with Brett.

6. The letters between them can be found in Frieda Lawrence (1982: 367–8).

7. *Reminiscences of D. H. Lawrence* appeared in January 1933. It includes the series of 'Reminiscences' that Murry had published in the *Adelphi* during 1930–1, but the larger part of the book is composed of Murry's detailed defence against Carswell's criticism of him in *The Savage Pilgrimage*. As part of his refutation of her charges against him, Murry also reprints here all of the reviews he had written of Lawrence's books.

8. Katherine Murry is here quoting from *Reminiscences* (1933: 16): 'I am speaking esoterically, for those who have ears to hear'.

9. It is in a matter such as this one that the reliability of Murry's journals as evidence comes once again into question. The gaps and omissions, the months or years missing from the collection of notebooks available to the public suggest active deletion. While pages remain that are crossed out – apparently in a fury by Murry's third wife, Betty (with some crude obscenities as her annotations) – it is likely that Murry himself eliminated some material. It goes without saying that any journal cannot be trusted completely, self-serving as it is, constructed to defend the actions of its subject at the same time as it offers the pretense of complete honesty.

10. Murry found much to agree with in Lawrence's treatment of male bonding in the *Fantasia*, and that agreement is evidenced by his choice of the name *Adelphi* ('Brotherhood') for his journal.

11. By the time Murry wrote *Son of Woman*, he had taken upon himself the role of a public exponent of sexually fulfilled marriage. See his article, entitled 'Modern Marriage', written in collaboration with Dr James Carruthers Young (who had been, ironically, Katherine Mansfield's doctor at Gurdjieff's Institute). Murry and Young here declare: 'Fundamental to a true marriage is complete biological fulfillment. Man and wife should have physical delight in each other' (Murry and Young 1929: 23). The article also suggests that lack of sexual fulfillment will cause a woman to 'divert . . . her tenderness to her children; the sex feeling that should flow towards the husband is diverted to them'. The analysis following about the dire results to the 'son, enveloped in this morbid maternal tenderness' is strikingly similar to Murry's account of Lawrence's upbringing in *Son of*

Woman, written more than a year later. Cassavant (1982: 91) notes that the article 'appropriated ideas' from Lawrence's *Fantasia*.

12. Elaine Feinstein observes that 'Lawrence believed that what made Murry so attractive to women was the knowing and insinuating sexuality which pleasured the female more than asserting the male – precisely the opposite of what Lawrence wanted to offer' (Feinstein 1993: 201).

13. This is not the place to discuss in detail Murry's tragic second marriage to a woman who tried to pattern herself after Katherine Mansfield – so much so that she remarked on hearing that she had developed tuberculosis that she was 'glad' because she wanted Murry to love her as much as he had loved Mansfield. It is a subject worthy of a book of its own. For information about this marriage, its genesis and development, see L: 122–78.

14. Murry quotes from a letter Frieda wrote to him in 1956, where she admits to that jealousy (MSX 4160: 167).

15. It is possible that Woolf read it a year later, however. A letter of 20 April 1931, written on board ship during her cruise to Greece mentions that she is reading 'a screaming gull called Middleton Murry' (LVW 5: 51), and her diary entry of 8 May 1931 also refers to reading Murry. The editor's note suggests that it was 'probably *Son of Woman*' (DVW 4: 96).

16. Murry's interest in Christianity and his different attitudes about it are also relevant to his varying views about Lawrence. These are outside the scope of this book, but much has been written about them; see, in particular, Griffin (1969b: 123–40). Murry's *Adam and Eve* (1944) has an interesting chapter on Lawrence in relation to Christianity, and *Love, Freedom and Society* (Murry 1957) takes up these religious concerns as well.

17. Murry joined the Independent Labour Party in December 1931. On Murry's Marxist phase, see L: 181–205.

Chapter 10

Circulating Murry

I

If Murry had more than two decades to come to terms with Lawrence's 'excessive sensibility' and to realise his 'genius' *without* 'ignoring the contradictions' (Murry 1957: 121), Lawrence would never be able to do the same for Murry. He died too soon, and his circulation of Murry during his last years was almost totally negative. The spate of fiction following Murry's romantic entanglement with Frieda in the autumn of 1923 contains representations of Murry that reveal Lawrence's animosity so blatantly that it must have been obvious to all their mutual acquaintances. Earlier, when Lawrence might have suggested aspects of his relationship with Murry in *Women and Love*, the physical and social attributes of Gerald Crich were so different from Murry's that their friends – and even Murry himself – did not recognise the connection when the book was first published. In contrast, the three stories Lawrence wrote in the winter and spring of 1924, 'The Last Laugh', 'The Border Line' and 'Jimmy and the Desperate Woman', are satiric portraits of Murry that seem calculated to evoke public ridicule of the man he had once asked to be his blood-brother. A fourth story, 'Smile', which was written a year and a half later, reveals how the passage of time did not dampen Lawrence's urge to ridicule Murry, even if it may have muted the element of sexual rivalry (no Lawrentian figure appears in that story).

Of course travelling in literary circles can be dangerous for anyone's reputation. Friends and families of writers frequently discover representations of themselves in fiction, and though occasionally they might be pleased to do so, usually they are not. Lady Ottoline Morrell, as we have seen, was furious with Lawrence over his portrait of Hermione in *Women in Love*, and Mark Gertler was troubled by Gilbert Cannan's use of him as the model for *Mendel*. But Murry had to endure the rarer experience of being forced to watch versions of himself appear *repeatedly* in works of fiction. We have already seen how artfully Mansfield had circulated her own versions of Murry in such stories as 'The Man Without a Temperament' and 'Je ne parle pas français', but her portrayals are complex and multi-faceted, serious attempts to understand and sympathise even when they reveal hurt and anger. So subtle was her technique that Murry –in his innocence or self-unawareness – responded more to their intimations of love than to their criticism. Lawrence's stories (as well as Aldous Huxley's later novel *Point Counter Point* [1928]) do nothing to redeem Murry.

Both Lawrence and Huxley draw attention to Murry's roles as editor and writer in their representations, unlike Mansfield, who ignores the public figure for the isolated, private one. In 'The Border Line', Lawrence makes the Murry figure, Philip Farquhar, a journalist (whose wife is named 'Katherine', but is, like Frieda, the 'daughter of a German baron'). He describes him as 'always throwing his weight on the side of humanity, and human truth and peace' (Lawrence 1976: 3: 587, 591). In 'Jimmy and the Desperate Woman' he is the 'editor of a high-class, rather high-brow, rather successful magazine', whose 'rather personal, very candid editorials brought him shoals, swarms, hosts of admiring acquaintances' (Lawrence 1976 3: 606). Similarly, Huxley's notorious Denis Burlap is the editor of a literary paper, and like Jimmy Frith, he attracts the attention of admiring readers, especially female ones. Since Huxley had once worked closely with Murry as his assistant editor on the *Athenaeum*, he could draw on aspects of Murry's behaviour in the workaday world that Lawrence would not have had the chance to observe, but both Lawrence and Huxley highlight characteristics of Murry's personality that were well-known among his friends and colleagues. For instance, they both remark upon his enigmatic smile, which Huxley describes as 'something mysterious, subtle, inward' (Huxley 1996: 62), and Lawrence as a 'malevolent half-smile', making him 'a mixture of faun and Mephisto' (Lawrence 1976 3: 623). Murry's well-known emotionality is clearly apparent in Huxley's description:

> That was the trouble with Burlap. You never knew where you stood with him. Either he loved you, or he hated. Life with him was a series of scenes – scenes of hostility or, even more trying . . . scenes of affection. One way or the other, the emotion was always flowing. (Huxley 1996: 62)

Huxley's satire emphasises the disjunction between Burlap's self-presentation as a suffering, beset, religious seeker (who nonetheless is 'a man whose excursions into the drawing rooms of the rich were episodes in a life-long spiritual quest might justifiably be regarded as the equivalent of Sunday-morning church') and his actual professional role as a powerful man who can manipulate and (in one particularly egregious instance) destroy the lives of his employees (Huxley 1996: 126).

Lawrence emphasises instead the relative passivity and weakness of the Murry figure in contrast to the Lawrence figure. His attention is drawn –not surprisingly – to the dynamics of the homosocial elements in his relationship with Murry, which is most apparent in 'The Border Line', where Lawrence describes Philip Farquhar as 'a little somebody in the world', who has a 'dark little body, [which] made him interesting to women' and who could 'give off a great sense of warmth and offering, like a dog when it loves you' (Lawrence 1976 3: 588, 589). In contrast, Lawrence describes Alan Anstruther, Katherine Farquhar's first husband who had died in the war, as 'that red-haired fighting Celt', a 'first-born lord', who 'was handsome in uniform, with his kilt swinging and his blue eye glaring' (ibid.: 588). Philip and Alan had been friends, although Alan disparaged the friendship to Katherine, telling her 'I never positively cared for the man' (ibid.: 590). It was Philip 'who had an almost uncanny love for Alan' (ibid.: 589). Moreover, Philip considered Alan to be 'the only real man, what I call a real man, that I have ever met'. Philip's passivity is underscored by his statement that his own 'strength lies in giving in – and then recovering [himself]' (ibid.: 590). Philip admired Alan for 'never [letting] himself be swept away', a trait unlike his own impulsiveness. (Murry's impulsiveness is noted by both Huxley and Lawrence.) Lawrence establishes the dichotomy between the two men by stressing the difference between the editor's 'subtle, fawning power' and that of the 'soldier, a ceaseless born fighter, a sword not to be sheathed' (ibid.: 592).

David Ellis draws attention to a subliminal homoerotic element in 'The Border Line' that becomes apparent when comparing Lawrence's second and third versions of the story. (The third version was not written until 1928.) In the second version, Philip's death is caused by suffocation when the ghost of Alan lies on top of him. Ellis suggests that this might be Lawrence's reaction to his earlier attraction to Murry. He surmises that Lawrence 'felt in some obscure part of his being that he had been physically betrayed by him, as well as by Frieda' (Ellis 1998: 164).

This difference between Murryean and Lawrentian types is again emphasised in 'Jimmy and the Desperate Woman'. Jimmy Frith, the more androgynous figure, is 'a rather small, shambling man' (Lawrence 1976 3: 611); his rival, Pinnegar, has muscles which are 'not large', but 'quick, alive with energy'. Pinnegar is 'like some pure-moulded engine that sleeps between its motions, with incomprehensible eyes of dark iron-blue' (ibid.: 618). Jimmy, in contrast, has 'beautiful dark-grey eyes

. . . with long lashes' (ibid.: 606). Lawrence emphasises these eyes by repeating and enlarging his description of them later in the story through the perception of Emily Pinnegar, the 'desperate' woman Jimmy plans to rescue from her miserable marriage. (Lawrence's focus on the long eyelashes should recall Murry's own reference to them in *The Things We Are*.) Huxley merely mentions 'grey eyes' that 'were very deeply set', and 'eyes that expressed nothing, but were just holes into the darkness inside his skull (Huxley 1996: 60, 156), which seems appropriate since his representation of Murry contains none of the subliminal erotic attraction that surfaces at moments in Lawrence.

Incidentally, both Huxley and Lawrence draw attention to Murry's beginning baldness: Huxley describes 'a natural tonsure as big as a medal showing pink on the crown of his head' (Huxley 1996: 60), and Lawrence, in 'The Last Laugh', remarks on Marchbanks's 'bald spot, just like a tonsure' (Lawrence 1976 3: 631). Both use this detail to intimate a basic duplicity in Murry: the monk and the satyr. Burlap is a 'mixture . . . of a movie villain and St. Anthony of Padua by a painter of the baroque, of a card-sharping Lothario and a rapturous devotee' (Huxley 1996: 60). Marchbanks, for Lawrence, 'seemed like a satanic young priest. His face had beautiful lines, like a faun, and a doubtful martyred expression. A sort of faun on the Cross' (Lawrence 1976 3: 631).

As in 'The Border Line', the homosocial rivalry between the male figures in 'Jimmy and the Desperate Woman' exudes a considerable charge of libidinal energy. In the final paragraph of the story, Lawrence describes the taxi ride from the station after Emily Pinnegar (who has finally left her husband) arrives in London to join Jimmy. In the taxi, Jimmy suddenly feels a 'perverse but intense desire for her', but this desire is complicated by his feeling 'so strongly, the presence of that other man about her, and this went to his head like neat spirits'. That 'other man', he senses, 'was actually bodily present, the husband. The woman moved in his aura. She was hopelessly married to him.' Excited by this realisation, Jimmy is left finally with the quandary: 'Which of the two would fall before him with a greater fall – the woman or the man, her husband?' (Lawrence 1976 3: 629).

Murry's hurt and angry reaction to these stories undoubtedly affected his construction of Lawrence in *Son of Woman*. As time passed, recurring reminders of Lawrence's caricatures would set off new self-defences and reinterpretations of his relationship with Lawrence. For instance, after Murry re-read Lawrence's 'Smile' in July 1953, he suddenly realised that it was a 'caricature' of his visit to Fontainebleau on the day that Mansfield died, and had not realised it earlier because he could not

believe that Lawrence would do anything like that. He acknowledged
that he had been hurt by Lawrence's depictions of himself in the other
stories, but not outraged in the same way. He also noted wryly that he
was 'three times killed by Lawrence in imagination' (MSX 4163: 13).

Clearly, sexual competition was an initiating force in Lawrence's fictional attacks on Murry, but we should not overlook the professional
competition suggested by the references to literary editorship in these
stories. As we have seen, Lawrence's disapproval of Murry's editorial
decisions had a long history. Even if Murry declared that he 'neither
desired, nor intended, to remain editor of [the *Adelphi*]' and believed
his role to be 'simply *locum tenens*, literally lieutenant, for Lawrence'
(RDHL: 100), he had immediately shaped the paper to his own interests.
Lawrence's reaction to the first issue was characteristically negative: 'It
seemed to me so weak, apologetic, knock-kneed, with really nothing to
justify its existence', he wrote to Koteliansky on 22 June 1923 (LDHL 4:
462).

From its beginning, the *Adelphi* had become a focus of anti-Murry
derision. It was, in fact, an attack on the *Adelphi* by Raymond Mortimer
in the *New Statesman* on 21 July 1923 that could be said to have initiated the years-long debate with T. S. Eliot over romanticism and classicism. Mortimer had called the *Adelphi* 'the last stand' (Mortimer 1923:
448) of romanticism, and Murry's response to that attack, 'On Fear; and
on Romanticism', in the September issue of the *Adelphi*, would be the
first sally in an ongoing battle that would continue to damage Murry's
reputation.[1] Lawrence had not yet returned to England when this essay
appeared, but Frieda had arrived near the end of August and her trip
with Murry to Freiburg would take place in September. At that moment,
Lawrence tended to be in agreement with Murry, and he wrote to him
from Los Angeles after reading the essay on 17 September 1923: 'This
classiosity is bunkum, but still more *cowardice*' (LDHL 4:500).

'On Fear; and on Romanticism' is one of Murry's most important
essays; it sets forth a definite position from which he will not waver,
neither in his debate with Eliot nor in his future life course. In this essay
he declares outright: 'I think it is very true that I myself am a Romantic'
(Murry 1924b: 80). The term already is loaded with the freight of historical argument.[2] Murry sets out to show that this self-attribution is not
merely a personal idiosyncrasy, but a stance that situates himself in the
line of cultural development which he calls the 'English' tradition:

> there is no point, in English conditions, in opposing Romanticism to
> Classicism. In England there never has been any classicism worth talking
> about: we have had classics, but no classicism. And all of our classics are
> romantic. That is to say, the *decorum* the great English writers naturally

observe is one that they fetch out of the depths in themselves. It is not imposed by tradition or authority. There is a tradition in English life and English literature, of course, but it is not on the surface; it is not formulated or formulable, any more than the tradition of English politics is formulated or formulable. It is something you have to sense by intuition, if you are to know it at all. The English writer, the English divine, the English statesman, inherit no rules from their forbears: they inherit only this: a sense that in the last resort they must depend upon the inner voice. If they dig deep enough in their pursuit of self-knowledge – a piece of mining done not with the intellect alone, but with the whole man – they will come upon a self that is universal: in religious terms, the English tradition is that the man who truly interrogates himself will ultimately hear the voice of God, in terms of literary criticism, that the writer achieves impersonality through personality. (Murry 1924b: 81–2)

Murry contrasts this 'English tradition' with the continental and decides that 'Romanticism as I have tried to describe it, is itself the English tradition: it is national, and it is the secret source of our own peculiar vitality. In England it is the classicist who is the interloper and the alien' (Murry 1924b: 82). This emphasis on the *English* tradition implicitly criticises what David Goldie calls the 'cosmopolitan catholicism' of T. S. Eliot's own editorial venture: the *Criterion* (Goldie 1998: 92). But there may also be some hints of allusion to the personal Eliot in Murry's diction. The terms 'interloper' and 'alien' might well have annoyed a man who despite all his efforts, was never really accepted as 'English'. Moreover, consider how Murry demeans the classicist by claiming that he

has always been an insignificant person over here. Sometimes he has been à la mode: he was so for some time in the eighteenth century, and I am perfectly prepared to believe he is in the swim again at this very moment. But that is no more important than an exotic fashion in trousers [can this be allusion to Prufrock?]. He *cannot* establish himself here; he may be a pastime for the *dilettanti*; his elegance may be attractive, but it is always the slightly excessive elegance of the outsider. (Murry 1924b: 82–3)

The hidden barbs in Murry's remarks would have been hard for Eliot to ignore, especially because – as David Goldie points out – Murry's essay 'appeared in the same month as a stinging attack by Murry on the arid intellectualism of *The Waste Land*' (Goldie 1998: 102).

Eliot's response came quickly; he published 'The Function of Criticism' in the *Criterion* the next month, and in it directly attacked Murry's position: 'With Mr. Murry's formulation of Classicism and Romanticism I cannot agree; the difference seems to me rather the difference between the complete and the fragmentary, the adult and the immature, the orderly and the chaotic.'[3] Eliot's ire was particularly aroused by Murry's reference to 'the inner voice':

The inner voice . . . sounds remarkably like an old principle which has been formulated by an elder critic in the now familiar phrase of 'doing as one likes'. The possessors of the inner voice ride ten in a compartment to a football match at Swansea, listening to the inner voice, which breathes the eternal message of vanity, fear, and lust. (Eliot 1975: 71)

Eliot's reaction to 'the inner voice' reveals a class bias that is in itself an assault not only against Murry's position, but against Murry himself and his supporters (many of them of lower-middle and working-class origins) at the *Adelphi*.[4] Apparently, Eliot had also been similarly ridiculing Murry to Virginia Woolf for her amusement, for it was at this time that he made the comment to her that I quoted in Chapter 8, comparing Murry 'to a half starved clerk spouting religious revival on a tub at Hyde Park Corner' (LVW 3: 80).

In 'The Function of Criticism' Eliot's use of highly judgmental binaries such as adult/immature and orderly/chaotic tends to undermine Murry's stance, making it appear flimsy, soft, subjective, and – as is characteristic of such pairings – feminine. This is a strategy similar to Lawrence's in the short stories where his use of oppositional binaries tends to demasculinise Murry. It cannot be purely coincidental that a resurgence of the intellectual competition that had long marked Murry's relationship with Eliot occurred at nearly the same time as the resurgence of sexual competition with Lawrence.

If Murry's relations with Eliot had been largely professional, unlike those with Lawrence, he still hoped to develop a genuine friendship amidst that professionalism. Lea quotes from a letter from Murry to Eliot in 1923 in which Murry expresses concern about Eliot's personal situation, asking him if 'there is *anything*' he can do to help him:

'Dear old boy, I don't know what to say to you. I never do. But in my way believe me I love you – I think of you and feel for you continually. And there is this queer feeling that you and Vivien and I are bound together somehow.' (L: 117)

This longstanding emotional concern for Eliot suggests that Murry might be afraid of alienating him, therefore in 'More About Romanticism', which appeared in the December issue of the *Adelphi*, Murry attempts to defuse the antagonism his first approach to the topic had aroused: 'The sooner the accidental and contingent elements are eliminated from this debate the better; for then we shall more quickly have a glimpse of the real nature of the issues that are involved' (Murry 1924b: 136). Murry takes special care at the start of the essay to refer to Eliot as 'the gifted editor of the Criterion' (ibid.: 134). He also enlarges the scope of his discussion in 'More About Romanticism', by now defining romanticism and classicism as 'perennial modes of the human spirit', instead of demarking them strictly as representative of English and continental values. He broadens the discussion by discerning the same dichotomy within the evolution of Christianity: the Catholic Church 'is essentially classical', but 'Christianity itself . . . is essentially romantic' (ibid.: 136), and interprets the Renaissance as a 'rebellion of a great Romanticism against a secular Classicism' (ibid.: 136).

The publication date of 'More About Romanticism' suggests that it must have been written after Murry had returned from his trip to Freiburg with Frieda, perhaps just as Lawrence was arriving in England. I mention this because it does seem as if two strands of Murry's increasingly complicated life become intertwined here. Murry's reason for travelling to Freiburg with Frieda – who was on her way to visit her family – was ostensibly for the purpose of 'consult[ing] a doctor on Vivien Eliot's behalf' (L: 117). Nonetheless, whatever gratitude Eliot might have felt regarding Murry's friendly intervention did not prevent Vivienne Eliot from later publishing a satirical piece on Murry's editorial style in April 1924, just about the same time as Lawrence was mocking him in 'Jimmy and the Desperate Woman' and 'The Border Line'.[5] Moreover, the fact that Eliot published 'Jimmy and the Desperate Woman' in the *Criterion* (October 1924) suggests that he might have enjoyed seeing Murry satirised while the debate was still in progress.

Despite the few instances of what might seem like personal animosity in Murry's debate with Eliot, apparently the two men continued to have – at least superficially – cordial relations. There never occurred an absolute rupture between them like the one between Murry and Lawrence. In his journal on 30 October 1930, the day that Murry finished *Son of Woman*, he mentions that the 'estrangement' between himself and Lawrence 'was just inevitable. We were made to attract & fly away from each other.' (This paragraph of the entry begins with a list of the people Murry had 'loved', including Marguéritte, Katherine, Gordon Campbell, Lawrence and a few others.) Musing about his relationships, he next considers – almost as an afterthought – his feelings about Eliot:

> I forgot. In some queer way I have almost loved Tom Eliot. This is a queer business. I have felt that I had some significance for him: some help to give. But it wasn't given, and I don't think it was my fault. There's still a bond of some sort between us. But what it is I don't know. I don't understand his poetry: don't even feel inclined to take the trouble of finding out whether I could understand it. (MSX 4148: 77)

Nonetheless, the personal element continued to intrude as Murry's debate with Eliot continued. One of the major accomplishments of

David Goldie's fine book *A Critical Difference* is to expose the contingency of their critical positions. Goldie recognises 'the presence of irrational components in Eliot's formulation of his critical scholasticism' and describes how 'he was spurred by a hostile personal reaction to Murry (and to people like Murry) into making assertions which proved in the long term to be unsustainable' (Goldie 1998: 4). Through a precise and nuanced analysis of each stage of the critical dialogue between Murry and Eliot, Goldie demonstrates convincingly that 'substantial parts of each writer's theory of criticism were not so much laid bare by these debates as actively constructed during them' (ibid.: 3).

At the heart of Goldie's book is his use of a remarkable 'find'. Tucked away in the mass of papers that make up the John Middleton Murry Collection at Edinburgh University Library is an unpublished typescript of Murry's 'The Classical Revival', apparently written around December 1925. The typescript contains numerous annotations in Eliot's own hand, evidence that Murry had passed the essay on to him, as he seems to have done with other essays as well. Goldie suggests that 'Eliot may have been prompted into his defence of classicism by a pre-publication reading of Murry's essay' (Goldie 1998: 157). Goldie recognises that such an assertion cannot be proved, but it is hard to resist the temptation to believe it when reading his penetrating explication of Murry's typescript and Eliot's marginal commentary. When Murry discerns a contradiction between Eliot's classicist principles and the methodology of *The Waste Land*, Eliot writes in the margin, 'No one ever said it was [classical]. "The Waste Land" makes *no attempt whatever to be classical*' (Goldie 1998: 157). This stunning example adds fuel to Goldie's central contention that the debates between the two men forced 'each to articulate a position that might otherwise have remained only implicit' (ibid.: 194). Eliot's comments appear to have led Murry to alter some of his statements in the later, published version of the second half of the essay, even if he did so without fully accepting Eliot's point.

It is in that essay, 'The Classical Revival', published in the *Adelphi* in February 1926, that Murry makes the notorious remark: 'Mrs. Woolf's "Jacob's Room" and Mr. Eliot's "The Waste Land" belong essentially to the same order. Both are failures; though "The Waste Land" is the more impressive, because the more complete and conscious failure.' In this particular critique, Murry makes what might be his most short-sighted prognostication: 'Fifty, ten years hence no one will take the trouble (no small one) to read either of these works' (DR: 178).[6]

As we have seen, Murry had been critical of Woolf's writing for a long time. Nearly two years earlier, she recorded in her diary a conversation in which he told her with a Lawrentian flourish: '"you won't begin with your instincts. You won't own them. With all your exquisite sensibilities – you're content to stay at that"' (DVW 2: 296). The date of this diary entry, 12 March 1924, coincides with Lawrence's writing of 'Jimmy and the Desperate Woman', which, according to Ellis's chronology of Lawrence's fiction (Ellis 1998: 549), was composed between 19 February and April 1924. It is amusing in that context to notice that Woolf, quite independently of Lawrence, takes note there of Murry's 'rolling lustful, or somehow leering eye' (DVW 2: 296).

Murry had so alienated himself from Bloomsbury after Mansfield's death that he was no longer considered even to be on its fringes. His editorship of the *Adelphi* had linked him with a different readership and a different set of colleagues and these were the sorts of people not likely to be found at Garsington or at fashionable parties amongst the intelligentsia. In the same diary entry of 12 March, Woolf says that she 'kept thinking how he'd come down in the world, spiritually, what tenthrate shillyshallying humbugs he must live among' (DVW 2: 297), and in an entry on 17 October she notes that Murry had married again and remarks: 'Thats a sordid page of my life by the way, Murry' (DVW 2: 317).[7]

Nearly thirty years later, Murry found himself forced to make some accommodation for Virginia Woolf's lasting fame and prestige. (Interestingly, when Woolf died in 1941, Murry made no comment in his journal. Instead, he only neatly pasted a newspaper clipping of her obituary onto one of its pages. This is striking, since he usually recorded his reactions to the deaths of people he had known.) His journal on 10 January 1954 reveals that he was reading *A Writer's Diary*, and was 'impressed . . . by her truly valiant effort at honesty', but surprised by 'how extraordinarily sensitive she was to criticism of any kind – exalted by praise, utterly depressed by a hostile judgement even though it came from a source for which she had no respect'. He then reiterated his long-standing belief: 'I do not feel there was much *positive* literary genius in V. W'. Yet now that all the complexities of their personal relationship were far removed to the past, he exclaimed:

> I must read more of her books. I stopped at *Jacob's Room*. But there is certainly nothing in this journal which convinces me that she had the gift. She had a finely educated sensitivity; but it was too intellectualized. Her descriptions, for example, do not live, do not get home to the reader's solar plexus . . . She lacked the pregnant 'superficiality' of the creative genius: that enables it to keep to the mystery of the real, to present the object in such a way that it is at once familiar, homely, yet rich and full of wonder: that gives writing the 'transparent quality' V. W. admired in K. M. (or *told* K. M. she admired, in a letter – there is no trace of such admiration in *A Writer's Diary*) . . . (MSX 4158: 332–3)

Murry continued this entry by telling himself that now he must read *The Waves*, *Three Guineas* and *Between the Acts*. (Oddly, he did not mention *Mrs Dalloway* and *To the Lighthouse*.) He ended this long entry on his responses to Woolf's writing with a discussion of the significance of his estrangement from Woolf, and Bloomsbury as a whole:

> *A Writer's Diary* forcibly reminds me how completely I slipped out of the V. W. circle, when *The Athenaeum* came to an end. First, through Katherine's increasing illness and her increasing dislike of Bloomsbury values; then, quite finally, through beginning *The Adelphi* after her death. I crossed the Rubicon, and burned my boats, with a vengeance. I was henceforward beyond the pale. And, of course, I was glad to be beyond it. But, since Bloomsbury became more and more the arbiter, I had put myself off the map. With a bit of myself I regret it, but with my essential self not at all. I just did not belong, and I should have become horribly false had I tried to maintain the connection. But breaking it was not all gain. There was a sort of discipline involved which would have done me good: by the violence of my reaction against what I felt was superficial & false in the Bloomsbury values, I became too unbuttoned, – too isolated, also. I had no one to criticise me, at all, at all. (MSX 4157: 332–5)

II

Murry's break with Bloomsbury also coincided with his positioning of himself on the 'wrong' side in his debate with Eliot, who was to emerge as the representative 'modernist' (even if the positions he maintained undermined much of the original spirit of pre-war modernism). But, as we have seen, Murry's own association with modernism had altered greatly since his enthusiastic embrace of it when he founded *Rhythm* in 1911. The debate with Eliot served, in a sense, as a final severing of his ties with the ongoing development of literary modernism, which through Eliot's domination, was achieving its 'classical' stage. In the years following Mansfield's death, Murry became increasingly disenchanted with the modernist project. He lost interest in Proust and Joyce and seemed unable to appreciate the significance of Eliot's and Woolf's innovations. As his criticism began to incorporate more fully the historical and cultural implications of literary movements, and he began to focus on the personal struggles of his spiritual 'heroes' (Keats, Blake, Shakespeare, Jesus), he alienated himself from the newer schools of criticism which were based on theoretical approaches to the study of literature. According to Goldie:

> By the end of the 1920s Murry had cultivated the individuality of his critical response to such an extent that no one felt impelled to listen, especially

the new generation of critics springing up through the academies of the Anglo-American world. (Goldie 1998: 190)[8]

Yet Murry's notoriety really cannot be adequately explained by his retreat from modernist writing nor his defence of romanticism, although these might have been contributing factors. More important was the disdain of the intelligentsia for his managing of the *Adelphi*, especially his emotional editorialising, his accounts of his mystical experience, and his use of it for the continuing promotion and public worship of Katherine Mansfield. Lawrence's and Huxley's satirical attacks contributed greatly to that notoriety, and Murry himself only increased it by publishing his two controversial books on Lawrence. Finally, there was his sudden conversion to Marxism, which, though short-lived, again evidenced his propensity for impulsive intellectual as well as emotional commitments.[9] As he admitted in a letter to Richard Rees: 'If ever there was a bloke who knew what it was to be "converted", I am he' (quoted in L: 194). Accordingly, Lea declares: 'By 1933, his reputation had touched bottom' (L: 213). In a much later reconsideration of Murry, Lea mentions that 'by the 1930s, an opinion poll taken at Cambridge was to reveal Murry as the most despised literary figure of the time' (Lea 1975: 168).

It cannot be coincidental that Murry chose that moment when his 'reputation had touched bottom' to write his autobiography, *Between Two Worlds*. As a reaction to the continuing accumulation of negative criticism, Murry might well have decided to use the autobiographical format to re-circulate himself in a more positive way. Not that he would portray himself as a hero, nor as a particularly admirable person, but he did seem to believe that coming to grips with the underlying forces that had turned him into someone who had aroused such contrary passions might 'help other people in the same way as [he had] been helped by the self-revelation of people before [him]' (quoted in L: 215).

As we have seen, the autobiographical impulse had already been a significant component of Murry's writing for some time, and it had been one target for his detractors' adverse criticism. But even his supporters were uneasy with his tendency to indulge in confessionalism, as is apparent in the following comments by Rayner Heppenstall, who wrote the first book about Murry, published in 1934:

> The greatest stumbling-block of all in Murry's work is his introduction from time to time, for no better reason than that he finds they will illuminate his thesis, of snippets of autobiography – innocent, at that, of any pretence to a decently obscuring symbolism. (Heppenstall 1934: 18–19)

Perhaps Murry's deficiencies as a poet and novelist, his inability to create 'a decently obscuring symbolism' (or an 'objective correlative', as Eliot might have put it), are the reverse side of his predilection for literally describing his own experiences and using them as empirical evidence to support his critical positions. Although his use of the personal relates to his larger concern with individual growth and creativity, which he analyses in his essays and books on literary figures, he also knew that he made his readers uncomfortable with his approach and felt that he must explain it. For example, he begins the first paragraph of *God* (1929) with these words: 'It seems that I cannot avoid beginning this book autobiographically' (Murry 1929). This apologetic tone seems designed to disarm his critics, especially when he goes on to explain his method as the result of his own mental weakness, a strategy that strives to make a sympathetic relationship with readers who also might find abstruse philosophical writing unpalatable:

> Had I a more powerful mind, it might be possible for me to expound its theses in orderly abstraction; and there have been many moments when I have fervently desired to do this. It is not comfortable to wear one's heart upon one's sleeve; and I am troubled by the thought that it would be a far more comely thing if I could develop my theses as a pure philosopher, in forms from which the taint of personality had been wholly removed. (Murry 1929: 13)

Autobiography, as a genre, is typically egocentric: the author must consider his or her life important enough for readers to want to know about it: thus the many accounts of famous people. Their egocentricity must be controlled so that it does not become offensive: indulgences in bragging. Many recent autobiographies, however, are studies in victimisation; they are outwardly directed to the forces which reduced the author to abjection – which then is overcome by heroic measures, either physical or psychological. Murry's approach to autobiography in *Between Two Worlds* is different from either of these types. What should appear egotistical is often undercut through his willingness to reveal his weaknesses and failures. If he describes the effects of social forces on himself, it is still clear that he was not a helpless victim, but a respondent in a process to which he contributed. Murry's journals during the period of his composition of *Between Two Worlds* reveal that he was troubled about the problem of 'truth' in autobiography.[10] He recognised that he could not be completely open about his sexual life, and was still affected by the same standards of literary decorum that revealed themselves in some of his reviews of Lawrence's novels. (He also had to keep in mind the dangers of writing about living people. Even on relatively trivial matters, he found himself censoring for the sake of not offending someone.)

In *Between Two Worlds* Murry is reticent about his physical attractiveness and its contribution to his early successes. Consequently, he only admits to have 'always been taken by surprise' whenever he found a woman attracted to himself:

> My instinctive presupposition has always been that if I like a woman, the woman will not like me . . . though I have to confess that my uniform experience has been that whenever I have liked a woman it has always turned out that she has liked me. (BTW: 138)

He only hints at the usefulness of his attractiveness when he mentions that he was a beautiful baby, and that his mother 'needed a beautiful baby to recompense her' for carrying such a heavy one (he weighed over eleven pounds at birth). Yet the placement of this reference to his 'beauty' in the first paragraph of the book suggests that it played a greater part in his later relationships than he could admit.

Now that he no longer cared about the judgments of the literary establishment nor felt the need to accommodate himself to the social standards of Bloomsbury, Murry might have felt free to examine the core of his essential difference from most of its members: his lower-middle-class origins. He focuses this issue not in terms of his later social difficulties with people like Lady Ottoline Morrell or Virginia Woolf, but on his experiences with the upper-class assumptions of the educational system he had entered as a child. By receiving a scholarship to Christ's Hospital, he now realised, how 'a subtle and evergrowing veil interposed' between himself and his parents: 'It was not my fault; I was caught up in a process: I was being lifted out of my own social class into another' (BTW: 43). That process had affected a child who 'had, from the beginning, an altogether peculiar fear of life'. Murry suggests that there was in him 'some original shrinking sensitiveness' that 'had been inordinately increased by [his] social instability'. Without support from the presence or the ingrained values of his parents, this sensitivity produced in him a profound sense of inauthenticity:

> I was for ever passing into new social environments, and being compelled to adjust myself to them. I had a perpetual sense that I was required to live, as it were, on false pretences; that I, a creature without a background, was deceiving others into believing that I had the same background as they. (BTW: 241)

Between Two Worlds can be read as a major document in the literary archive of the phenomenon of 'passing'. Murry's description of the psychological damage it inflicted upon him makes his autobiography at least as valuable for its analysis of the insidious characteristics of passing and the anxieties of class identification as it is for its documentation of his relations with Mansfield and Lawrence, which take up the latter half of the book.

Murry emphasises the emotional burden of his superior education. He seems to take no genuine pride in recounting that by most measures of achievement he had been a child prodigy. He learned 'to read at two' and by the age of seven was 'at the top of a superior sort of board school . . . with a handful of boys much older than [himself]' (BTW: 10–11). Now that he has a son of exactly the same age as he was then, he says that he would 'be truly appalled if he knew what I knew at his age . . . algebra up to quadratics, a good deal of chemistry and geology', and that he had even written an essay on Gothic architecture. Of these achievements, Murry writes:

> It is a grim process to reflect upon – this early education of mine; grim in itself, for it involved the complete obliteration of a child's childhood; for which, when I later came to know of what I had been deprived, I used to blame my father: grimmer still, when later I realized that in my father's eyes, and perhaps also in fact, there had been for me but one way of escape from a life of squalor and futility, and I ceased to blame him, and acknowledged with gratitude that he had done all he could for me. (BTW: 11–12)

The text of *Between Two Worlds* takes up 496 pages and yet only covers Murry's life up to the moment of the armistice and his concurrent realisation that Katherine Mansfield would not survive her illness. He was at that point only twenty-nine years old. Although I have quoted often from this book, it has always been with a cautious sense that its interpretation of events needs to be balanced with other information from different sources. Nonetheless, it contains many important details about Murry's interactions with Lawrence and Mansfield in their formative stages, and consequently, it has been of great use to biographers and critics of both authors despite its limitations. Much of what I have discussed in this book does not appear in Murry's autobiography: the last years of Mansfield's struggle to live; his editorship of the *Athenaeum;* the final breakdown of his friendship with Lawrence; his complicated relationship with Eliot; and the difficulties of his relations with Bloomsbury. (It is noteworthy that the names of T. S. Eliot and Virginia Woolf do not appear anywhere in its pages.)

Murry decides to end the book with his sense of emotional/spiritual 'devastation' in 1918, when he could describe his life as 'now divided into . . . moments of solitary vision' and a 'waking dream':

> Between the two worlds there was now an abyss. In the world of vision I was at home, because I was not; in the world of act and suffering, of love and friendship, I was, and was in anguish or in insentience. (BTW: 496)[11]

His decision to end the book where he does is an interesting move both thematically and strategically. If he had continued its narrative even up through the following year, he would have had to describe his ascension to power as the editor of the *Athenaeum*, which would have severely undermined the atmosphere of angst and indecision towards which the book's momentum seemed to lead. It also made it unnecessary for him to have to face his problems in interacting with Bloomsbury. In fact, the absence of Bloomsbury tends to insinuate its insignificance in Murry's intellectual and emotional development. Instead, his book can emphasise that the most important figures in his adult life were Mansfield and Lawrence. The publication of *Between Two Worlds* cannot be said to have done anything to redeem Murry with Bloomsbury, not that any of its members might have enjoyed finding themselves depicted in it. While Virginia Woolf was reading it, she wrote to Ottoline Morrell, on 17 July 1935: 'I read Murry on Murry because carrion has its fascination, like eating high game' (LVW 5: 418).

Murry's circulation of himself continued for the rest of his life; even his journals seem calculated – in sections at least – for some posthumous definitive interpretation of the meaning of his life's journey. This continual process of self-examination he understood to be the result of his broken roots, his sense of never fitting in anywhere. In *Adam and Eve*, a decade after finishing *Between Two Worlds*, he was still contemplating the matter and was now ready to position his life's trajectory within a larger theory about the movement of English social history: 'I myself am a scientifically perfect product of that period of extreme social dislocation' (Murry 1944: 35). He clearly recognised how much any person's life was shaped by cultural factors outside his or her control.

Murry would continue to interpret his own experiences through the various lenses of his altering ideological perspectives. What he might not have appreciated as fully as we can today is how much his seemingly 'unfashionable' movement away from the centres of intellectual power in the metropolis might actually have placed him in the vanguard of a similar movement later in the twentieth century. His career can be said to demonstrate the same kind of withdrawal from cosmopolitan modernism to a localised, England-centred 'shrinking island' that Jed Esty discerns in the writings of the later Woolf and Eliot.[12] Murry's formerly enthusiastic cross-channel adventures, such as his youthful forays into artistic life in Paris, which had brought him into contact with Fauvism and subsequent developments in modern art and literature, were overshadowed finally by the harsh experiences on the continent he had undergone with Mansfield in those last years of intense suffering. After her death in 1923, Murry's travelling days were essentially over. He would never live abroad again. His concerns were centred in English life and English culture. His increasing focus on romanticism in his literary criticism kept his attention close to home as well, but this focus only added to his isolation from the changing currents of European cultural movements.

Murry's activities during the more than twenty years remaining to him after he completed *Between Two Worlds* are outside the parameters of this book. They are so varied and complex that they need a book of their own to illuminate how such political work as his establishment of the Adelphi Centre (which became a nexus for people devoted to social change through the principles of communalism), and his commitment to pacifism (exemplified by his editorship of *Peace News*), influenced his continuing production of essays, reviews and books on an array of subjects. What becomes apparent in studying Murry's journals, however, is the persistent presence of Mansfield and Lawrence throughout all of these years. One entry, that of 3 August 1956, might stand for a nearly final statement (Murry died the following year) of the meaning of his connection with them, and I will quote it so that Murry has the last words in this book:

> I have the feeling that I have been completely outside the main stream of literature: that I don't 'belong' and indeed never have belonged. My concern has always been that of a moralist, and I have never been sufficient of the artist to be diverted from it. And yet the stubborn feeling persists that my 'concern' was shared in the old days by Lawrence & by Katherine: that I was, in some sense, their critical counterpart, and that the *kind* of seriousness we had has been lost. That distinguished us, absolutely from the Bloomsburies. Eliot came nearer to it: but from him, too, there was an inevitable separation. None of us was, or ever could have become, capable of accepting dogmatic Christianity, as Eliot did. I am the sole remaining representative of our particular integrity, our particular concern. We were all socially outsiders, quite without the social and domestic tradition which the Bloomsburies, Aldous Huxley, and expatriate – *plus royaliste que le roi* – Eliot inherited. And, I think, experience came more naked and direct to us than to the others. To us, there was a sense in which they were all 'phoneys' (in the nuance of *The Catcher in the Rye*). Love meant more to us: we needed it more.
>
> It is *just* possible that I shall regain some significance: that my 'concern' and the contemporary 'concern' will meet. It is just *possible*. (MSX 4160: 160–1)

Notes

1. The essay appeared in the *Adelphi* on 4 September 1923 and Murry reprinted it under the title 'On Editing and Romanticism' in *To the Unknown God* in 1924.

2. See Goldie (1998: 96–100) for details about the historical dimensions of the romanticism/classicism controversy that preceded Murry's and Eliot's debate.

3. Eliot's essay appeared in the *Criterion* in October 1923, and is reprinted in the *Selected Prose of T. S. Eliot* (Eliot 1975: 68–76).

4. Jason Harding also reminds us not to 'overlook . . . the extent to which the exchange was not simply a contribution to intellectual debate, but an important means of providing good copy for both periodicals' (Harding 2002: 26). See his discussion of the competition between the *Criterion* and the *Adelphi* (ibid.: 26–43).

5. See F. M. [Vivienne Eliot] (1924), 'Letters of the Moment II', *Criterion* 2, 7 (April): 360–4. It is not certain that Murry would have known the identity of 'F. M.'.

6. Woolf's diary entry of 8 February 1926 records her reaction to this statement: 'Murry says my works won't be read in 10 years time – Well, tonight I get a new edition of the V[oyage]. O[ut]. from Harbrace – this was published 11 years ago' (DVW 3: 58). And to Vita Sackville-West she writes on 3 February: 'Murry, by the way has arraigned your poor Virginia, and Virginia's poor Tom Eliot, and all their works, in the Adelphi, and condemned them to death' (LVW 3: 238).

7. There is a complicated history to Virginia Woolf's negativity towards Murry, some of it related to Leonard Woolf's professional experience with him. One instance involved Murry's negative review of Leonard Woolf's joint translation (with Koteliansky) of Chekhov's notebooks: 'Leonard said how he'd never met a worse man than Murry', Virginia Woolf wrote on 7 June 1921 (DVW 2: 124). Ironically, in light of Murry's own practice, this was the review in which Murry rashly claimed it to be 'almost a crime to make public fragments of an author's manuscripts which he obviously did not mean to show to the world' (*Nation and Athenaeum*, 4 June 1921, 365).

8. Goldie's 'no one' apparently does not include the vast numbers of less sophisticated followers of Murry, such as J. H. Watson, a Durham blast-furnaceman, who began to subscribe to the *Adelphi* in 1923, and found himself and his co-workers 'stirred by what was an unknown world, the world of books and literature. Keats and Shakespeare, Tchehov and Hardy, Lawrence and Murry, opened up a new way of living for me, firing the brain and freeing the tongue . . . Quite a large number of us gathered round to discuss the ideas and books mentioned in the *Adelphi*, and we faithfully read through Murry's *Keats and Shakespeare* with the reverence usually reserved for Holy Writ' (Watson 1959: 51).

9. *The Necessity of Communism* had appeared in 1932.

10. Composing *Between Two Worlds* seems to have depleted some of the energy Murry typically expended upon writing in his journals, which is not surprising given the intensity of self-probing it demanded. He mentions on 8 November 1933, that 'the impulse to keep up this diary seems to fail while I am writing the *Autobiography*' (MSX 4150: 111). Yet what he does manage to include in it about his daily life reveals that it was as chaotic as ever, and that his miserable marriage to his third wife, Betty (to whom, nonetheless, he dedicated the book), had become 'steadily more hopeless'.

The unpleasant domestic atmosphere produced by this disintegrating marriage is vividly presented in the books written by Murry's children from his previous marriage. See Colin Middleton Murry, *I At the Keyhole* (C. M. Murry 1975), and Katherine Middleton Murry, *Beloved Quixote* (K. M. Murry 1986).

11. As its epigraph also makes apparent, the title of Murry's autobiography was taken from Matthew Arnold's poem 'Stanzas from the Grande Chartreuse', lines 85–6: 'Wandering between two worlds, one dead/The other powerless to be born'. The title might also retain a deeply submerged memory of Lawrence's use of the phrase in 'Whistling of Birds' in the *Athenaeum* in 1919. For the influence of Matthew Arnold on Murry's criticism, see Woodfield's introduction to *Defending Romanticism* (Murry 1989: 16–17).

12. See Jed Esty, *A Shrinking Island: Modernism and National Culture in England* (Princeton: Princeton University Press, 2004).

Bibliography

Ackroyd, Peter (1984), *T. S. Eliot*, London: Hamish Hamilton.

Alpers, Antony (1953), *Katherine Mansfield: A Biography*, New York: Knopf.

Alpers, Antony (1980), *The Life of Katherine Mansfield*, New York: Viking.

[Baker, Ida] (1972), *Katherine Mansfield: The Memories of L. M.*, New York: Taplinger.

Baldrick, Chris (1996), *Criticism and Literary Theory 1890 to the Present*, London: Longman.

Bibesco, Elizabeth [1922] (1989), 'An Obituary and a Portrait', in Leighton Hodson (ed.), *Marcel Proust: The Critical Heritage*, London: Routledge, pp. 185–7.

Bishop, Alan (1988), *Gentleman Rider: A Life of Joyce Cary*, London: Michael Joseph.

Boone, Joseph Allen (1998), *Libidinal Currents: Sexuality and the Shaping of Modernism*, Chicago: University of Chicago Press.

Bradshaw, David (1991), 'John Middleton Murry and the "Times Literary Supplement": The Importance and Usage of a Modern Literary Archive', *Bulletin of Bibliography* 45, 4: 199–212.

Bradshaw, David (1996), 'The Best of Companions: J. W. N. Sullivan, Aldous Huxley, and the New Physics', *Review of English Studies* 47, 186: 188–206; 47, 187: 352–68.

Bromwich, David (1985), 'Reflections on the Word "Genius"', *New Literary History* 17, 1: 141–64.

Burgan, Mary (1994), *Illness, Gender, and Writing: The Case of Katherine Mansfield*, Baltimore: Johns Hopkins University Press.

Byrne, Janet (1995), *A Genius for Living: The Life of Frieda Lawrence*, New York: HarperCollins.

Cannan, Gilbert (1916), *Mendel: A Story of Youth*, London: Unwin.

Carswell, Catherine (1932), *The Savage Pilgrimage: A Narrative of D. H. Lawrence*, New York: Harcourt.

Carswell, John (1978), *Lives and Letters: A. R. Orage, Beatrice Hastings, Katherine Mansfield, John Middleton Murry, S. S. Koteliansky, 1906–1957*, New York: New Directions.

Cassavant, Sharron Greer (1982), *John Middleton Murry: The Critic as Moralist*, Tuscaloosa: University of Alabama Press.

Delany, Paul (1978), *D. H. Lawrence's Nightmare: The Writer and His Circle in the Years of the Great War*, New York: Basic Books.

Dunbar, Pamela (1997), *Radical Mansfield: Double Discourse in Katherine Mansfield's Short Stories*, New York: St Martin's Press.

Eliot, T. S. (1931), 'Books of the Quarter', *The Criterion* 10: 7, 769.

Eliot, T. S. (1975), *Selected Prose of T. S. Eliot*, ed. Frank Kermode, San Diego: Harcourt.

Eliot, T. S. (1988), *The Letters of T. S. Eliot, Volume I: 1898–1922*, ed. Valerie Eliot, San Diego: Harcourt.

Ellis, David (1998), *D. H. Lawrence: Dying Game, 1922–1930*, Cambridge: Cambridge University Press.

Esty, Jed (2004), *A Shrinking Island: Modernism and National Culture in England*, Princeton: Princeton University Press.

Faderman, Lillian (1981), *Surpassing the Love of Man: Romantic Friendship and Love Between Women from the Renaissance to the Present*, New York: Morrow.

Farr, Diana (1978), *Gilbert Cannan: A Georgian Prodigy*, London: Chatto & Windus.

Feinstein, Elaine (1993), *Lawrence and the Women: The Intimate Life of D. H. Lawrence*, New York: HarperCollins.

Freud, Sigmund [1930] (1989), *Civilization and Its Discontents*, trans. James Strachey, New York: Norton.

Gertler, Mark (1965), *Selected Letters*, London: Rupert Hart-Davis.

Gilbert, Sandra and Susan Gubar (1988–94), *No Man's Land: The Place of the Woman Writer in the Twentieth Century*, 3 vols, New Haven: Yale University Press.

Girard, René (1965), *Deceit, Desire, and the Novel*, Baltimore: Johns Hopkins University Press.

Glenavy, Beatrice, Lady (1964), *'Today We Will Only Gossip'*, London: Constable.

Goldie, David (1998), *A Critical Difference: T. S. Eliot and John Middleton Murry in English Literary Criticism, 1919–1928*, Oxford: Clarendon Press.

Griffin, Ernest G. (1969a), 'The Circular and the Linear: The Middleton Murry–D. H. Lawrence Affair', *D. H. Lawrence Review* 2, 1: 76–92.

Griffin, Ernest G. (1969b), *John Middleton Murry*, New York: Twayne.

Gross, John (1969), *The Rise and Fall of the Man of Letters: Aspects of English Literary Life Since 1800*, London: Weidenfeld and Nicolson.

Hankin, C. A. (1983), *Katherine Mansfield and Her Confessional Stories*, New York: St Martin's Press.

Harding, Jason (2002), *The Criterion: Cultural Politics and Periodical Networks in Inter-War Britain*, Oxford: Oxford University Press.

Hardy, Dennis (2000), *Utopian England: Community Experiments, 1900–1945*, London: E & FN Spon.

Heppenstall, Rayner (1934), *Middleton Murry: A Study in Excellent Normality*, London: Cape.

Heppenstall, Rayner (1960), *Four Absentees*, London: Barrie and Rockliff.

Hignett, Sean (1984), *Brett: From Bloomsbury to New Mexico, A Biography*, London: Hodder & Stoughton.

Huxley, Aldous [1928] (1996), *Point Counter Point*, Normal, IL: Dalkey Archive Press.

Irigaray, Luce (1985), *This Sex Which is Not One*, Ithaca: Cornell University Press.

Kaplan, Sydney Janet (1991), *Katherine Mansfield and the Origins of Modernist Fiction*, Ithaca: Cornell University Press.

Kaye, Peter (1999), *Dostoevsky and English Modernism, 1900–1930*, Cambridge: Cambridge University Press.

Kimber, Gerri (2008), *Katherine Mansfield: The View From France*, Oxford: Peter Lang.

Kinkead-Weekes, Mark (1995), 'Introduction and Notes', in D. H. Lawrence, *Women in Love*, London: Penguin.

Kinkead-Weekes, Mark (1996), *D. H. Lawrence: Triumph to Exile, 1912–1922*, Cambridge: Cambridge University Press.

Kinkead-Weekes, Mark (1999), 'Rage against the Murrys: "Inexplicable" or "Psychopathic"?', in George Donaldson and Mara Kalnins (eds), *D. H. Lawrence in Italy and England*, New York: St Martin's Press, pp. 116–34.

Kirkpatrick, B. J. (1989), *A Bibliography of Katherine Mansfield*, Oxford: Clarendon Press.

Lawrence, D. H. (1972), *Phoenix: The Posthumous Papers of D. H. Lawrence*, ed. Edward D. McDonald, New York: Viking.

Lawrence, D. H. (1976), *The Complete Short Stories*, 3 vols, New York: Penguin.

Lawrence, D. H. (1978), *Phoenix II: Uncollected, Unpublished, and Other Prose Works*, ed. Warren Roberts and Harry T. Moore, New York: Penguin.

Lawrence, D. H. (1979–2000), *The Letters of D. H. Lawrence*, ed. James T. Boulton et al, 8 vols, Cambridge: Cambridge University Press.

Lawrence, D. H. [1920] (1987), *Women in Love*, ed. David Farmer, Lindeth Vasey and John Worthen, Cambridge: Cambridge University Press.

Lawrence, D. H. [1922] (1988), *Aaron's Rod*, Cambridge: Cambridge University Press.

Lawrence, D. H. (1998), *The First 'Women in Love'*, ed. John Worthen and Lindeth Vasey, Cambridge: Cambridge University Press.

Lawrence, Frieda (1982), *The Memoirs and Correspondence*, ed. E. W. Tedlock, New York: Octagon Books.

Lea, F. A. (1959), *The Life of John Middleton Murry*, London: Methuen.

Lea, F. A. (1975), *Voices in the Wilderness: From Poetry to Prophecy in Britain*, London: Brentham Press.

Lilley, George P. (1974), *A Bibliography of John Middleton Murry, 1889–1957*, Toronto: University of Toronto Press.

McDonnell, Jenny (2009), '"Wanted, a New Word": Katherine Mansfield and the *Athenaeum*', *Modernism/modernity* 16, 4: 727–42.

McEldowney, Dennis (1985), 'The Multiplex Effect: Recent Biographical Writing on Katherine Mansfield', *Ariel* 16, 4: 111–24.

Mansfield, Katherine (1927), *Journal of Katherine Mansfield*, ed. J. Middleton Murry, New York: Knopf.

Mansfield, Katherine (1930), *Novels and Novelists*, London: Constable.

Mansfield, Katherine (1945), *Collected Stories of Katherine Mansfield*, London: Constable.

Mansfield, Katherine (1954), *Journal of Katherine Mansfield*, ed. J. Middleton Murry, London: Constable.

Mansfield, Katherine (1984–2008), *The Collected Letters of Katherine Mansfield*, ed. Vincent O'Sullivan and Margaret Scott, 5 vols, Oxford: Clarendon Press.

Mansfield, Katherine (1987), *The Critical Writings of Katherine Mansfield*, ed. Clare Hanson, New York: St Martin's Press.

Mansfield, Katherine [1997] (2002), *The Katherine Mansfield Notebooks: Complete Edition*, ed. Margaret Scott, 2 vols in 1, Minneapolis: University of Minnesota Press.

Mansfield, Katherine and John Middleton Murry (1988), *Letters Between Katherine Mansfield and John Middleton Murry*, ed. Cherry Hankin, London: Virago.

Meyers, Jeffrey (1978), *Katherine Mansfield: A Biography*, New York: New Directions.

Moore, James (1980), *Gurdjieff and Mansfield*, London: Routledge & Kegan Paul.

Moran, Patricia (1996), *Word of Mouth: Body Language in Katherine Mansfield and Virginia Woolf*, Charlottesville: University of Virginia Press.

Morrell, Lady Ottoline (1964), *Memoirs of Lady Ottoline Morrell: A Study in Friendship, 1873–1915*, ed. Robert Gathorne-Hardy, New York: Knopf.

Morrell, Lady Ottoline (1974), *Ottoline at Garsington: Memoirs of Lady Ottoline Morrell, 1915–1918*, ed. Robert Gathorne-Hardy, London: Faber & Faber.

Mortelier, Christiane (1994), 'The French Connection: Francis Carco', in Roger Robinson (ed.), *Katherine Mansfield: In from the Margin*, Baton Rouge: Louisiana State University Press, pp. 137–57.

Mortimer, Raymond (1923), 'New Novels', *New Statesman* 21, 536: 448.

Murry, Colin Middleton (1975), *I At the Keyhole*, New York: Stein and Day.

Murry, John Middleton (1916), *Still Life*, London: Constable.

Murry, John Middleton (1919), *The Critic in Judgement; or, Belshazzar of Baronscourt*, Richmond: Hogarth Press.

Murry, John Middleton (1920a), *Aspects of Literature*. New York: Knopf.

Murry, John Middleton (1920b), *The Evolution of an Intellectual*, New York: Knopf.

Murry, John Middleton (1921), 'Marcel Proust', *Nation and Athenaeum* 30, 6: 218–19.

Murry, John Middleton (1922a), *Countries of the Mind: Essays in Literary Criticism*, London: Collins.

Murry, John Middleton (1922b), *The Things We Are*, London: Constable.

Murry, John Middleton (1923), 'Proust and the Modern Consciousness', in C. K. Scott Moncrieff (ed.), *Marcel Proust: An English Tribute*, London: Chatto & Windus, pp. 102–10.

Murry, John Middleton (1924a), *Discoveries: Essays in Literary Criticism*, London: Collins.

Murry, John Middleton (1924b), *To the Unknown God: Essays Towards a Religion*, London: Cape.

Murry, John Middleton (1924c), *The Voyage*, London: Constable.

Murry, John Middleton [1922] (1925), *The Problem of Style*, Oxford: H. Milford.

Murry, John Middleton (1928), *Things to Come: Essays*, London: Cape.

Murry, John Middleton (1929), *God: Being an Introduction to the Science of Metabiology*, London: Cape.

Murry, John Middleton (1931), *Son of Woman: The Story of D. H. Lawrence*, London: Cape.

Murry, John Middleton (1932), *The Necessity of Communism*, London: Cape.

Murry, John Middleton (1933), *Reminiscences of D. H. Lawrence*, London: Cape.

Murry, John Middleton (1935), *Between Two Worlds: An Autobiography*, London: Cape.

Murry, John Middleton (1944), *Adam and Eve: An Essay Towards a New and Better Society*, London: Dakers.

Murry, John Middleton (1952), *Community Farm*, London: Nevill.

Murry, John Middleton (1956a), 'Coming to London – VIII', *London Magazine* 3, 7: 30–7.

Murry, John Middleton (1956b), 'The Living Dead – 1. D. H. Lawrence', *London Magazine* 3, 5: 57–63.

Murry, John Middleton (1957), *Love, Freedom and Society*, London: Cape.

Murry, John Middleton (1959), *Katherine Mansfield and Other Literary Studies*, foreword by T. S. Eliot, London: Constable.

Murry, John Middleton [1916] (1966), *Fyodor Dostoevsky: A Critical Study*, New York: Russell & Russell.

Murry, John Middleton (1983), *The Letters of John Middleton Murry to Katherine Mansfield*, ed. C. A. Hankin, London: Constable.

Murry, John Middleton (1989), *Defending Romanticism: Selected Criticism of John Middleton Murry*, ed. Malcolm Woodfield, Bristol: Bristol Press.

Murry, John Middleton (various dates), 'The Diaries and Notebooks of John Middleton Murry', MS-Group-0411, Alexander Turnbull Library, Wellington, New Zealand.

Murry, John Middleton and James Carruthers Young (1929), 'Modern Marriage', *Forum* 81, 1: 22–6.

Murry, Katherine Middleton (1986), *Beloved Quixote: The Unknown Life of John Middleton Murry*, London: Souvenir Press.

Murry, Mary Middleton (1959), *To Keep Faith*, London: Constable.

New, W. H. (1999), *Reading Mansfield and Metaphors of Form*, Montreal: McGill-Queen's University Press.

Philip, Jim (1979), 'John Middleton Murry and "Adelphi" Socialism, 1932–1938', in F. Barker et al. (eds), *Proceedings of Essex Conference on the Sociology of Literature, July 1978: Practices of Literature and Politics*, Colchester: University of Essex, pp. 218–31.

Read, Herbert (1960), 'Book Reviews', *London Magazine* 7, 1: 64.

Rees, Richard (1963), *A Theory of My Time: An Essay in Didactic Reminiscence*, London: Secker & Warburg.

Sassoon, Siegfried (1946), *Siegfried's Journey, 1916–1920*, New York: Viking Press.

Scottish Arts Council (1985), *Colour, Rhythm & Dance: Paintings &*

Drawings by J D Fergusson and His Circle in Paris, Edinburgh: Scottish Arts Council.

Sedgwick, Eve Kosofsky (1985), *Between Men: English Literature and Male Homosocial Desire*, New York: Columbia University Press.

Séllei, Nóra (1996), *Katherine Mansfield and Virginia Woolf: A Personal and Professional Bond*, Frankfurt: Peter Lang.

Seymour, Miranda (1992), *Ottoline Morrell: Life on the Grand Scale*, London: Hodder & Stoughton.

Simpson, David (1995), *The Academic Postmodern and the Rule of Literature: A Report on Half-Knowledge*, Chicago: University of Chicago Press.

Smith, Angela (1999), *Katherine Mansfield and Virginia Woolf: A Public of Two*, Oxford: Clarendon Press.

Smith, Angela (2000), *Katherine Mansfield: A Literary Life*, Basingstoke: Palgrave.

Smith, Angela (2009), 'GUTS – Katherine Mansfield as a Reviewer', *Katherine Mansfield Studies* 1: 3–18.

Squires, Michael and Lynn K. Talbot (2002), *Living at the Edge: A Biography of D. H. Lawrence and Frieda von Richthofen*, Madison: University of Wisconsin Press.

Stead, C. K. (2004), *Mansfield: A Novel*, London: Vintage.

Stillinger, Jack (1991), *Multiple Authorship and the Myth of Solitary Genius*, New York: Oxford University Press.

Sullivan, J. W. N. (1932), *But For the Grace of God*, New York: Knopf.

Tomalin, Claire (1988), *Katherine Mansfield: A Secret Life*, New York: Knopf.

Watson, J. H. (1959), 'A Good Workman and his Friends: Recollections of John Middleton Murry', *London Magazine* 6, 5: 51–5.

Wellek, René (1986), *A History of Modern Criticism: 1750–1950. Volume 5: English Criticism, 1900–1950*, New Haven: Yale University Press.

Wellens, Oscar (2001), '"The Brief and Brilliant Life of *The Athenaeum* under Mr. Middleton Murry" (T. S. Eliot)', *Neophilologus* 85, 1: 137–52.

Whitworth, Michael (1996), 'Pièces d'identité: T. S. Eliot, J. W. N. Sullivan and Poetic Impersonality', *English Literature in Transition 1880–1920* 31, 2: 149–70.

Whitworth, Michael (2001), *Einstein's Wake: Relativity, Metaphor, and Modernist Literature*, Oxford: Oxford University Press.

Woodeson, John (1972), *Mark Gertler*, London: Sidgwick & Jackson.

Woolf, Leonard (1972), *Beginning Again: An Autobiography of the Years 1911 to 1918*, New York: Harcourt.

Woolf, Virginia (1925), *The Common Reader*, New York: Harcourt.

Woolf, Virginia [1929] (1963), *A Room of One's Own*, New York: Harcourt.

Woolf, Virginia (1965), *Contemporary Writers*, New York: Harcourt.

Woolf, Virginia (1975–80), *The Letters of Virginia Woolf*, ed. Nigel Nicolson and Joanne Trautmann, 6 vols, New York: Harcourt.

Woolf, Virginia (1977–84), *The Diary of Virginia Woolf*, ed. Anne Olivier Bell and Andrew McNeillie, 5 vols, New York: Harcourt.

Index